On the
MEANING OF LIFE

An ANTHOLOGY
of Theological Reflection

by
Clarence Bauman

Printed in USA
by Evangel Press
Nappanee, IN
1993

To
PILGRIM

TABLE OF CONTENTS

PREFACE

ALWAYS BE PREPARED TO ANSWER EVERYONE WHO
REQUESTS FROM YOU THE REASON FOR YOUR HOPE.

This anthology of theological reflection on life's meaning is my
response to St. Peter's judicious counsel.

These statements of faith were for the most part presented as lectures in the various courses developed during thirty years of teaching theology and ethics at the Associated Mennonite Biblical Semi-
naries. What qualifies these essays for presentation in this form is
their introductory character and exploratory nature. Though these
reflections pretend to be neither academic nor exhaustive and bear
no ecclesiastical imprimatur, they nevertheless claim to be authentically definitive. These thirty essays represent points of light inform-
ing the horizon of our theological awareness and ethical concern
from the perspective of the Anabaptist Vision.

Thanks be to God, to Alice, and to Art Block for making this publication possible.

INTRODUCTION

The most fundamental human need is to find a MEANING FOR BEING: one that transcends existential pessimism and the shallowness of arbitrary opinion, that gives life memory and future, cohesion and continuity, that provides the resources to love and to care, to give and to forgive, that achieves peace within ourselves and others, that enables one to survive the catastrophes of life and history without losing hope and without being swept along by the sheer momentum of global turbulence.

The human race is caught in a crisis of meaning—all too painfully evident in the fear, anger, anxiety, and despair that saturate our awareness through mass informants. The challenge confronting ancient humanity was 'how to die' in a world which reflected the heavenly peace to which they were destined. The challenge facing the modern self is 'how to live' in a world devoid of meaning or purpose.

Meaning signifies coherence and unity through those events that compose our life. When we say that something is 'meaningful', we indicate that it forms something larger or superior to itself, that it is a vital link or function within a comprehensive whole. Meaning requires the condition of order within this world while signifying something beyond mere existence: either an end and aim, or the notion of form. Hence, two modes of meaning can be distinguished: meaning as purpose or goal, and meaning as form or order. Meaninglessness or 'non-sense' begins wherever we fail to comprehend a self-transcending and self-fulfilling reason for being. Search for meaning is search for the ultimate order to which one can relate the experiences and events of life. We seek light on the mystery of life and power for its mastery. Our theological reflections on life's meaning are inspired by the yearning of our minds for some explanation of the universe and our place within it and for a way or rule of life in harmony with the holy life and perfect will of God Himself.

The quest for life's meaning poses many existential questions: What can I KNOW? What may I BELIEVE? What might I HOPE? What shall I DO? Who am I? Who was Jesus? Why did he die? How might his death save us? Does the meaning of Jesus lie in his life or in his death? Can I believe what Jesus believed, live what he lived by, and die what he died for? What means Christ for us today? And what are the implications of following him closely? How will we find the answer to both the real Jesus and the true self?

We need to discern how our realization of life is informed by our awareness of death and how this awareness leads to transvaluation of values. In what sense is death the key to the door of life? What remains after we die: a love? an identity? a contribution? a purpose? a meaning? a memory?

We need to understand the various historical traditions of spiritual ascent and how one experiences Divine Presence through the noödynamics of prayer.

We need to know whether it is possible, feasible, and desirable to recover the Anabaptist Vision. If so, on what moral grounds and by what spiritual resources? What is the price for going the way of peace? What shall we make of Luther's *Zwei-Reiche-Lehre* and of the logic by which Christendom continues to justify 'holy war'?

Therefore, we ask ourselves: What is the real meaning, actual purpose, or vital significance of this life? How can my life acquire a meaning big enough to live by and great enough to die for? How can we as Christians recover for ourselves inner integrity within the world as it is and within the Church as it ought to be? How can one gain perspective on what is ultimately worth doing in any given manner and time? How do I discern my divine calling and vocation? And to what extent should my calling coincide with the self-understanding and self-evidence of the established Church, its books and its laws? What constitutes a divine imperative? And how does one become enlightened, holy, perfect? How does the study of theology inform our quest for true being? In what sense is knowledge of God possible, personal, objective, subjective? How does God reveal Himself? Is revelation of God mystery? history? miracle?

Do Jews and Christians worship the same God? Do they form one people of God? If not, what is the nature of their hope? If so, what is the meaning of their being? How does the integrity of the Jews who reject Jesus compare with the hypocrisy of Christians who claim him as Lord but do not what he says? What do men live by? What are the ethical implications of theology and what is the theological basis for ethics? What are the levels or stages of moral consciousness within the secular mind? And what are the definitions of morality between intention and result?

What is the nature of our economic struggle between having and being? How might the conditions of our economic involvement become a means of grace? Is God always on the side of the poor? Can one inherit the Kingdom only if one is poor with Christ? How can we resolve the religious tension between the desire to survive and enjoy the amenities of culture and still live in the integrity of Christian spirit wholly committed to the claims of love and community?

Since the meaningfulness of life is inseparable from the quality of personal wholeness within our most fundamental primary interrelationships of family and community, we need to ask ourselves what it really means to be married. Is marriage a natural affair

4

(Luther), a religious sacrament (Catholic), or a spiritual friendship (Puritans)? Did Jesus ever counsel divorce? How might marriage fulfill the fidelity of God's own covenant love?

Since our best insights on meaningful life derive from Scripture, we also ask: What constitutes the mystery and miracle of the Bible? Does the holiness of the Bible lie in its content or in the manner of its communication? How does God's Word become man's word in the Bible? Why does the Church need the Bible?

What does the story of philosophy contribute to the quest for meaning? How do the classics of Western thought from Homer to Jaspers deal with conflict of conscience? How does Homer—in contrast to Job—resolve 'the terrible mystery of God's capricious will'? Does 'Perpetual Peace' depend upon 'The Science of Right' (Kant)? Can civilizations be maintained only by executing the 'Articles of War' (Melville)? Does the resolution of life's conflicts lie in lowering the demands of the Christian superego—for therapeutic reasons (Freud)? How does the 'Way to Wisdom' (Jaspers) compare with the counsels of evangelical faith?

Our response to these questions constitutes the agenda of this anthology. Thus, in 'answering that of God in Everyone', we realize that the meaning of life is not synonymous with the fact of existence but *confronts* our existence. The meaning of life is not merely the self-expression of existence nor is it a projection from experience. We may discover or recover life's meaning, but we do not invent it.

In the final analysis, we are left with the intuitive awareness that in theological reflection silence has the last word. Only the word issuing from the depth of silence says something, for "silence constitutes the mystery surrounding every word and sustains the truth within the word." Consequently, "what can be said at all, can be said clearly, and, about what one cannot speak, one must keep a holy silence to witness the Mystery manifesting itself" (Wittgenstein).

THE QUEST FOR MEANING AND BEING

On this occasion I wish to share some reflections on the Quest for Meaning and Being.

As a point of reference I allude to those hard sayings of Paul: "See to it that no one makes a prey of you by philosophy and empty deceit, according to human tradition, according to the elemental spirits, and not according to Christ. . . . Let no one pass judgment on you . . . Let no one disqualify you . . . Why do you submit to regulations? . . . These have indeed an appearance of wisdom (in promoting rigor of devotion . . .), but they are of no value" (Col. 2:8ff.).

Paul argues: Do not be exploited by tradition—it is all too human. If one seeks the meaning of one's being in blind conformity to others, one has no authentic basis for one's own existence. One is unstable in all one's ways—drifting like flotsam with the tide of social convention and driven by the winds of ideology—without meaning or destiny. As for the "elemental spirits," Paul identifies only their function of deceiving men into thoughtless, meaningless conformity.

On the lower levels of social existence, the shape of this conformity is determined by utilitarian concern for survival. The self-interest of the group becomes the collective conscience to which the individual naturally conforms. On the upper echelons of society, one's authenticity is exploited by the lure of cultural benefits. Paul decries conformity to the world as "empty deceit," for the meaning of one's being lies neither in nature nor in culture.

But Paul referred primarily to religious conformity, the kind that promotes "rigor of devotion." That is what makes this text so hard—and so relevant. What is more restrictive than the prim propriety of religious establishment and what more stifling to spiritual creativity, more debilitating to personal growth than unquestioned conformity to "human tradition," perpetuated within the narrow horizon of an ingrown religious order by the exaggerated self-awareness of what is piously proper. The phenomenon of religion in all its plurality and diversity is, to a larger extent than its respective adherents realize, a strange intermingling of nature and culture. That also applies to the Christian religion which owes more to the conforming "elemental spirits" than to the nonconformist Jesus spirit. The church—including the Mennonite Church—is, to a larger extent than its own pillars and scholars dare to admit, enslaved by the precepts and doctrines of its own historicity. The existential question therefore is: How can we as persons recover for ourselves authentic meaning and being? How can we recover for ourselves inner integrity and authenticity within the church as it is and within the world as it ought to be? It is the urgency of this quest for Meaning and Being that compels our self-examination.

Most people live for finite aims and by the means to obtain and retain material benefits. They labor for the necessities of life and, beyond that, for leisure and pleasure. Whether they work or play or pray, most persons conform unquestioningly to the patterns and expectations of their immediate associates in order to avoid the embarrassment of censure and the insecurity of ostracism. Such empirical existence is largely unenlightened existence and therefore largely meaningless existence. Unless I recognize in that to which I conform a transcendent revelation of the meaning of all existence, my life lacks an underlying rationale. Whenever I allow my life to be conditioned by the unexamined will or unquestioned authority of others, I permit my inmost self to be reduced to a meaningless token. To yield to the will and power of others without discerning

WHY is to a large extent "empty deceit."

We need to recover for ourselves a certain independence of mind and soul if we are not to be altogether consumed by the technological busyness of the world or overwhelmed by its ideological inanity. Somehow we must extricate ourselves from this all-consuming technological and ideological machinery that governs our empty labor and empty leisure if we are to recover what is human and truly fulfill ourselves. Our cybernetic age is characterized by a great loss of soul—a loss of genuine individuality.

Such deficiency also permeates the religious aspect of life. We need to gain a new integrity of belief and confession. Here, the integral course of action is to confess openly our reservations about what we do not comprehend and to pursue all the more fervently what we do comprehend of the Christian tradition so that it may become the vital and constructive force of our personal and social life. Christian faith is not appropriation of what is intellectually incomprehensible but is obedience, reverence, and trust in God—the God who leaves no person without divine witness within his conscience. From the Jewish prophets, from Jesus, and from Paul we discern what it means to cultivate an independence of conscience and to follow our own inner convictions. The only authority to which we should subject ourselves is one which stimulates and develops spiritual independence. We must not fear to trust our own judgment and intuition—particularly in matters religious. Tolstoy once countered his critics: "The justification for thinking with my own head is that I have none other with which to think." No endorsement of a body of ecclesiastical doctrine can obviate our responsibility for developing our own thoughts.

When we speak of the need for a certain independence of mind and soul, we do not mean a false, irresponsible independence that assumes indifference to an intolerable situation. We each stand with the other in relation of mutuality. Each of us is dependent on others because we are all interlocked in a common world. It is an illusion to abandon the world to work out our own salvation. This world is the place where God speaks and acts—always with many meanings, some of which become clear to us in existential moments although none can be generalized.

Despite our dependence on others, there is great personal value in achieving a certain inner independence: "To have as though we have not" (Paul), "to have but not be had" (Aristippus), "to be free to perform the task but not strive after its fruit" (Bhagavad Gita). True independence manifests itself not as indifference, imperturbability, or immunity but signifies attachment to the world and involvement in the world through transcendence of the world. To achieve personal independence means to become master of our own thoughts and our own historicity—of our origin and meaning. We achieve that as we learn to discern all things, listen to all contemporaries, and remain open to all possibilities.

We experience true independence as we become enlightened. Enlightenment is the path by which one comes to oneself. Those who fear enlightenment accuse it of destroying the sacred traditions upon which all life rests. They say enlightenment dissolves faith and leads to nihilism, disorder, and anarchy and that it absolutizes reason, exalts man, and denies God. These accusations apply to those who strive only to know but not to believe and who absolutize the insights of understanding while disavowing its factual limits. However, when we reject on principle the necessity of examining our faith and life and fail to cultivate a critical awareness of the quality and limit of every insight, we tend merely to defend man-made contents of our faith—its institutions and rules of conduct—on the dubious assumption that they are the ultimate forms of truth. Because folly and wisdom are so inextricably interwoven in all things human, only the examined life can be worthwhile.

We achieve authentic independence as we recover the lost inner journey of the soul. Beyond the necessity of performing practical tasks, we need to take time to evaluate our relations with others—our experiences of trust and betrayal, bliss and pain. We need to spend our time thinking through fundamental problems and not take for granted the catastrophes in human life and human relations. If we are to ascend the way of wisdom and recover the lost territory—that great wasteland of the barren soul—we cannot survive without daily moments of profound reflection to evaluate our relation to ourselves, to others, and to God. The reflective life is that process of the inmost self in which thought and being become identical. This is the meaning of the *Selbstbewusstsein* and *Gottesbewusstsein* (self-awareness and God-consciousness) of Jesus and the hope of those who follow him closely.

The point of this discipline is to gain perspective on what I should do in the present time—what is ultimately worth doing in any particular day and way—and in what relation my daily life stands to the whole of meaning and being. To a limited extent that is accomplished through ritual prayer or liturgical worship—by concentrating on holy objects in holy places. We recover our true depth, however, not so much through fixed spiritual exercises as by free contemplation in solitude.

The meaning of our being lies in discerning the unconditional imperative or inner voice. To the extent that we discern the voice, word, will, or spirit of God, our empirical existence becomes the soil that realizes the fruit of love, joy, peace, and abounding goodness. To the extent that we heed the beat of our internal drummer—that of God within us—our life evidences a unique quality of integration and well-being together with a mysterious sense of vocation, direction, and destiny.

This is how Jesus differed from men of his day and ours. Conscious of his calling and destiny, he went his way undeterred by passions of anger, hatred, despair, or self-righteousness. From Jesus we learn that an authentic person is one who knows he exists in relation to God as a child in relation to the father. Jesus said: "You shall know the truth and the truth shall make you free and you shall be free indeed." This knowledge of being sons and daughters of God constitutes our authentic freedom which fully opens us to the world while enabling us to be independent of the world. Jesus was completely free in all the forms of humanity: free to be a homeless infant in a cave in Bethlehem, a wandering prophet over the hills of Galilee, a dying criminal on a cross in Jerusalem. He was free to be a nobody and therefore free to be Messiah, free to be son of man as son of God, to find his life and fulfill his life in the constant awareness of God's guidance. Jesus pronounced that it is not only possible but normal for us to live in constant awareness of God's guidance.

This guidance need not take on tangible form as the appearance of a burning bush, an angel, or an oral commandment—though it can and may do so. For the most part, however, the unconditional imperative (cf. Karl Jaspers) remains hidden. Even in the records of Jesus' life there are but few references to an audible voice or visible sign (as at baptism and transfiguration) apart from which his divine determination remained a well-kept secret right to the very end. Usually, only in extreme situations—at the crucial crossroads of life or when we are in danger of becoming untrue to ourselves—does the unconditional imperative through a silent decision determine one's destiny as it determined Abraham's decision along the road to Moriah to sacrifice his son and as it determined Jesus' decision along the Nablus Road to Jerusalem to sacrifice himself. Though it governs one's whole life, this divine determination can never be consciously demonstrable apart from a discernment of the fruit of that spirit. Even these fruits, however, are not demonstrable proofs but, like Jesus' parables, are intimations of divine self-transcendence.

The mystery of divine guidance is not demonstrable; it does not yield to scientific analysis—except to be classified as a kind of divine madness. Socrates realized this when he confessed: The man of spirit is filled with a divine madness. Hosea confirmed it in his own words: "The prophet is a fool, mad is the man of spirit" (9:7). And Dostoevski depicted Jesus as "The Idiot."

What gives life its meaning one can find and lose, but never possess. God's guidance never becomes our own possession. The spirit blows where it wills. Only in our most sublime moments do we hear the sound thereof. Only in such moments do we recover a glimpse of something for which to live, something great enough for which to die. Nevertheless, it is out of and toward such moments that we authentically live in the conscious freedom of and spontaneous obedience to our inner calling.

This calling may coincide with the established church, its books and laws, but that it does so is by no means self-evident. We, like the prophets and Jesus, often hear God's voice most convincingly when it conflicts with all objective authority. Nevertheless, it is our individual responsibility to listen to the whole of reality, for it is through such listening that children of humanity become children of God. The more faithfully one listens to the voice within, the better one hears what is sounding outside.

This compelling divine awareness comes to us not as a bliss to behold, but as a decision to act. Whenever one heeds the unconditional imperative, one effects an unconditional decision, that is, a decision in true freedom without regard for consequences. Unconditional decisions always appear as costly decisions. In extreme situations the call of the unconditional leads to loss of life as the price for authenticity. Nevertheless, the will of God never comes to us as an external threat to be overcome but as an internal intuition I may affirm with my whole being in the recognition that it sustains what is authentically my best self and lifts me out of a life of indecision to become what I know I am meant to be. I intuitively recognize that the decision God unconditionally demands of me is in my best interests and identical with my highest aspirations. One's life is meaningful to the extent that it is unconditional. By awareness of and obedience to the unconditional, a human being partakes of the Eternal and becomes one with God as Jesus was one with God. Evil is the life of one who remains in the sphere of the contingent, drifting with the tide, whose being has no transcendent repose but subsists as the product of the flux and unrest of meaningless change.

Decision between good and evil constitutes the existential substance of life. One's enlightenment consists in the quality of one's discernment of good from evil, and one's commitment consists in the depth of one's identity with what one knows to be true. Good is unconditional love—the ultimate will to reality. Evil is unrestrained hate—the perverted will to destruction. Love impels to being, hate to nonbeing. Love operates as a quiet building in the world, hate eventuates in loud catastrophe. In each case an alternative is revealed, a decision required.

At the onset, awareness of the distinction between good and evil may be obscure, but in the course of unconditional obedience to what I know to be true the awareness becomes lucid. The problem of evil is not that we are unable to discern good from evil but that we are unwilling to decide to do the truth and, instead, vacillate and stumble through a life of indecision. To become authentic we must continually recapture ourselves from indecision, choose the good, and live by love.

The intention, *telos* or goal, and climax of our life is the point at which we ascertain God. Every person within his or her own historicity stands in an immediate and independent relation to God. What matters is not so much our knowledge of God as our particular attitude to God, that is, the extent to which we are open and ready for God and able to comprehend Him directly. The great Shema Israel is the attestation of the self-identity, definition, and calling of a people who hear and know God in their hearts and hence are known as "People of God." The awareness of God transcends all definition of God, all speech about God, all images of God. Awareness of God is an experience of inner silence and awe, without further questions and answers, when thought dissolves into radiance and repose from all wanderings of mind and soul.

That we have not yet reached this *telos* is obvious from the fact that we are still studying theology, still looking for the way to wisdom, still discerning what others knew and did and what we can believe and hope. Let us then pass our time—the time that we have to pass—and pass it well in the awareness that through this process, this "happening," we are to become what we were meant to be with and for one another within the whole of humanity all over this round world.

Only to the extent that I have found myself and conquered myself am I able to point the way to others and become with them the "People of the Way"—as followers of Jesus were first called. The truth begins with two; yet each of us must venture out on our own to complete our own cycle, to win our own authenticity, and to achieve in common with all our own unique destiny.

The point at issue is that life was meant to be reflective, a process of the inmost self, an inner journey in which thought and being become one. Theological education was not meant to be a process of accommodation and accreditation 'by degrees' but, rather, authentic illumination and growth into being.

At a decisive stage in his spiritual quest Dag Hammarskjöld prayed, "What I ask for is absurd: that life shall have a meaning.

What I strive for is impossible: that my life shall acquire a meaning." Seized by the same unrest I am impelled to the same request:

"Give me (O God) a pure heart—that I may see Thee,

A humble heart—that I may hear Thee,

A heart of love—that I may serve Thee,

A heart of faith—that I may abide in Thee."

(*Markings*, 100)

THE MEANING OF LIFE AND DEATH

The will to meaning is life's primary volitional force. If one has a WHY to live, one can bear with almost any HOW. Without the struggle for meaning, life disintegrates within an existential vacuum of conformism and boredom.

Seen from the perspective of the last day, the life of most people is so terrible because it is so ordinary, so superficial, so conventional. So that even on the last day it would seem improper and therefore be impossible to ask whether one's whole life had been wrong!

In this life we were meant to achieve mastery over our destiny to a much greater extent than is commonly evident from being nominally Christian. Inasmuch as this does not happen, we are wasting our precious life and time (irrespective of how many credits we accumulate on transcripts), and we may be well-advised to become a hermit and withdraw from the nonsense of the world or, as Moses and Jesus, to climb a mountain or get lost in a wilderness for forty days and nights to fast and have a hard think on what it really means to be or not to be in order to ascertain why we are in our world at all in such a time as this.

No one lives in this body forever, nor for very long. Most people do not fully realize this. Jesus did. Therefore, he said: "We must do the work of Him who sent us while it is day; the night comes when no one can work."

Jesus differed from others in that he was master of his destiny: he accomplished in his world and time what he intended—even under most adverse circumstances. When his time was up his task was finished and he left his body behind, which of course did not mean that he ceased to exist—nobody does. Because Jesus did what he came to do we think of him as unique, as a very rare exception— rare indeed! But we are very slow to grasp the point of his teaching, which was not to impress his disciples with his own uniqueness but to enable them to "go and do likewise"—the true essence of Easter. Through him we too are endowed at the horizon of our potential self with the spiritual capacity to tune in to that same divine frequency, so that we too can accomplish our divine calling and vocation and not merely fumble and stumble along mindlessly within our own time and space without orientation, direction, or fulfillment.

Much of life's misery is due to its meaninglessness, and most of our own suffering is caused by our spiritual ignorance. Most people for most of their lives fail to realize that time and space are not ends in themselves but means towards an eternal and transcendent intention. Once the veil of ignorance is removed, it appears obvious that every material extension somehow embodies a spiritual intention even as it appears self-evident that the manifest part of our tangible life between birth and death is but a small fragment of an infinitely larger invisible whole, as though the brief span of our life were but a comma in a vast sentence which has no period. Inasmuch as we recover intuitive awareness of our essentially spiritual nature, we are liberated from the meaninglessness which underlies most of our carnal suffering.

The meaning of life does not consist in vague generalizations but in a specific awareness of what I am to live by and for. It does not emerge from our existence but confronts our existence. It is not something we can invent, but it is something we may discover. It is not a compulsion that drives us but an invitation that calls us. It is not to be found within our own psyche but within the world of human relations and tasks. Its essence is not self-actualization but self-transcendence. It may be more active or more passive meaning—to be realized through contemplation, action, or suffering. We discover the meaning of life as we assume loving responsibility for another person or as we commit ourselves to an unfinished task. Apart from finding our redemption through human love and shaping our destiny through human action, we may discover that the meaning of life consists simply in the cross that is laid upon us and in the attitude by which we endure what we cannot change.

Each task and each destiny is unique, and there is only one right answer to any problem posed by any situation. Even our suffering is unique, for none can bear it for another or tell us what its purpose is. Life's meaning always changes but never ceases. What gives life its meaning one can find and lose but never possess. Each person must find it for himself, often without being able to tell another, for as one cannot look directly at the sun or death, so one cannot speak the whole truth in words, though one often expresses more than one intends.

We have lived inasmuch as we have suffered, and we are saved inasmuch as we have loved. Life is so precious in all its interrelationships and so rich in all its consequences. The real tragedy of life is not biological but spiritual death through alienation, depersonalization, loss of meaning and being.

On the cultural and national level, the all-pervasive fear of death and the neurotic compulsion to deny it indicate absence of a lifeview that transcends death. Ironically, the fateful weapons deployed for our security constitute our greatest liability, since the logic of their proliferation almost invariably spells nuclear death.

Our real enemy is not communism but the death instinct within ourselves which, by the vicious cycle of our own unfreedom, provokes our competitors into being our opponents. What hope there is for survival from this scenario of mutual destruction must come through our enemies by a self-transcendence of which we are admittedly incapable.

Meanwhile, we try to cover up our schizophrenic psychosis with the make-believe of a good life—we pay our insurance premiums, clutter our lives with cultural trivia from golf clubs to electric toothbrushes, and hope against hope somehow to perpetuate this meaninglessness on borrowed time.

Within the biblical worldview, human being in covenant with God has a cosmic identity, potentiality, and responsibility. Once this cosmology of the Judeo-Christian faith is lost, what remains to displace it is the Freudian romantic cosmology of two, in which each demands from the other redemption from meaninglessness. When this delirium of eros and thanatos has run its course and it has become obvious that overinvestment in sex fails to reap Utopia, the result is depression.

Other attempts at self-transcendence include the quest of the creative artist to embody immortality in visual form only to realize that all materialization is impermanent and ambiguous and borders sometimes on madness. Finally, when every anguished search for self-transcendence seems to end in demise or deceit, modern man drugs himself out of awareness or spends his time shopping which is the same thing.

But awareness of death was meant to lead not to despair of life but to transvaluation of values, enabling spiritual integration and sanctification. The psychic pain of one's life cycle with its ailments and depressions can be seen as a positive dynamic through which personality is deepened and matured. The very process of suffering is meant to be spiritual formation via cross and resurrection to a higher ethical consciousness in tune with the intimations of what lies beyond this bodily existence. Our life struggle between creation and redemption was meant to embody a dynamic balance between the Western will to assertion and the Eastern wisdom of submission. Since life at its highest demands a Jewish struggle for spiritual maturation through participation in the pain of God, Christians should not too cheaply resolve all conflict with the consolation of atonement theology. Besides halfheartedly singing the old sacred hymns in simple country churches to perpetuate the hope of apocalyptic bliss beyond this sinful vale of tears, we need in our struggle for meaning to invest more heavily in the fullness of life, for the Gospel proclaims a way of triumph through this world which God created and loves and for which Jesus lived and died.

What happens when we die? Within three days our bodies decompose into ill-smelling substances which are recycled within a closed system near the place from which they were borrowed. What about the mental, emotional, and spiritual components of our personal identity? Being nonphysical, our psyche is not subject to decay but is conserved within a larger infinite spiritual accountability. Just as our decayed body is reabsorbed by this planet without loss of energy, so our mental and spiritual components are transposed into that realm of universal mind over matter which ultimately determines the origin and destiny of all knowing and being. That nothing of informational consequence is ever lost is evidenced from the power of recollection inherent in the prophetic and messianic consciousness intent on fulfilling the divine intention of creation through progressive human regeneration.

When we take a closer look at reality, we find that its physical and spiritual dimensions are not as disparate as commonly assumed by theology and science. Naturalistic philosophy failed to see the spiritual within the material, while supernaturalistic religion failed to see the material within the spiritual. For opposite reasons both science and religion underestimated the noödynamic inherent in physical reality. In the light of new insights into the essence of reality the old dualistic controversy over nature versus spirit appears unfounded.

Psyche and matter are innately coextensive within an integral framework of meaning and being. This is evident from the fact that physical substance is almost as intangible and ethereal as spiritual reality. When we look at a piece of bone through a supermicroscope and focus on its atoms, what do we find? We find that its microreality consists of vast space within which a tiny nucleus (in a ratio of 1 to 10,000) is rapidly pulsating many million times per second. So that, instead of common-sense solid matter, we have a vast network of empty spaces filled with oscillating fields of various kinds of energy interacting with one another, all pulsating in harmony with their respective rates and spreading their influence infinitely throughout the cosmos.

An organism or organ beating or vibrating out of tune may be harmonized by applying a strong rhythm to it—which may be the principle of chemical and psychic healing. Sanctification and contemplation enable the respective components of our personal identity to function as integrative circuits in harmony with the isodynamics of the micro- and macrocosmos or, to say it theologically, in resonance with the mind and will of God and the noödynamics of shalom. Since God is not only very far away but also very near at hand, not merely beyond but also within all dimensions of His creation (the physical and metaphysical), the spiritual and material aspects of our life actually comprise one integrative reality embodying the mystery and light of the divine omnipresence.

Light travels around our planet seven times per second, so

fast that it is not really in motion but at rest in almost all places at once. Since time is a measure of motion, whatever travels faster than light is, strictly speaking, no longer temporal but partakes of eternal omnipresence. So that, if by implication we could expand our consciousness, we too could be where we ought to be without running so hard to get there!

Jesus said: "When your eye is single, your whole body is full of light." By virtue of this inner light we become what we were meant to be in our own presence within God's omnipresence. Somehow the whole meaning of life from the lithosphere to the noösphere manifests itself in its elemental constitutional dynamic as enlightened consciousness in which the subjective and objective aspects of soul and body, mind and matter, knowing and being are spiritually integrated in harmony with both our immediate nature and our ultimate destiny. The very nature of this vital connection determines our epistemology, ontology, soteriology, and ethics.

Death is the key to the door of life. Awareness of impending death enables us to transcend the prevailing superficiality of our accepted value systems and to become an authentic individual for God. Facing death opens us to the truth of life. Denial of death accounts for much of the emptiness and purposelessness of life—the façade, confusion, disorientation, and disillusionment. Only as we comprehend the precious finality of each temporal moment do we dare live it fully, dearly, and freely—without inhibitions or reservations.

As we catch an intuitive glimpse of what lies beyond, we become acutely aware that this life was meant to be invested as richly as possible with LOVING and LEARNING, with cultivation of the spiritual faculties of the heart and the mind, for that is why we are in this body within this world and time. Whatever we can divest to achieve this inner fulfillment of our being is the greatest conscious investment we can make towards our own blessedness in this life and in the life after life, for it is the embodiment of God's will for the universe both in time and throughout eternity. Through such transcendent awareness we recover a profound peace within ourselves and boundless resource to love others in such a way that their fear too will be transformed into faith and hope and their finite selfish anxiety into spiritual caring. As we fulfill ourselves in this freedom, we become what we were meant to be, now and forever.

May the mystery of God's Silent Presence inspire in us the strength to love and the authority to proclaim His Peace. *Baruch ha-Shem*!

Reprinted by permission from *The Mennonite,* July 28/81, 437f.

SPIRITUAL FORMATION THROUGH PRAYER

1. VARIOUS TRADITIONS
2. THE MODERN DILEMMA
3. SPIRITUAL DYNAMICS

SPIRITUAL FORMATION

Spirituality derives from the consciousness that God is Spirit, and spiritual formation embodies the process of becoming spiritual through the inspiration (inhaling) of God's own life force (*ruach*) whereby one comes to be "a live soul" (Gn. 2:7).

Within this creation it appears that every life form from the lithosphere to the noösphere undergoes within its own cellular and cosmic life cycle existential transformation, as its elemental energy mass is recycled within the dynamics of a larger process and meaning, transcending the objectivity and subjectivity of individual birth and death and somehow perpetuating itself indefinitely in the hope of ultimate renewal. However that may be, it appears that at the upper echelon of consciousness the process of ontic-noetic formation is, by divine initiative and definition, more spiritual than natural and, in turn, more integrative and deliberate. It involves the highest awareness and the deepest commitment, embodying the spirituality of the patriarchs and prophets and that special messianic consciousness of Jesus himself.

Somehow, within the cosmic parameters of this creation and its consummation and amid the narrower existential limits of our own emerging consciousness from cradle to grave, God intends for each of us to achieve a level of clarity and to assume a measure of responsibility for our own history and destiny that claims the divine authority of God's own knowledge and power. This is what re-creation, incarnation, and regeneration are all about—the human transformation at every stage by divine inspiration.

This special awareness characterized Jesus who differed from other men not in his physiology but in his spirituality: in that he knew WHO God was—most people do not; and in that he knew WHO he was—most people do not; and in that he knew his CALLING and VOCATION—most people do not. This knowledge of God and self in the concreteness of life constitutes sonship and discipleship, effecting the difference between a spiritual person who has found in God a reason to live by and for and a carnal person who perpetuates his relatively meaningless existence at all costs and often against all others.

The spirituality we seek is embodied in the mystery and wonder of Jesus. To FOLLOW him is to recover his WAY through his WORD. But the attempt to do so has resulted in many spiritualities, and whatever is manifold is disturbing because it is not simple to resolve. The wise speak of two ways and indicate which one is right. Consequently they are heard by many, for the choice they present is clear, even though the way they point to may not be easy. But those who speak of many ways often confuse many people and seldom help more than a few (cf. Buber, *I and Thou*). We therefore limit our typology to a few historical landmarks of inspiration, those representing reflective rather than active spirituality.

I. *VARIOUS TRADITIONS*

EASTERN ORTHODOX SPIRITUALITY confronts one with the transparency of God's reality through a way of knowing that is more intuitive than analytic. It is deeply rooted in the Greek Fathers as documented in the *Philokalia* and represents the passionate piety of the Russian soul. The Orthodox Church is primitivist and biblicist in character, and its spirituality reflects the light-metaphysics of the fourth Gospel in Neoplatonic terminology. The aim of Orthodox spirituality in its liturgical, contemplative, and ascetic emphasis is union with God and deification. The recent study by John Meyendorff on *St. Gregory Palamas* conveys the beauty and complexity of this spiritual tradition. The recent biography by Valentine Zander of *St. Seraphim of Sarov* (1759-1833) describes the spiritual formation of holy men living for many years as hermits in the deep solitude of the forest before assuming their calling as spiritual directors. *The Way of the Pilgrim,* unique among spiritual classics, documents the emphasis on the Jesus Prayer in Orthodox spirituality; and the legacy of Catherine Doherty in *Poustinia, Sobornost,* and *Strannik* captivates for our time the relevance of this spiritual adventure. Eastern Orthodox spirituality embodies the first beatitude of Jesus in childlike simplicity and spontaneous humility, the secret to the wondrous unfolding of the mystery of God's grace and love in the hearts of His people.

ROMAN CATHOLIC SPIRITUALITY is a field where many flowers bloom. One of the most enduring and influential is *The Rule of St. Benedict* (480-543). Its seventy-three chapters cover all aspects of spiritual living including work, prayer, and study, with treasured admonitions on the merits of silence, obedience, humility, and those other virtues that render a monk a saint. The Rule has become for all time the blueprint of monastic spirituality.

Then there are the beautiful *Little Flowers* of St. Francis

(1182-1226), whose simplicity, poverty, and joy transcend all legalism and egoism and for whom the natural and the supernatural comprise one indivisible whole. The spirit of St. Francis so closely resembles that of early Anabaptism that Ritschl and others were convinced it was St. Francis who initially inspired the Anabaptist vision of discipleship. Another timeless religious classic (6,000 editions in 50 languages) is *The Imitation of Christ* by Thomas à Kempis (1380-1471), who explores the implications of *imitatio Christi* for spiritual formation.

The genius of medieval MYSTIC SPIRITUALITY is Meister Eckhart (1260-1328), whose scintillating mind pondered with great profundity the mysteries of knowing and being that underlie the reality of spirituality and the wonder of spiritual formation in the eternal birth of the Son. A well-known spiritual guide for the practice of prayer is *The Way of Perfection* by St. Teresa of Avila (1515-82), foundress of many Carmelite convents. Her celebrated masterpiece *Interior Castle,* in probing the psychology of prayer, integrates the various levels and aspects of the devout consciousness. In John of the Cross (1542-91) we have a Spanish Carmelite whose incomparable *Ascent of Mount Carmel* and insightful *Dark Night of the Soul* probe that ocean of spiritual darkness which haunts sensitive souls in their quest for spiritual unity. From the Carmelite tradition derives also a beautifully simple treatise on *The Practice of the Presence of God* by Brother Lawrence (Nicholas Herman, 1611-91), who concluded that times of business should not differ from times of prayer. Therefore, he "quitted all forms of devotion and set prayer" to cultivate "by a simple attention . . . the actual Presence of God . . . by an habitual, silent, and secret conversation of the soul with God."

DESERT SPIRITUALITY from the hermitage of Charles de Foucauld (1858-1916), exemplified in his *Silent Pilgrimage to God,* marks a turning point in the modern revitalization of Catholic spirituality. Even Thomas Merton (1915-68) singled out from his many books *The Wisdom of the Desert* as one of the most important. These Catholic mystics inspire us to cultivate a more intuitive sensibility that leads to loving God with our whole self, a mentality whose uniqueness transcends the psychological positivism that tends to strangle our modern understanding and experience of spirituality.

PROTESTANT SPIRITUALITY has, since the Reformation, taken form in many traditions, one of which was PURITANISM, whose philosophy of life is captured by *The Pilgrim's Progress*, an allegorical spiritual autobiography of John Bunyan (1628-88) who was for many years imprisoned in England because he refused to stop preaching about sanctification of life and discipleship. The desperate loneliness of this agonizing symbolic inner journey from the City of Destruction to the Palace Beautiful has left its mark upon the Separatist mentality.

Another nonconformist, William Law (1686-1761), expelled from theological studies at Cambridge for refusing to swear the oath of allegiance to the Crown, applied his lucid mind to writing provocative books on spiritual formation, such as *A Serious Call to a Devout and Holy Life*. Law counters cheap grace and demands integrity of life according to the Sermon on the Mount. In addressing every aspect of the human condition he recommends voluntary poverty and "the refinement and exaltation of our best faculties" towards living a disciplined, pure, humble, joyful, and grateful life to the glory of God. The influence of this book over the past two centuries has transformed the lives of many nominal Christians. Law, in turn, also inspired in John Wesley (1703-91) this emphasis on entire sanctification in pursuit of Christian perfection.

Within contemporary EVANGELICALISM there appears a new openness and concern for spiritual formation through a sanctification of life that integrates the positive elements of Pietism, whereas, in the more liberal Anglican, Reformed, and Lutheran traditions, the pejorative historical attitude towards Pietism apparently still prevails.

QUAKER SPIRITUALITY is rooted in the conscience of George Fox (1624-91), that spiritual giant known for his overpowering individuality. Four years he wandered from town to town seeking spiritual counsel. An ancient priest in Warwickshire had him chew tobacco and sing Psalms. Another advised taking physic and having his blood let by leeches. Nothing helped. Then, according to his *Journal,* he began to receive "pure openings" directly from the Light which cut across all religious convention. The Lord opened unto him that being bred at Oxford or Cambridge does not fit and qualify one to be a minister of Christ. Next, it was opened unto him that God does not dwell in temples. Guided by these openings, he kept speaking truth to power and refused to be silenced even though beaten and imprisoned. In effect, the Lord's power was truly over all. Fox lived what he preached and founded a Society of Friends committed to "walking cheerfully over the world, answering that of God in everyone." The *Journal* of John Woolman (1720-72) exemplifies the cultivation of that spiritual resourcefulness from which protests of conscience proceed without malice, pride, or disturbance of personal integrity and social respect. *A Testament of Devotion* by Thomas R. Kelly (1893-1941) establishes that "Life from the Center is a life of unhurried peace and power. It is simple. It is serene. It is amazing. It is triumphant. It is radiant."

Mennonites feel threatened by Quaker spirituality: they do not know what to make of the Inner Light, that Divine Presence in silent worship without preachment, sacrament, or Sunday School lesson. Nor do they feel comfortable with a Quaker view of Scripture. When it comes to speaking truth to power, Mennonites are put to shame by Quakers and silenced as Fox silenced the Puritans.

ANABAPTIST-MENNONITE SPIRITUALITY is an entity

too close to home to define objectively in few words. Resource for
the task has been provided by much historical research in sixteenth-
century sources and in attempts to comprehend the essence of that
movement in the light of its spiritual antecedents (e. g., *Anabaptism
and Asceticism,* 1974 by Kenneth R. Davis). But, in this matter of
interpretation, so much of the result depends on the presupposition.
(My own persuasion lies in the hope of establishing the legacy of
Hans Denck as normative rather than marginal.) For the American
scene, Harold S. Bender provided in *Two Centuries of American
Mennonite Literature* (1929) an indispensable bibliography from
1727 to 1928. John C. Wenger issued in *Separated unto God* (1951)
a definitive plea for simplicity and nonconformity. And Robert Friedmann produced in *Mennonite Piety, Its Genius and Its Literature*
(1949) a resourceful analysis.

   In the spiritual development of Mennonitism, Friedmann identifies three negative trends: 1) Pietism, 2) Formalism, and 3) Secularism. The decisive difference between Pietism and Anabaptism is
seen as a shift in focus from Paul's doctrine of justification to Jesus'
teaching on the Kingdom of God. Paul starts with the experience of
sin, while Jesus began with the demands of *Nachfolge.* "The ultimate
meaning of the concept of justification implies 'enjoyment'
(Geniessen)" (86), whereas, "The idea of the Kingdom of God ultimately leads us to work and to suffer" (87).

   In the absence of religious persecution and the presence of cultural adaptation, the dominant motif in Mennonite spirituality
became this Pietist emphasis on edification and ENJOYMENT
(based on "Train yourself in 'godliness' " of I Timothy 4:7, translated
'Gottseligkeit' and interpreted as *'gottselige Gemütsübung'* or, literally, 'pious mood-training', a subjectivism peculiar to the German).
This Pietist emphasis included glorious expectations after death and
concern over the certainty of qualifying for them. In effect, Pietist
Erbauung (edification) displaced Anabaptist *Nachfolge* in the inner

history of Mennonite spirituality (104). Friedmann discerns the successive stages of this inner process of adaptation by Mennonitism to Pietism in his study of the origin and influence of Mennonite prayer books. He noted the unresolved tension between the fixed text and the living inspiration, between providing prayer texts for those unskilled in the art of prayer and stifling the spontaneity of the Spirit by so doing.

This awareness pertains to the second liability Friedmann identified as "the problem of 'formalism', the tendency to retain stiffly and with little thought the traditional heritage, unquestioned, untested, and without any inner dynamic" (225). In reflecting on the Anabaptist vision, Paul Peachey keenly observed: "As long as their genius had not crystallized into cultural tradition they were creative, but their prophetic impact waned when they developed externally transmissible sub-culture systems" (*Recovery*, 339). Once ethnic cohesion displaces spiritual vitality, the church ceases to be an existential community. "If (says Peachey) we transform the vision into a terminal cultural value, we shall go down with all the other pharisaisms of history" (340). According to Jesus, that happens through misuse of prayer (Mt. 6:5f.).

The problem of secularization (to which Friedmann alluded without comment) has far-reaching implications precisely for our understanding of prayer, its reality and spirituality. There has been considerable confusion within PROTESTANT traditions of our culture between psychological counseling and spiritual guidance, a confusion that has blurred the decisive differences between the self-understandings implicit in 1) psychotherapy, 2) pastoral counseling, and 3) spiritual direction in their respective focus, content, process, attitude, and practice. Widespread tendency to overpsychologize spiritual direction has contributed to this confusion. It has caused thousands of clergy to leave their parishes for secularized psychological practice, and it has left all those people without guidance whose spiritual questions and concerns remain yet unredeemed when treated with "therapy."

The medical model with its emphasis on psychoanalysis and the pastoral counseling model with its focus on interrelationship have together largely displaced the agenda of spiritual directive, that is, the recovery of a right relationship with God and the subsequent discovery of the spiritual resources for personal renewal, healing, and growth through prayer, repentance, and forgiveness.

In marked contrast to the psychological interest in building "ego strength," egotistic self-importance is not an asset but a liability in the development of the kind of spirituality exemplified by Jesus' first beatitude: "Blessed are the poor in Spirit." Jesus taught his disciples to pray not "MY will be done" but "THY will be done." This secularized ambiguity regarding the formative dynamic of prayer invariably reflects a much deeper underlying dilemma we need to identify.

II. *THE MODERN DILEMMA*

1) The modern person lives in a desacralized world in which prayer has no place inasmuch as the realm of mystery has been exposed by science so that the departmentalization into sacred versus secular realms no longer applies. The person of today has no need to pray and hence no desire to do so; in fact, he does not even know how to pray. This is also the world of many Christians who protest the traditional metaphysical presuppositions of praying ever since alert spirits such as the honest bishop John A. T. Robinson divulged (in his provocative *Honest to God*) that God is no longer 'up there' somewhere in celestial remoteness. Therefore, rather than 'lifting up the receiver' of the heavenly telephone to tap the hotline, we need only to 'elevate our minds' by accepting the consequences of Rudolf Bultmann's *Entmythologisierungsprogramm.* This reluctant revolution

comes as relief to those who were never turned on by devotional practices in seminary and whose only consolation was the awareness that they were by no means alone in their secret guilt over their spiritual inadequacy. For the modern 'enlightened' Christian, prayer is no longer what one does when DISengaged from the business of the world to 'be with God' in the sacramental or supernatural way of monastic or pietistic withdrawal or contemplative concentration. The moment of truth consists instead in unconditional ENGAGEMENT with life itself in the dynamics of practical decision-making. The conclusion is that one prays best FOR people precisely when one agonizes WITH them rather than withdrawing FROM them on the assumption that prayer, like love, is most fruitful when not disengaged from life.

2) The crisis of prayer is exposed by linguistic analysis. The predominantly essentialist character of traditional prayer language has lost its credibility in existentialist society where reality is no longer a fixed ontological superstructure but a process of becoming. Even the use of personal language in conversing with God, just as though He were a man, reduces prayer to a language event with no evident difference in content from that of ordinary conversation—except for that incomprehensible vocabulary of glossolalia. Furthermore, prayer has no informational content about which it makes sense to talk to a God who knows everything.

3) Then there is the modern awareness of the impracticability of prayer. (Cf. Jacques Ellul's *Prayer and Modern Man.*) Biblical prayer assumed that one has power over demons, sickness, nature, and other people. Even when it failed to work that way, the eventual hope of its efficacy always seemed within reach when human resources failed. But, as in the cure for cancer, so in all other areas of life, relevance of this remote resourcefulness of prayer to vitally affect the conditions of life has, for all practical purposes, become altogether extinct, since almost everything can be accomplished by scientific technique. Con-

sequently, prayer as efficacious means has been made superfluous by the technology that replaced it, except, perhaps, inasmuch as it is considered good for one's psychological health.

4) No less problematic is the naturalistic assumption that the influence of a mighty ocean, a majestic mountain, a glorious sunset, or a terrible storm 'naturally' inspires worship of a Supreme Being. For the modern human has been educated by Marx, Nietzsche, and Freud to distrust his instinctive projections and oceanic feelings and to psychoanalyze that body of unexamined assumptions out of which transcendent moods are fabricated.

5) Nor have the many little technical advices and devices on breathing, fasting, journaling, and jogging convinced skeptics that the whole fuss and fumble is more than a subjective preoccupation.

6) Religious art, too, fails to convince those who see through it. Reynold's painting of "Little Samuel" depicts a charming child with dimpled face and pretty curls in a lovely blouse kneeling with chubby hands folded in graceful gesture as eyes are raised in ecstacy toward heaven, all of which reduces the drama of prayer "to the level of the pleasant, the consoling, the sweet, the banal, the ordinary. The prayer of little children is so nice" (Ellul, 8)—nice enough to serve bourgeois mentality as a sentimental cover-up for the reality of encountering God. Even Millet's "Angelus" appears problematic. In a field we see a dropped hoe, a half-filled sack of potatoes, and two peasants who momentarily interrupted their work to heed the call to prayer at the sound of the church bell. What can they produce but a brief automated formula ready for instant recitation, despite Jesus' disdain for "vain repetition"?

7) Most disconcerting of all is the pious misuse of prayer as a cheap evasion of the moral responsibility to be a true neighbor to one's fellow being.

III. *SPIRITUAL DYNAMICS*

PROPO-
SITIONS

We have reviewed ancient traditions and modern dilemmas of prayer. In what follows, we elucidate the spiritual dynamics of prayer within Jewish-Christian faith and faithfulness in the form of fourteen propositions, the inspiration for some of which derives indirectly from Buber and Heschel, especially, *Man's Quest for God*, as quotations indicate.

SPIRIT-
UAL
OBEDI-
ENCE

1) Prayer is an act of spiritual obedience. The prayer of faith, "Thy will be done," is incorporated into the freedom and determination of God. While we cannot fully resolve the dynamics between God's sovereignty and our responsibility, we do know that God loves us and desires our personal fellowship and therefore wills that we should pray—"without ceasing" (I Thes. 5:17).

BREATH
OF GOD

Praying is the event of being touched by the breath of God and thus becoming a living soul, the actuality of a spiritual "I" in relation to the "Thou" of God. In prayer, our relationship to God is both unconditionally exclusive and inclusive: the relationship of absolute intensity and purity into whom everything is potentially included and integrated in the ultimate awareness that the whole world is full of God—our God, who is at once wholly other and wholly present. God's reality implies the primacy of literal meaning beyond all metaphor and symbolism. Consequently, we address our prayers to the transcendent God beyond ourselves, not to an immanent good within ourselves. To stand before God means not only to believe that one believes but to know Whom one believes. When we know before Whom we stand, we also know with an incontrovertible inner certainty who we must be and what we must do in the world in God's Name.

Words of prayer are building blocks of spiritual reality; they do not describe a situation, they constitute it. For when I pray, I am the

SPIRIT-
UAL
REALITY reality I express. To speak to God is to fulfill the intention of the word by finding one's identity within it. Prayer is the mystery of God's word becoming man's word and the history of man's word becoming God's word. This primal language-event (*Wortgeschehen or Sprachereignis*) is awesome and overwhelming in its creative power and limitless claim.

EGO
TRAN-
SCEND-
ENCE 2) To pray in the Spirit is to transcend our ego and our mind in reach for what is of supreme importance: God Himself. To truly worship is to forget one's self and to rise to a higher level of existence in order to see the world from God's point of view. We have lost the power to pray inasmuch as we have lost the immanent awareness of God's reality and presence; and therefore we cling so desperately to our own.

SELF
SUR-
REN-
DER Through prayer we become detached from the triviality of our egoistic self to discover and recover our ultimate attachment to God. In this transition from self-consciousness to self-surrender we fulfill our highest spiritual aspiration of being at one with God and all his creatures. We are granted this grace as we acknowledge the simplicity and holiness of the good in all its dimensions and intentions in this life and in all its primal and infinite interrelationships.

CON-
SCIOUS-
NESS
OF GOD Through prayer the scattered rungs of our confused mind are ordered and the broken ladder of our dissipated consciousness is repaired, enabling our thoughts to mount to God in sacred participation in His redemptive will that informs and enlightens all our knowing and being with the radiance of His meaning and blessing.

THE
LIGHT
OF THE
HOLY In prayer we see ourselves in the light of the holy and understand our world and time from the perspective of eternity. This awareness frees us from the narrowness of self-interest to discern the vital from the futile, to clarify our most profound hopes, discover our true aspirations, and confirm our highest

intentions of knowing and doing God's will.

3) One who prays experiences fundamental transformation of the ego. The identity of the self no longer consists in self-perceptions, self-understandings, self-aspirations, or self-activities bounded by one's own abilities and liabilities. For in praying I experience the

EGO
TRANS-
FORM-
ATION

boundless: the boundlessness of creation and the boundlessness of relation. In prayer the whole meaning of my being is defined in relation not to myself but to God's self. Consequently, prayer frees me from the necessity to have or be something by which to define or defend my existence at all costs or over against all others. Prayer relieves one of the anxiety to survive by opening up the wonder of an awareness transcending personal fate.

4) To pray is to cultivate mindfulness of God. A Jewish rabbi pondered the dilemma of a shoemaker whose poor customers owned

MIND-
FUL-
NESS
OF GOD

but one pair of shoes which he repaired all night before they returned to work next morning. Finding no time for morning prayer, the devout shoemaker remorsefully sighed: "Woe is me, I haven't prayed yet!" The rabbi surmised that wholehearted regret is better than perfunctory performance if it awakens mindfulness of God at the margin of the soul.

To pray is to dwell on the edge of the cosmic mystery that sustains our world and to absorb the secret stillness that envelops our life before birth and after death, an awareness that fills us with pro-

COSMIC
MYS-
TERY

found gratitude for the inconceivable surprise of living. Through prayer we discover that the whole world is full of God in grateful praise, a fact so evident in the boundless imagination of the clouds, the unconquerable majesty of the mountains, the humble beauty of the flowers, and the eloquent melody of the birds.

Awareness of God at the boundary of existence also evokes in us first the desire and then the ability to answer that of God beyond

AWARE-
NESS
AND
RE-
SPONSE

and within us, even when there is no song in our heart. Even when our soul is wasting in weariness or woeful turmoil, we can still cry for help. And, as we do, we too arrive as latecomers in creation's choir to fill our place at the border of God's Presence, to be relieved of all our heaviness and all that keeps us from fully entering that celestial realm.

5) Prayer is not expedient, practicable, or useful. It is not a special utilization of supernatural means employed towards natural ends for

ONTO-
LOGI-
CAL
NECES-
SITY

the preservation or enhancement of life. "The purpose of prayer is not to satisfy an emotional need. Prayer is not a need but an ontological necessity, an act that constitutes the very essence of man. He who has never prayed is not fully human" (Heschel, 78). "To live without prayer is to live without God, without a soul. No one is able to think of Him unless he has learned to pray to Him" (59). "You need God in order to be and God needs you—for that which is the meaning of your life" (130). Prayer may not save us, but it will make us worth saving. Prayer is not just good for something, it is good in itself. Therefore prayer should not be misrepresented by social activism nor misused as a political function. Prayer as dialogue of the spirit is the highest expression of life. As we live and pray in the spirit, we respond with our whole being to the Thou of God while confirming and confronting that Thou in others in God's Name. *Yes!*

6) Prayer is an act of self-purification. It enables us to be honest, to stand for what we believe, to integrate our thought with our conscience, and to confirm our faith in the purity of truth and our trust

SELF-
PURI-
FICA-
TION

in the simplicity of the good. Prayer overcomes envy and fear, conquers despair and resentment, and resolves anguish and grief— melting by its warmth what is so hard in our life, relieving by its strength what weighs so heavily upon our heart, and dispelling by its light the shadows that tend to darken our pathway. Prayer is a light that makes visible the right, that reveals what is dubious and unworthy, that empowers us to recover the pearl of great price.

The purpose of prayer is not to inform God of our needs but to invite Him to rule our lives. Prayer is not a sermon addressed to God but an invocation to participate in His life. The intention of prayer is not to simplify our ideas so as to make them relevant to others, but to purify ourselves to make God relevant to us. The language of prayer consists not in the transliteration of words but in the transformation of selves, so that our prayers may be the soul's embodiment of the spirit in holiness and truth. Prayer is not simply a way of speaking but a spiritual openness to the Almighty to inform and transform us within the meaning of our whole being from God's point of view.

HOLI-NESS AND TRUTH

The discovery of prayer as the wellspring of life may come through affliction or tragedy that takes us out of life's presumptuous self-evidence, forcing us to the edge of precarious existence and compelling us to reexamine the meaning of our being from the perspective of the last day of our historicity. It is more natural, however, when contemplative prayer emerges as the very essence of spiritual life: as the fruit of a plant whose seed has matured in the soil of devout living and whose roots are anchored deeply in the ground of faith and faithfulness.

WELL-SPRING OF LIFE

7) However and whenever it happens, prayer is always the realization of our ultimate aspiration but never the product of our own inspiration. The awareness and nearness of the divine Presence is not our own achievement. Communication with God is not an act of our will but is the subject of His will. We may yearn and wait for it, but we do not and cannot bring it about. God is not at our disposal as an object of our thought. We can make ourselves communicable before God, but, when communication with God happens, it is the result of His, not our initiative. We participate vitally—not so much in knowing God as in being known by Him, not by elevating our thoughts and projecting our wills but in becoming part of God's

NOT OUR POSSES-SION

thought and will. Our inner participation is vital, but its nature is more passive than active.

To the thinker God is an object; to the pray-er God is the subject, the One to whom and by whom we are known and judged, affirmed and sustained within the dynamic quintessence of our own vital knowing and being. Our will enters this interrelationship in a

GOD IS decisively significant way, yet not as the primary effective factor.
SUBJECT We may open the gates, but we do not determine the entry. We
OF OUR experience the inspiration to pray, but we do not inspire its event.
PRAYER We produce the words we utter but not the enlightenment of the consciousness for which we yearn. Without this vital transition from the physical dimension to the metaphysical intention, even our highest words and thoughts ramble and roam aimlessly about our outer and inner world without finding God or being addressed by Him. In prayer we offer God the highest meanings of our simple thoughts and words which, transformed by His blessing and anointing, comprise the wisdom, faith, and faithfulness by which He sustains and redeems our world and life.

8) Our relation to God and others was meant to be unmediated.
UN- Mediation implies unfulfillment and estrangement requiring intra-
MEDI- vention to resolve contravention. Because God is one in His know-
ATED ing and being, all primary relations are immediate relations. This
PRES- *Unmittelbarkeit im Gottesverhältnis* marks the spiritual uniqueness
ENCE of Yeshua's *Sendungsbewusstsein* and constitutes the heart of the *kerygma*.

Through appropriation of the divine Presence we ourselves become present where we are on the ground of promise and fulfillment. The
ONE- present of God's Presence through our own happens as we become
NESS open and ready for God and for others in His Name. In the mystery of history our own potential oneness was meant to be included in God's essential oneness.

9) In praying through words we need to recover the dignity of words. The original function of speech was to address God directly and that of God in others indirectly. The self-consciousness of doing so arises at the point where the unity of the self in its primal identity is divided into subject and object, a division which, in sundering our speech, leaves us with sacred language that is largely irrelevant and with secular speech which is mostly irreverent.

DIGNITY OF WORDS

Words are meant to embody the fruit of spiritual insight and commitment (and not to be a mere mouthful of dust or refuse in the backyard of intelligence). Words of prayer are not made of dust or paper but are repositories of the living spirit, provided we rekindle the divine Light within the word and encounter the divine Presence within it. Words were not meant merely to describe a situation but to constitute it. In common speech it is we who speak the words, but in prayer the words themselves speak as they incarnate the spiritual power of the person. Words of prayer do not simply fall off one's lips as dead leaves fall off a tree in autumn but are meant to soar like birds of life from our heart through the universe to God.

WORDS AND SPIRIT

The words of prayer comprise an island of spiritual meaning which we rediscover and reinhabit as we develop the interrelationship between the concepts of the divine which transcend the bounds of our consciousness with the thoughts and feelings that comprise the habitation of our own souls. Just to express the unspeakable Name of God is to force our consciousness almost beyond its bounds, for that word itself is so much greater than our mind and the very moment we utter it we are overwhelmed by our unworthiness in the awareness that we have said so much more than we are capable of knowing or feeling.

SPIRITUAL MEANING

In the experience of praying we may intuit thoughts and feelings beyond our power of expression or empathy as God's own spirit fills our words with groanings that cannot be uttered. At such moments we realize that worship of the heart exceeds understanding with one's mind and that the highest function of the word is to serve as a messenger summoning us to meet God face to face. Our praying words should be consonant with the self if they are to reflect the concern of the self, but their goal and intention are to lead beyond all self-expression to the translation and transfiguration of the self in relation with and attachment to God. This spiritual formation transpires through the sanctification of our language.

10) Liturgy conducted with dignity, precision, and decorum can become monotonous, cold, stiff, and dead if it lacks the spontaneity of life itself. Everything may be on schedule as predicted in the bulletin except for that adventure of the soul in which one may shed a tear or invest a sigh. How can we prevent our churches from becoming the graveyard where the spontaneity of the spirit is buried? Heschel observes: "There are many who labor in the vineyard of oratory; but who knows how to pray, or how to inspire others to pray?" (50). He claims that "if the vast amount of time and energy invested in the search for ideas and devices for preaching, if the fire spent on the altar of oratory were dedicated to the realm of prayer, we would not find it so difficult to convey to others what it means to utter a word in the presence of God" (79). "Preaching is either an organic part of the act of prayer or out of place." "Preach in order to pray. Preach in order to inspire others to pray. The test of a true sermon is that it can be converted to prayer" (80).

SPONTANEITY AND LITURGY

In resorting to fixed liturgical prayers to compensate for our own lack of personal inspiration, there is always the danger of relying too heavily upon the text and of forgetting that no word from outside can replace or represent the spontaneity of our own soul. Limiting the expression of our spirituality to the repetition of liturgical prayers is like limiting our conversation of life to the rereading of old letters from deceased friends. It is more important to utter a few liturgical words with deep inner participation than mechanically to

THE TEXT AND THE SOUL

perform a long and impressive ceremony. "Ceremonies end in boredom, and boredom is the great enemy of the spirit" (114). A Jewish proverb says: "Better a little with *kavanah* (empathy) than much without it." Sometimes it may be necessary to stand still within the soul of a single word or expression that addresses us rather than recapitulate the whole pilgrimage of *Heilsgeschichte*, lest we become familiar with all the words but intimate with none.

TEXT AND FORM

When praying becomes an institution it ceases to be life. Institutions are necessary to give constancy to form. They constitute the cradle in which life transpires, but they cannot produce that life. Worship requires both the spontaneity of the spirit, without which the body is a corpse, and the discipline of the body, without which the spirit is a ghost. "The problem is not how to revitalize prayer; the problem is how to revitalize ourselves" (77). "A revision of the prayer book will not solve the crisis of prayer. What we need is a revision of the soul, a new heart rather than a new text" (84).

I-THOU RELA- TION

11) Private prayer requires for its survival and health the larger context of spiritual life within a community of prayer, for even though we pray as individuals, we represent before God the community of His people. Through prayer, awareness of God becomes the basis of authentic relation to all others. In those FOR whom I pray, I recognize and call forth the divine potential to which I address myself. And in those WITH whom I pray, I confirm my own identity in the formative oneness of God's own people. Those who pray for one another become spiritual friends, and those who pray together, stay together. This reality of meeting is not the result of search or research but the event of spiritual encounter. Furthermore, at the heart of every spiritual community there is meant to be a house of prayer or Poustinia, even as every Christian home needs at its formative center a specially consecrated prayer room.

12) To pray FOR the world means to believe IN the world. Since

HOLY WORLD-LINESS God's love embraces the whole world there is nothing within it that can separate us from Him. We are not saved apart from or out of this world but in, with, and through it. This world is the place where God speaks and acts always with many meanings. It is here that we are to discern our calling and vocation, not as an otherworldly awareness demanding that we step out of this world but as an inner-worldly presence of spiritual coexistence and coinsistence that transpires in the lived actuality of holy worldliness with the redemptive intention of conforming the whole of reality in His Name.

EXIS-TENTIAL SPIRIT Spirituality is always essentially an innerworldly affair involving the unsolved antinomy of being in but not of this world, a polarization that makes life dynamic with existential meaning. If we love the world as God loves it, we will not opt out of this committed *Gegenseitigkeit* prematurely by baptizing the whole world or spiritualizing only a part of it. Nor may we abandon the world by cultivating a pious inwardness on the assumption that God has been edged out of the real world into an otherworldly transcendence from which the church mediates divine sanction in the event of suffering, guilt, and death. That metaphysical and moral departmentalization of life exemplified by thinking in two spheres and living in two compartments on the strength of an otherworldly identity ignores Bonhoeffer's awareness—"Die mündige Welt ist gottloser und darum vielleicht gerade Gott-näher als die unmündige Welt"—and denies the incarnational truth that spirituality does not fragment man but makes him whole (*Widerstand und Ergebung*, 246).

SILENCE AND SPIRIT-UAL INTU-ITION 13) The ultimate response to the Thou of God in unbounded freedom of the spirit is silence. All other response binds that Thou into the It-world of verbal objectification. In the final analysis, genuine prayer begins where expression ends. It derives not from words but from spiritual intuition. Our words are but surface waves of a mighty incommunicable oceanic awareness of the incomprehensible mystery of God. To cultivate this awareness of God at the heart of our being we need to create an atmosphere of spiritual stillness, not just around us, but within us; not by talking about it, but by living in it.

One can imagine a world without speech, but one cannot imagine a world without silence. Silence constitutes the mystery surrounding

SILENCE every word and sustains the truth within the word. Without silence
MYS- there is no communication and no community—no forgetting, no
TERY forgiving, and no loving. Silence heals and makes whole what is
& fragmented and dissipated. In silence one recovers the autonomous
TRUTH meaning of one's being. Silence becomes holy as one returns the word to God and receives it back again as the original wonder of dialogical re-creation.

Verbal prayer aspires to dialogical encounter with God as person. Silent prayer ascends to a state of being in God beyond the realm of the senses. Words are crutches for the mind. The intention of true

DIVINE prayer is to get to God beyond our words. God is silent and it is
SILENCE through silence that we participate in His Being. God is silent and
IN THE His word expresses that event. *Gott redet auch dann wenn Er*
HUMAN *schweigt*! Only a word coming out of silence says something. Our
WORD speech was meant to express the divine silence in the human word. But, when the silence within the word is violated and the silence between the words is obliterated, the word itself is destroyed together with the faith, hope, and love it was meant to convey.

Standing between the silence from which we derive and that silence to which we return, our understanding is confronted by the

THE divine imperative: "Be silent before the Lord God" (Zep. 1:7 &
DIVINE Zec. 2:13), "Let all the earth keep silence before Him" (Hb. 2:20),
IMPER- "Be still and know that I am God" (Ps. 46:10), "Commune with
ATIVE your heart . . . and be still" (Ps. 4:4). May we understand what this
TO BE means and become still enough—especially in our worship—to
STILL hear God and to listen each other into life. "For God my soul waits in Silence" (Ps. 62:5).

14) The reality of prayer cannot be defined or contained. Even prayer "without ceasing" cannot contain God. The whole world full

SPIRIT- of God cannot contain Him, for God's strength is not a content at
UAL DY- our disposal nor His Presence a continuum within our control.
NAMICS What gives life its meaning one can find and lose but never possess. The pure relation of spirituality which permeates and embodies the whole stuff of life as dynamic community is not available as self-evident continuity. There is no guarantee for the contiguity of true being apart from real living.

The noödynamic of prayer in its perpetual movement, concentra-

SPONTA- tion, and direction never comes to rest as the available "isness" of
NEITY an "It" in cultic or creedal form, for the purpose of all spirituality is
OF LIFE to get beyond "it." Therefore, its highest symbols may not be reduced to its lowest terms. The spontaneity of dynamic life transcends all established order. Law holds the world together but love moves it forward.

Prayer is not an experience and when I pray it is not my experience.

SPIRIT- Prayer is an epistemological and ontological event in which I real-
UALITY ize and fulfill the meaning of my being in Almighty God, my Cre-
THEO- ator and Redeemer, who wills ultimately and therefore needs and
PHANY binds me im-mediately in gracious covenant to Himself. Conse-
ULTI- quently, our whole calling and mission as lived prayer becomes the
MACY & event of His theophany and our spiritual formation, on earth as it is
IMMED- in heaven. The ultimacy of all spirituality depends on its intrinsic
IACY immediacy—the secret dynamic of all spirit and life.

Spiritual formation transpires in the noödynamics of God's love as our worldly form embodies His eternal life.

Adapted with permission from my article entitled: "How Then Shall We Pray." *The Mennonite,* June 21/83, 292f.

OUR LORD'S PRAYER

FORM

Matthew 6:9-13 has the full address and seven petitions with a commentary on the fifth (vv. 13 & 14). The best MSS (B & X) omit the doxology. The three "thou" petitions followed by four "we" petitions reflect the pattern of the Decalogue with its two tables of duties to God and to men. In Matthew's version, the first couplet corresponds to the fifth, and the second to the fourth, while the central request for bread has no parallel and is the only statement not beginning with a verb.

Luke 11:1-4 omits the full address, the third and seventh petitions, and the doxology, and has variations in the fourth petition (e. g., *hēmeran*) and in the fifth (e. g., *hamartias*) with numerous poorly attested additions, such as the invocation of the Holy Spirit to cleanse us attached to the second petition.

The difficulty of harmonizing rhyme and meter in the reconstructed Aramaic *Vorlage* of both versions argues against a common source.

CONTEXT

Matthew placed the Lord's Prayer in his Sermon on the Mount within the didactic triad on Alms, Prayer, and Fasting (6:1-18): the basis for a new integrity in relation to God as one prays, to others as one gives, and to oneself as one fasts. In Matthew 6:5-8

Jesus contrasts the secrecy and brevity of true prayer with hypocritical publicity and Gentile verbosity.

According to Luke 11:1-4, the Lord's Prayer is Jesus' response to a disciple's request: "Teach us to pray, even as John taught his disciples." (The *Didache* [8:3] adds, "Three times daily shall ye pray thus.")

Matthew's version was for Jewish believers whose prayers had become routine. Luke's version was for Gentile Christians who needed first to learn how to pray.

Were the prayers of John, of the Essenes, of the Synagogue (e. g., the *Shemoneh Esreh*), and of the Psalms not accessible to the disciples or acceptable to Jesus?

OUR FATHER IN HEAVEN

Jesus instructed his disciples to pray not to himself but to God. Jesus was a Jew and prayed as a Jew. His Christian followers, however, are divided from Jews precisely by their prayers inasmuch as they pray to or through, rather than as, Jesus.

Deity is addressed as Father in Homer and in Sumerian prayers long before Moses and the prophets. The Old Testament speaks of God as Father on fourteen occasions. Malachi 1:6 reproves Israel for not giving God the honor a father deserves from his son. Isaiah 63:16 cries, "Thou, O Lord, art our Father, though Abraham does not know us and Israel does not acknowledge us."

Abba (Daddy) replaces the mystery of the Hebrew tetragram JHWH with the intimacy and trust of an infant. As a Jew, one would hesitate to address God in this familiar way. Jesus did it always—

except in his cry, "My God, why . . . ?" For him, the God far away ("in heaven" denotes transcendence, not location) was near at hand. According to Jesus, one enters the Kingdom only as a child (Lk. 18:17). "The Spirit bearing witness with our spirit" inspired the bilingual Aramaic-Greek usage of *abba 'o pater* (Rom. 8:16, Gal. 4:6) in both Jewish and Gentile churches.

1. HALLOWED BE THY NAME

"Exalted and hallowed be His great Name in the world He created according to His will"—so reads the ancient Hebrew prayer, the Kaddish (Holy), with which the synagogue in Jesus' day con-cluded its service. Together with the Jewish synagogue, the Chris-tian congregation anticipates the fulfillment of Ezekiel 36:23, "I will vindicate the holiness of my great Name . . . the nations will know that I am the Lord, says the Lord God, when through you I vindicate my holiness before their eyes."

"Hallowed be thy Name" expresses the paradox of Christian being both as imperative ("Ye shall be holy," Lv. 11:45) and as indicative ("Ye are holy in Christ"). God is holy, and by His Holy Spirit we become what we are in the wholeness of holiness through the cleansing of our lips and the transformation of our heart.

Jesus prayed, "Consecrate them in the truth . . ." (Jn. 17:19). Through ceremonial washing, anointing, and sacrificing it was to become clear that it is God and not man who sanctifies and conse-crates Israel, including places, objects, and persons. Beyond separa-tion from the unclean, sanctification implied re-creation, re-stora-tion, and re-demption within the covenant context through which the hidden mystery of God's holiness is revealed as the ideal of Israel—ontologically and existentially realized through Christ in the holy worldliness of sonship and discipleship.

2. THY KINGDOM COME

What does this second "thou" petition mean, and when and how is it to happen? How may we resolve the *schon jetzt aber noch nicht* (yet, not yet) of living in its presence while awaiting its appearance? Is it a unique once-for-all event or a universal truth? Does God Himself bring it about? If not, why not? If so, in what sense are we to work toward its realization?

How do we interpret and harmonize the following texts? The Kingdom of God is at hand (*eggiken*, Mk. 1:14). The Kingdom is within (in the midst of) you (*entos*, Lk. 17:21). My Kingdom is not of this world (Jn. 18:36). Blessed are the poor (in spirit) for yours (theirs) is the Kingdom (Lk. 6:20, Mt. 5:3). The sons of the Kingdom will be thrown into outer darkness (Mt. 8:12). Do not hinder (the children) for to such belongs the Kingdom of God (Mk. 10:14). Unless one is born anew he cannot see the Kingdom (Jn.3:3). Through many tribulations we must enter the Kingdom (Acts 14:22). Flesh and blood cannot inherit the Kingdom (I Cor. 15:50).

In the words of the Kaddish, the Jewish soul prays: "May He rule His Kingdom in your lifetime and in your days and in the lifetime of the whole house of Israel, speedily and soon."

3. THY WILL BE DONE ON EARTH AS IN HEAVEN

This third "thou" petition (only in Mt.) reflects the agony of Gethsemane. Luther called it *"ein schrecklich Gebet"* (a fearful, terrible prayer). With these words, Paul declared his readiness "not only to be imprisoned but even to die at Jerusalem for the name of the Lord Jesus" (Acts 21:13). These were the last words of Polycarp and countless other martyrs. When Jonah during that storm at sea was asked by the ship's captain why he alone did not pray, Jonah allegedly replied, "There is no prayer . . . that my God will hear unless I am prepared to do His will" (*The Burden of Nineveh*).

Compare Socrates' last words before he drank the hemlock, "Leave me then, Crito, to fulfill the will of God, and to follow where He leads" (Great Books 7:219), with those of Jesus in Gethsemane: "Abba, Father, all things are possible to thee; remove this cup from me; yet not what I will, but what thou wilt" (Mk. 14:36).

If all things exist and happen by God's will (Rv. 4:11), even to birds and lilies (Mt. 6:26ff.) and to the hairs of our head (Mt. 10:30), why is there this "terrible" conflict of will expressed by Jesus? Is this petition so "frightful" because we presume to be persons of good will? Must one's will be broken or suppressed in order that God's will "be done on earth as in heaven"? If not, why not? If so, does this petition not thwart our personality and lead to resignation and fatalism?

Paul said: "He has made known to us . . . the mystery of His will . . . to unite all things in Him, things in heaven and things on earth" (Eph. l:9f.).

Peter said: "It is God's will that by doing right you should put to silence the ignorance of foolish men. Live as free men, yet without using your freedom as a pretext for evil; but live as servants of God" (I Pt. 2:15f.). "Let those who suffer according to God's will entrust their souls to Him" (I Pt. 4:19).

John said: "The world passes away . . . but he who does the will of God abides forever" (I Jn. 2:17). "This is the confidence which we have in Him, that if we ask anything according to His will He hears us" (I Jn. 5:14).

4. GIVE US . . . OUR BREAD

In Matthew the first "we" petition reads: "Our bread for tomorrow give us today." Luke substitutes for the aorist imperative *dos* (which denotes a single action) the present imperative *didou* (which means "keep on giving") thereby expanding "this day" to "each day," a generalization which literally means "Keep on giving us our daily bread for tomorrow" in keeping with the request, "Give us this bread always" (Jn. 6:34).

Origen (d. 254) interpreted this petition metaphysically as a plea for spiritual bread (on the assumption that *epiousion* was derived from *epi ousia* which, with some imagination, could be translated "ground of being," implying that "bread" was a metaphor for *logos*).

Jerome (d. 420) emphasized the eschatological dimension of the petition on the assumption that it focuses not so much on the next day as on the great Tomorrow of the final day. Accordingly, "bread for the coming day" (from the Aramaic *mahar*) means "bread of life" and points to the "bread of heaven" which those whom Jesus appointed will eat with him at the messianic banquet (Lk. 22:30) in his Kingdom which has already come near (Mk. 1:15) and is present in the Eucharist. This petition then urges us to realize today (Mt: *sēmeron*) and daily (Lk: *hēmeran*) the eschatological reality of that Tomorrow (*epiousion*), for "daily bread" acquires its Christian significance from the "Last Supper."

Gregory of Nyssa (4th cen.) and Chrysostom (d. 407) interpreted this petition to mean that Christians may ask only for the bare necessities of the body, only for the rough barley loaf required to satisfy one's hunger, whereas, Luther held that it includes everything that furthers nourishment and physical well-being for one's self and one's friends!

Do we assume that Christians owning property, bank accounts, insurance policies, and retirement funds can as sincerely and authentically pray for "bread" as if they were careless about such investments?

For breaking bread with tax collectors and sinners Jesus was derided by the Orthodox as "a glutton and a drunkard" (Mt. 11:19). To them he responded: "Many will come from the East and the West and sit down with Abraham, Isaac, and Jacob in the Kingdom of heaven, while the sons of the Kingdom will be thrown into outer darkness" (Mt. 8:11f.). Why do we celebrate "communion" only with saints when Jesus himself communed with sinners?

5. FORGIVE US . . . AS WE FORGIVE

Matthew 6:12 reads: "Forgive us our *debts* as we also have forgiven (perfect) our debtors." Verses 14 and 15 qualify what is to be forgiven, in both instances, as "trespasses." In Matthew 5:24 Jesus urges: "First be reconciled to your brother" before coming to the altar.

Luke 11:4 records: "Forgive us our *sins,* as we ourselves forgive (present) every one who is indebted to us."

Mark 11:25 states: "Forgive if you have anything against any one; so that your Father also who is in heaven may forgive you."

Is the emphasis of this petition upon obtaining or proclaiming forgiveness?

Does the reference to human activity (only here in the Lord's Prayer) intend a comparison, imply a condition, or indicate an effect?

In what sense is true forgiveness (God's and ours) conditional or unconditional? What about insisting on genuine repentance?

6. LEAD US NOT INTO TEMPTATION

If the causative verb has a permissive nuance implying, "Let us not fall into temptation" for "God tempts no one" (Jas. 1:13), how are we to understand the divine initiative in the temptation of Abraham (Gn. 22) and of Jesus (Mt. 4:1)?

What constitutes "temptation"? Should we pray for exemption from it or perseverence in it?

7. DELIVER US FROM EVIL

What is the nature (external/internal) of "the evil" (one) from which we seek deliverance, and how do we enable God to answer our petition?

DOXOLOGY

"For thine is the Kingdom and the power and the glory for ever, Amen" occurs first in the *Didache* (2nd cen.) as the triumphant response of believers affirming the realization of these petitions in their lives. May our witness confirm theirs.

Reprinted by permission from *The Mennonite*, Oct. 30/79, 644f.

RECOVERING JESUS' WORD AND WAY

1. WHAT WE KNOW ABOUT JESUS

We know that Jesus was a Jew, that he was a child of Jewish parents, that he was brought up in a Jewish home, that he spoke the Jewish language, was reared in Jewish tradition, lived all his life among Jews, and that all his followers were Jews.

We know that Jesus' life was relatively short and that it ended in great suffering and violent death. There is great mystery about the nature of the beginning of this life and about the reason for its ending, and, unless we intuitively comprehend something of this mystery, we shall never really know anything about Jesus.

Jesus differed from other men in that at an early age he found a reason to live by and die for. Most people try to outlive Jesus, try to live as long and as well as possible. And even at a late age most do not find a reason for living—a meaning big enough to live by and great enough to die for. Consequently, most people merely exist to maintain their vacuous existence at any cost and in hopeless conflict with others.

Jesus differed from other men in that he really knew WHO God was (most people do not) and because he really knew WHO HE himself was (most people do not). Jesus knew who SENT him and hence knew his CALLING and VOCATION (most people do not). This knowledge of GOD and SELF in the concreteness of life constitutes SONSHIP and DISCIPLESHIP.

What we really know about Jesus biographically is very little. We have no picture of him, no letters, not even a fragment of his own handwriting. We have no description of his appearance or size, no particle of his clothing, and no indications of his habits or preference in food, shelter, or attire. All those things which matter so much to most people seemed to matter so little to him. What we know about Jesus in these respects is very little— and it matters very little—for the greatest of spirits cannot be described in the smallest of terms.

But, about what really matters in life, about what really mattered to Jesus, about what he lived by and died for and about what we can believe and hope, about THIS we know a GREAT DEAL from Jesus. We know this through his teaching, especially in the Sermon on the Mount.

2. THE MOUNTAIN SAYINGS

The Sermon on the Mount (or *Berglehre Jesu*) is the most important, most quoted, and most debated text of the Bible. Matthew's version (chaps. 5-7) and Luke's (6:20-49) differ as to what Jesus said, when he said it, from where, to whom, and why. Its original content was inseparable from its context, and questions concerning its making, manner, and matter are all interrelated even as our understanding of what Jesus meant is interrelated with our own self-understanding and that of those to whom these words were first addressed.

Jesus was in Galilee, teaching in the synagogues, proclaiming the Kingdom, and healing the sick; and, as his fame spread widely, great crowds gathered from everywhere. Seeing the multitudes, he went up a mountain. His disciples came to him, and he taught them. Jesus' mountain teaching had a profound effect both on his disciples and on the multitudes.

3. SELIGPREISUNGEN

The Sermon on the Mount begins with Beatitudes (*Selig-*

preisungen) or, simply, "Beautiful Words" of which there are eight in Matthew and four in Luke. In Matthew the first four blessings are upon the poor (the poor "in spirit," the mourners, the meek, and those who hunger and thirst). The next three blessings (upon the merciful who shall obtain mercy, upon the pure in heart who shall see God, and upon the peacemakers who shall be called sons of God) concern relations between God and man and between fellow beings. The final blessing is upon the persecuted. In Matthew, the Kingdom of heaven is associated with the poor in spirit and with the persecuted.

Luke omits the five beatitudes of character (the mourners, the meek, the merciful, the pure in heart, the peacemakers) and supplies four woes parallel to the four blessings of condition (blessed are the poor, the hungry, the weeping ones, and those who are hated; woe to the rich, the full, the laughing ones, and those of whom it is well-spoken).

These blessings are very profound and convey a wealth of meaning. They are not mere pious sentiments, but they intrinsically embody the reality of hope realized through Jesus. The blessedness promised is the life of God Himself revealed in the character of Jesus, who becomes poor, meek, lowly, pure in heart, a peacemaker and man of sorrows. But Jesus is speaking not only about himself. The reality he professes is also that of his disciples who are so "poor in Spirit" that they have nothing but Jesus and so blessed that in him they have everything.

The first blessing immediately raises many unfathomable questions: Is God always on the side of the poor? Or did Jesus refer to spiritual poverty? If so, is the Spirit the object or the subject of poverty? Are we to be poor in self-esteem, self-reliance, self-confidence? How would that qualify us for the Kingdom? Are the poor blessed in that they are '*geistreich*', especially endowed with Holy

Spirit? Why then speak of this as a 'second' blessing when it is the first? In what sense are these blessings meant to inform our faith and affect our life? To WHOM do they apply, HOW, and WHEN? Does one understand JESUS when one understands his blessings? Or the reverse? WHEN does one understand THAT one understands? WHAT does one understand WHEN one understands? HOW does one understand WHAT one understands? WHOM does one understand when one understands JESUS? What does it MEAN to understand HIM?

4. PIETY, SIMPLICITY, AND INTEGRITY

In Matthew 6:1-18 Jesus establishes the basis of a new integrity in relation to God when one prays, in relation to others when one gives, and in relation to the self as one fasts so that charity is no longer a matter of social prestige "in order to be seen," so that prayer is no longer performed with an eye to public scrutiny, and so that fasting is more than an exercise in public relations. Hence, charity, piety, and asceticism assume intrinsic meaning and acquire real character in the life of a disciple of Jesus.

Throughout the *Berglehre*, Jesus addressed himself to various aspects of life. The sayings on Treasures (Mt. 6:19-21), on the Single Eye and on Serving Two Masters (vv. 22-24), and on Cares (vv. 25-34) concern the simplicity and integrity of authentic living. The sayings on Judging (Mt. 7:1-5), on the Pearls (v. 6), and on the Golden Rule (v. 12) concern the relation of disciples to unbelievers. Others, such as those about the Two Ways (vv. 13-14) and the False Prophets, articulate the great divide. There are warnings against the self-deception of those who cry "Lord" but do not what he says (vv. 21-23) and admonitions to build one's life upon a solid foundation (vv. 24-27)—all of which amazed and astonished the people witnessing his teaching and authority.

5. SIX ANTITHESES

Jesus came not to relax or abolish the Law but to radicalize and fulfill it. The extraordinary qualities or characteristics of the new obedience he demands are expressed in six Antitheses (Mt. 5) regarding 1) Wrath or Reconciliation, 2) Adultery or Purity, 3) Divorce or Fidelity, 4) Swearing or Truthfulness, 5) Retaliation or Nonresistance, and 6) Enmity or Brotherhood. In each case the higher way is indicated.

"It was said," Do not MURDER, "But I say," Do not ANGER! (5:21-26). Jesus prohibits insult, scorn, and disdain, for anger leads to murder; Jesus declares sacrificial rites pointless so long as unforgiving relationships prevail and urges offenders to be reconciled quickly before they appear before the Great Judge.

"It was said," Do not ADULTERATE, "But I say," Do not LUST! (27-29). The Torah forbade adultery of the body. Jesus forbade adultery of the eye, for, when one's eye becomes an instrument of impurity, one cannot see God. Lust is impure because it is unbelief which leads to Gehenna, not to life in God's Kingdom. With this Antithesis to the seventh commandment, Jesus intends a whole new world of positive interrelationships in which men and women are no longer objects of lust and exploitation but coheirs of the grace of life.

"It was said," Divorce only LEGALLY, "But I say," Divorce NOT AT ALL! (31-32). Moses provided legal documents to protect divorced women. Jesus appealed to the will of the Creator who enables husbands and wives to live in covenant faithfulness. Jesus did not permit divorce under certain circumstances, for he did not provide exception to God's will. Jesus denounced the Mosaic concessions to human weakness which allowed Jewish husbands to justify their unfaithfulness by legalizing it. Jesus forbade divorce and denounced remarriage of divorcées as adultery. Many do not like what he said. Only few admit it. The rest distort his words to suit their intentions.

"It was said," Do not swear FALSELY. "But I say," Swear NOT AT ALL! (33-37). Let your 'yes' be yes and your 'no' no, for oaths are imposed for wicked ends. "It was said," An eye for an eye and a tooth for a tooth, "But I say," Resist NOT with evil, turn the other cheek, go the second mile (38-42). Finally, "It was said," Hate your enemy, "But I say," Love your enemy (43-48) and make no distinction between countrymen and foreigners, for God is kind to all, and we are to be like Him.

6. MODIFICATIONS AND MISINTERPRETATIONS

One way to live with these 'hard' sayings is to MODIFY them. Tolstoy observed that in the fifth century the text of Jesus' first Antithesis was tampered with by redactors who inserted (in v. 22) the qualification, *eikē*, meaning "needlessly" or "without a cause." Thus, Jesus' UNconditional statement ("Whoever is angry with his brother shall be liable to judgment") was modified to a CONDITIONAL statement ("Whoever is angry . . . without a cause"). Tolstoy was amazed to note that the Fathers in expounding this text concentrated mostly on defining those causes for which anger could be legitimized by citing in support of their opinions instances of the anger of apostles and saints. As a result, each person became his own judge as to whether his own anger was justifiable and not "without a cause," to the effect that, inasmuch as anger is caused, each person claimed his own anger to be both lawful and necessary.

Similarly, Jesus' third command, "Do not divorce" has been altogether obscured. Almost without exception, the so-called Matthean 'except clause' has, in the history of interpretation, been

misinterpreted as an exception to Jesus' unconditional prohibition of
divorce. In contrast to Moses, Jesus did not sanction divorce in case
of unchastity. He did not assume that one infidelity justifies another.
Jesus did not make concessions to human sinfulness. Jesus said that
the husband who dismisses his wife thereby "makes her an adulteress"—except when she herself commits adultery, in which 'exceptional' case, she herself is at fault. Even then, Jesus counsels neither
divorce nor stoning but repentance and reconciliation. But most
interpreters annul the contrast between Jesus' demand and Moses'
concession so as to accommodate existing evils.

As for "Swear not at all," most commentators insist that this
commandment is not obligatory and that it never applies to the oath
of allegiance which every responsible Christian is obliged to swear.
The problem of conscience is mostly absolved by swearing upon the
Bible, thereby kissing this text instead of obeying it.

Most Christians concur that Jesus' teaching is an impossible
ideal which, if taken too seriously, would drive us mad and which, if
applied too literally, would destroy the social, political, and economic institutions of our life which we have set up so well and hold so
dear. It is commonly assumed that the Sermon on the Mount, if
applied too consistently, would surely threaten our life, destroy our
liberty, and interfere with our pursuit of happiness.

7. THE DOUBLE STANDARD

A notable effort to preserve the radical character of the Sermon on the Mount without being threatened by its implications is
the classical DOUBLE STANDARD approach. In this way the
Constantinian Church of the fourth century declared Jesus' words to
be a counsel of perfection for a select few, not an unconditional
command for all. Those who could not reconcile their conscience
with compromise solutions were advised to retreat out of the world

into the monastery and there to live their Christian life uncompromisingly. The poverty, chastity, and nonviolence which were so impracticable for the masses thus became the meritorious achievement of a few. By an ingenious division of labor the laity could fight the carnal wars while the clergy fought the spiritual battles. The laity produced earthly goods and received in exchange spiritual blessings—each contributed according to his ability and each received according to his need to meet all the demands of nature and spirit and to guarantee the symbiosis of Church and State in their cultural function.

8. LUTHER AND CALVIN

Martin Luther rejected the two-level ethic of Roman Catholic morality as a mock solution threatening the unity of the Christian conscience. Luther left the monastery and returned to the world, not because the world was better but because the cloister itself had become a subtle form of self-deceit. Luther insisted that every Christian must do what is necessary to maintain the world within the secular office. Since man needs protection for himself, his family, and his country, Luther exempted the political office (the *Amt*) from having to conform to the Rule of Christ. Though sensing a certain uneasiness about requiring Christians to kill rather than to love their enemies, Luther argued that soldiers too can be saved. The assumption that the state is somehow 'ordained' of God sufficed to guarantee that for Christians military service qualified as *Gottesdienst* (Christian service). "Not I beat and stab and kill (said Luther) but God and my Prince, whose servant my hand and my life are." Within Luther's *Zwei-Reiche-Lehre* the two-level ethic of Catholicism is internalized, resulting in the schizophrenic departmentalization of the Christian person.

Calvin did not allow the sentiments of Jesus to interfere with whatever seemed expedient within the theocracy of Geneva. He resolved the conflict between love and war (in his *Institutes*) by giving priority to the examples of Israel's judges over the teaching of Jesus.

The Reformers assumed the intact symbiosis of Church and State within the *corpus christianum* and did not expect the only partially Christian society to practice the ethic of Jesus. Given the sinfulness of the world and the impracticability of the way of absolute love, secular proximations of relative justice were given priority over distinctly Christian principles. Protestantism offered a reformulation of the problem but no solution.

9. APOCALYPTICISM AND DISPENSATIONALISM

Johannes Weiss and Albert Schweitzer developed the ingenious theory that Jesus intended his Antitheses as INTERIM-ETHIC valid only for the brief moment of history before the imminent Kingdom of God would be realized supernaturalistically, when the dead believers would be resurrected, living believers metamorphosed, and all unbelievers judged and destroyed. Since Jesus was mistaken and none of that happened, we should not apply his teaching to present circumstances and tasks which he never envisioned and for which his words were not intended. Though Jesus may guide our faith, he cannot rule our life.

An inverted version of this eschatological evasion is the DISPENSATIONALIST view which relegates the imperatives of Jesus not to the past but to a future millennium when Jesus' teaching is to be applied by unbelieving Jews after all the Christians have been raptured. This sophistry allows Fundamentalists the advantage of defending a literal interpretation of Jesus' commands while postponing the application of loving one's enemies until a future millennium when there are not supposed to be any. From the Gospels, one does not gather the impression that Jesus intended for those whom he called to postpone their obedience that long.

10. MISUNDERSTANDINGS AND EVASIONS

Rudolf Bultmann informed us that Jesus did not tell us
WHAT to do (that would be sheer legalism) but HOW to do it,
namely, completely and unreservedly. Jesus' Antitheses, we are told,
do not demand new content, only new thoroughness. He who knows
THAT also knows HOW, for "The moment of decision contains all
that is necessary for the decision." It is assumed that Jesus, being an
'existentialist', gave us no specific commands, no criteria for right
action, no values, no content at all, no ethic at all. While it is true
that Jesus' demand for personal integrity exceeds that measure of
response expressed by formulated commandments, this spiritualistic
refusal to concretize discipleship in history paves the way for a "situation ethic" which no longer feels the need to be instructed and
corrected by the Word. As Bultmann applied to Jesus his own modern, non-Jewish dialectic, so countless philosophers and theologians
have imputed to Him their own half-truths and prejudices so as to
justify their own mentality by identifying it with the Jesus upon
whom they superimposed their own self-understanding.

In surveying the history of the interpretation of the Sermon on
the Mount, one is overwhelmed by the church's theological ingenuity in developing almost convincing explanations why, for example,
Christians should not or could not love their enemies. All these
learned explanations for why Jesus' teaching applies either to a different time than now or in a different way than then create the dubious impression that Jesus either did not say what he meant or did not
mean what he said, as if Jesus, though wanting to say the right thing,
did not know how! The complexity of biblical hermeneutics can
create the specious impression that the difficulty is in the area of
intellectual comprehension rather than in the realm of personal commitment. Upon hearing people complain how hard it is to understand the Bible, Mark Twain allegedly confessed that he was both-
ered more by those parts he understood than by those he did not.

The difficulty of understanding Jesus is not unrelated to the difficulty of following him.

11. WORD AND WAY

The plain teachings of Jesus on The Way have been divorced from life and are mostly held to be either inaccessible or irrelevant. In the lectionaries and liturgies of the great churches the sayings of Jesus have been largely replaced by dogmatic creeds taught and read as prayers. The emphasis is not on the teaching (*didache*) OF Jesus but on the preaching (*kerygma*) ABOUT Christ. Jesus' teaching on the WAY (*'odos*) of the Cross has been replaced by Paul's proclamation of the WORD (*logos*) of the Cross with the effect that the offense of the Cross has been transferred from the existential to the epistemological plane so that the personal command to FOLLOW JESUS has become an intellectual problem of BELIEVING in CHRIST. That following Jesus is presumptuous and unnecessary is implicit in the logic of most atonement theories which distract from the fact that the meaning of Jesus is to be sought in his own teaching, the truth of which "is not too hard for you, neither is it far off. It is neither in heaven nor beyond the sea. It is in your mouth and in your heart, so that you can do it" (Dt. 30:11f.).

To follow Jesus is to recover his WAY through his WORD.

THE QUEST FOR THE REAL JESUS

As a basis for discussion I wish first to present a Jewish understanding of Jesus, then to examine how Christian understanding differs, and finally to indicate the direction my own quest is taking.

I

Jesus was a Jew. He was a child of Jewish parents. He was brought up in a Jewish home. He was reared among Jewish traditions. All his life he lived among Jews. BUT his teaching was anti-Jewish. He advocated beliefs no Jew could hold. Therefore, the Jews rejected him and reject him still. Our first task is to discern with utmost clarity the reason for this rejection.

Jesus lived in a century of violent political conflict. From 165 B. C. (beginning of the Maccabean wars) up to 36 A. D. (end of Pilate's procuratorship), 200,000 Jews—the prime of the nation physically, intellectually, and culturally—had fallen in persistent conflict with Rome.

Those who survived and still possessed strength and vitality joined the Zealots (as did Barabbas, Judas, and Simon) while the weak, vapid, and halfhearted (who like Jesus were "not of this world") turned their eyes from political realities to preoccupy themselves with religious speculation and mystical vision. They studied Torah for its own sake and comforted the people with their knowledge of God and with hope of salvation from some meteoric miracle. In so doing, they undermined Jewish national religion and gave rise to that otherworldly spiritualism known as Christianity.

Those who had returned from exile did so on the promises of
Jeremiah and Second Isaiah that kings would be their nursing moth-
ers and providers. Instead, they suffered only slavery to foreign
powers. There was to have been universal peace, but they knew only
tumult and bloodshed. All nations were to bow down to them and
pay lowly homage. Instead, Judah remained subject to her enemies
under the ruthlessness of Edom. Jerusalem's foundations were to
have been sapphires as Judah was to thrive on the riches of the Gentiles. Instead, she experienced only oppressive economic exploitation by Roman tax and tribute. Instead of Messiah son of David
there was only Herod the Edomite, who exploited the nation's very
life and blood to satisfy his boundless lust for fame and glory.
Instead of the bright prophetic ideal, there was only the dark political reality.

The situation was beyond endurance. In the young and able
this antithesis between the ideal and the real evoked an unsuppress-
ible national zeal. They became fearless Zealotic freedom fighters,
while Jesus, as the Essenes at Qumran, concentrated on the shining
spheres of perfection in another world. Unable to cope with the realities of the present they concentrated on the future, spinning golden
threads of messianic hope and promise for the meek, poor, destitute,
lost, outcast, miserable, and penitent.

It was from these circles of the meek that the teaching of
Jesus sprang. Lacking the resources to resist denationalization, the
simple and downtrodden found release from their sufferings in this
world in the proclamation of a Kingdom of heaven by a son of a
carpenter from Galilee.

The common masses, having been brought up on pseude-
pigrapha replete with messianic apocalypses, imagined they saw in
every wonder-worker and preacher their prospective ruler and saviour. At first, these disillusioned people also saw in Jesus their

King-Messiah—their supernatural political saviour from the Roman yoke which pressed so hard upon them, that bondage which constituted an insult to the God of Israel. But, once Jesus advised giving to Caesar what is Caesar's and proclaimed a Kingdom not of this world, he lost his popularity. Since Jesus betrayed their expectation, the masses fell back to the bar Kochbas and Barabbas who in self-sacrifice pitted themselves against the kingdom of Rome. Their one crime was that they acted according to conscience, their own misfortune that they were no match against the world's greatest power.

Jesus broke down Jewish faith and undermined Jewish loyalty. He lacked patriotic feeling and hence became a stranger to his people in their longing for freedom from Roman subjection. The Jewish soul abhorred a son of man who shared their identity but not their national sorrow or hope.

In Judaism the Kingdom of heaven never conflicted with national security, political progress, and economic prosperity. Jesus simply lacked that fundamental quality of Jewish optimism. In his love for poverty and austerity, dislike of oaths, and specialization in exorcism he was a typical Essene, except for their scruples about cleanliness.

Like Hindu and Egyptian priests, Jesus cared only about the afterlife, ignoring the demands of this life and its social order. Nothing mattered to him but heaven and the future life, so he went to meet it willingly without any responsibility for his people or nation. He loved those who murdered him because they benefited him by killing him who was not of this world.

Judaism is a way of life on earth. Jesus offered a hope only for heaven. He prepared us not to live in this world but to die for the next world. Judaism is concrete and realistic. Jesus was abstract and theoretical. In Judaism religion, people, and land constitute an inseparable whole. Jesus emphasized only spiritual not economic or political redemption, thereby isolating religion from its national roots and national destiny. Judaism insists on human dignity. Jesus preached a pusillanimous passivity that resists not evil but invites murder and massacre.

How can a state endure if it abolishes the oath? How can a culture prosper when its investors are condemned for being camels that cannot squeeze through the needle's eye of austerity? How can a people survive when its eunuchs are idealized? Jesus' teaching intended the ruin of national culture, the ruin of national politics, the ruin of national civilization, and the ruin of national life. Jewish religion sought to save the tiny nation, guard its great ideals, keep it from sinking into paganism, and slowly enable it to realize in the civil life of the Jewish state and nation the moral teaching of its prophets. But, by an incongruity of circumstances, Judaism produced Jesus, who with a deadly kiss sought to kill the very life and hope of his people. Therefore, the Jews rejected him and reject him still.

The Jews had already suffered enough. They could not follow a shepherd who led his flock to the slaughterhouse of Edom. "So the chief priests and Pharisees gathered the council and said 'What are we to do? . . . If we let him go on thus, everyone will believe in him, and the Romans will come and destroy both our temple and our nation' " (Jn. 11:47-48). Given the option of sacrificing either Jesus or the national cause, the 'responsible' Jews concluded that it were better that one man die for the people and that he die for his own convictions as messianic pretender to the throne of David—an indictment no Roman governor would fail to take with utmost seriousness.

What the Jews understood about Jesus is this: that to follow him is too costly. This is the integrity of Jews in rejecting Jesus over against the hypocrisy of Christians who claim him as Lord but do not what he says. That, however, is not the only difference between Christians and Jews.

II

How then does the Christian understanding of Jesus differ from that of the Jews? At first, the only difference was that the Jews believed the Messiah was still to come, while the Christians believed he had already come.

The Jews awaited a Messiah like Moses, who would redeem his people not through defeat but through victory, not in weakness but in strength, not by his blood but by his power. In the Old Testament the content of hope, like the claim of covenant, is not theoretical but concrete. Redemption is not otherworldly but historical, not metaphysical but economic, not merely spiritual but also political. Israel's redemption from Egypt and Israel's calling to practice righteousness, peace, and brotherhood in Canaan were deeply rooted in the promise of the land, not in hope of heaven, in the givenness of the earthly Jerusalem, not in a vision of a heavenly Jerusalem. But Jesus did NOT redeem Israel politically. He suffered and died as a criminal. Therefore, Christians concluded that Jesus never meant to deliver Israel in any other way than spiritual—for his Kingdom was not of this world. Does the conclusion follow?

Contrary to all expectations, Jesus suffered a most scornful death. From this, Christians concluded that God willed his death as a ransom. Does the conclusion follow? To explain the purpose of such a will of God, Jesus' suffering was held to be vicarious and his death atoning to redeem mankind from original sin. Since the Messiah could not end in shameful death, Christians proclaimed that God raised him from death and that he, unlike others, is immortal. "Though we once regarded Christ from a human point of view we regard him thus no longer" (II Cor. 5:16), the Jesus "who was put to death for our trespasses and raised for our justification" (Rom. 4:25), for in this way "God was in Christ reconciling the world to himself" (II Cor. 5:19).

Jews believe one is saved by repentance and good works. This is what John the Baptist preached, and this is what Jesus preached. There was nothing otherworldly about that! But Paul concluded that, since the people killed the prophets and rejected Jesus and since he himself persecuted Jesus' disciples, all human works are evil and Jesus alone did the one good work, the supernatural work, of dying for our sins. Hence, man is justified not by works but "through faith in Jesus Christ" (Gal. 2:16), *sola fide, sola gratia.* Does the conclusion follow?

Jesus often spoke of his Father in heaven in poetic, figurative language typical of Judaism. Gentiles interpreted this to mean that Jesus was genetically related to God who fathered him—a belief expressed in the doctrine of his virgin birth, that is, Mary's conception by the Holy Spirit.

The great divide concerns the meaning of SON of God. Jews regard this a functional designation equivalent to SERVANT of God and referring primarily to the servant PEOPLE and hence in no way conflicting with the fundamental premise of Jewish faith: Monotheism—"The Lord our God is one" (Dt. 6:4). However, in their polemic against the Jews, Christians extended the claim that Jesus is the Messiah to imply that Jesus is God, that is, both God and man, having two natures, divine and human, unmixed, unchanged, indivisible, inseparable. In this way the great councils of Christendom replaced Jewish personal and functional meanings with hellenistic metaphysical and ontological categories.

Since Jesus did not eradicate evil and restore mankind, Christians hold that he will return to do in the future what he failed to do in the past. This hope for the future Jews and Christians have in common except that for Jews the coming Redeemer can be God alone, for Christians he must be Jesus alone.

Jesus, as John the Baptist, proclaimed "The Kingdom of God is at hand" (Mt. 3:2). But, since it did not come during Jesus' life, his disciples expected it at his death and were disillusioned when world and time continued. Paul undertook to explain why the King came but not his Kingdom, though he hoped to witness it during his life-time and admonished the churches, "Brethren the appointed time has grown very short" (I Cor. 7:29). But, when Paul also died without witnessing it, scoffers were everywhere saying, "Where is the promise of his coming? For since the fathers fell asleep all things have continued as they were from the beginning" (II Pt. 3:4). Peter then took up the defense with the consoling explanation, "With the Lord one day is a thousand years" (v. 8)—an explanation not soon to be outdated but hard to reconcile with Jesus' promise. "Truly I say to you, there are some standing here who will not taste death before they see the Son of Man coming in his Kingdom" (Mt. 16:28).

This survey of theological problems suffices to show how Christians differ from Jews in their dogmatic understanding of WHO Jesus was and WHY he died.

III

Despite all these differences, what Christians have in common with Jews is their rejection of Jesus' teaching. In surveying the history of the interpretation of the Sermon on the Mount, one is overwhelmed by the church's theological ingenuity in developing explanations why Christians either should not or could not love their enemies. The teachings of Jesus are either idealized as impossible (Naumann) or secularized as irrelevant (Fletcher), either eschatologized as *Ausnahmegesetzgebung* (Schweitzer) or dispensationalized as futuristic (Chafer), either legalized as *praeparatio evangelica* (Luther) or spiritualized as mystic experience (Spener), either individualized as personal ethic (Niebuhr) or universalized *Lebensweisheit* (Fichtner), either demythologized as *Selbstverständ-*

nis (Bultmann) or divinized as *Sakrament* (Städeli), either historicized as *zeitbedingt* (Windisch) or categorized as hyperbole (Scott), either clericalized as concilia (Augustine) or popularized as universal truth (Harnack), either rationalized as internal law (Kant) or theologized as grace (Barth), either visualized as christology (Thurneysen) or modified as folly (Calvin), either internalized as *Gesinnung* (Herrmann) or eternalized as otherworldly (Dibelius). For all its learned explanations why Jesus' teaching applies either to a different time than now or in a different way than then, this hermeneutical language game creates the impression that Jesus either did not say what he meant or did not mean what he said, as if Jesus, though wanting to say the right thing, did not know how.

The problem with Christianity is that, while it upholds the highest claims as to the deity of Christ, it fails altogether to live according to the teachings of Jesus. (As a case in point, most churches resemble more a horror museum with their military glory tableau than a community of love and suffering.) We ought not ignore the deeds and words of Jesus while reducing his life to birth, death, and resurrection in order to make these bare facts yield elaborate theories of vicarious atonement and sacramentalism. Supernaturalistic explanations as to WHY Jesus died and HOW his death saves us largely evade the historical implications of messiahship and discipleship along the via dolorosas of life. The meaning of Jesus lies in his life, not merely in his death. (If Jesus' life does not save us from actual sin, it is doubtful whether his death saves us from original sin.)

Jesus differed from other men in that he really knew WHO GOD was and hence WHO HE was. Jesus knew who SENT him and hence knew his CALLING and VOCATION. This knowledge of God and self in the concreteness of life is what constitutes sonship and discipleship. A Son of God is one who is open and ready for God. That—and not a doctrine of *perichōrēsis*—is the elemental presupposition of christology. The spirit and will of Jesus are expressed in the paradox of working to save the lives of others while possibly losing our own in the process and thereby realizing life's supreme meaning as a material means to a religious end. The answer to the question WHO is Jesus? is simultaneously the answer to the question WHO am I? For he who discerns who sent HIM is thereby committed to his calling and vocation. The true meaning of our life and death is inseparable from the actual meaning of his life and death. He who FOLLOWS Jesus will find the answer to the quest both for the REAL Jesus and the TRUE self.*

---

*Cf. my book, *The Sermon on the Mount, The Modern Quest for its Meaning*, Mercer University Press, 1985.

THE HISTORICAL JESUS AND THE ANABAPTIST VISION

John Miller has discovered an intrinsic parallelism between Anabaptist studies and Jesus studies* and claims that there is a direct, implicit, and necessary connection between recovering the Anabaptist Vision and recovering the historical Jesus. Albert Schweitzer predicted that the future of theology or the theology of the future would be *Leben-Jesu-Forschung*, and Rufus Jones prophesied that the hope for a new type of Christian society was to be found in the Anabaptist movement. According to John Miller, the hour has now come to explore and evaluate the meaning of this convergence for our own theological *Selbstverständnis* and for our sense of mission.

The logic of the matter lies in his interrelation of three issues: Authority, Christology, and Lifestyle. Who shall rule over us? John Miller answers: no living pope or paper pope, but the Nazarene; the words he spoke, the example he left, the spirit he manifests shall rule over us. This, says John Miller, is what motivated the first believers, this is what they clung to, remembered, proclaimed, lived by, and died for. Then something happened. As the oral Jesus traditions were transcribed, translated, and edited, not only was the original *Sitz-im-Leben-Jesu* reinterpreted and the original mold, context, or setting reshaped or recast, but, beginning with the latter part of the second and into the third century, Paul, John, Hebrews, and Revelation came to occupy a place of authority in the Church and eventually displaced the authority of the Jesus tradition. Because Pauline and Johannine thought appeared so much more theologically profound than that of Jesus himself, the priority Jesus' sayings had claimed in the life and thought of his followers gave way to abstract questions of a philosophical nature. Sixteenth-century Anabaptism arrested this development and returned to Jesus and his word. This has now become the current theological trend, and John Miller implies that our true identity is with the contemporary Jesus questers rather than with the great systematic theologies of Christendom. If Jesus rules our life, he also rules our theology.

This raised the second question: WHO is this Jesus? The great councils said: Jesus is God. John Miller says: Jesus was and is a man, a teacher, prophet, martyr raised to life, not a dying and rising God. John Miller implies that this emphasis on the humanity of Jesus is not foreign to nor incompatible with Anabaptism. In exploring the implications of these insights, John Miller identifies three propositions: 1) According to Christian theological tradition, the chief work of Jesus was his death. John Miller says the meaning of Jesus lies in his teaching. How then did Jesus differ from other rabbis? Jesus was more aggressive: other rabbis waited till students came to them; Jesus took the initiative and called disciples. While the elders of Israel counseled to study Torah, Jesus said: Follow me! 2) How are we to understand his death? Regarding this event, says John Miller, Jesus and Anselm have nothing in common. Jesus forgave sinners and taught his followers to do so. Anselm taught that God demanded an atoning death for sin. But Jesus understood his crucifixion as a martyr's death, the rationale for which is the boundless love (not wrath) of God. 3) Jesus intended his work to be continued. How? Through an expanding disciple community whose *Gemeinde*-structure would share his authority (to bind and loose without distinction of spiritual rank) and would duplicate his ministry. Finally, what then is the Christianity of the future? To build a Church upon the foundation of the Gospels in accordance with Jesus' original intentions.

What John Miller says raises many theological questions, and theological questions are often disturbing questions. It is particularly serious to ask questions about Jesus, for, once that kind of question can be asked, no holds are barred, everything is up for reevaluation, including the meaning of history and our identity, security, and hope. As long as the central question about Jesus can be kept closed, everyone can do business as usual, everyone can be secure. But, once that question is asked, nothing else matters. It is a threatening experience, for, as Bonhoeffer reminds us, when pressed to its logical conclusion it leaves only two options: either the one who asks it must die or he kills Jesus.

John Miller asks: WHO IS this Jesus? To Pilate's inquiry, Jesus replied: *su legeis* (you say it). At Caesarea Philippi, Jesus charged his disciples to tell no one. To those who must know he said: Follow me! Hans Denck comments, "Die jünger Christi verliessen bald haus und hof, weyb und kind umb Christus willen und wussten noch nit, wer er war." (The disciples of Christ left house and home without delay, wife and child for Christ's sake, and did not yet know who he was.) And then Denck adds, "Nyemandt mag (Christus) warlich erkennen, es sey dann, das er im nachvolge mit dem leben. Und nyemandt mag im nachvolgen, dann sovil er in zuvor erkennet" (Fellmann edition, 44-45). (No one can truly know Christ except he follow him with his life. And no one can follow him except insofar as one previously knows him.) The mystery and wonder of this epistemology of obedience inspired Schweitzer to write: "As one unknown and nameless he comes to us, just as on the shore of the lake he approached those men who knew not who he was. His words are the same: Follow thou me! And he puts us to the tasks which he has to carry out in our age. He commands. And to those who obey, be they wise or simple, he will reveal himself through all that they are privileged to experience in his fellowship of peace and activity, of struggle and suffering, till they come to know, as an inexpressible secret, WHO he is" (*Out of my Life and*

Thought, 56-57). In his own challenging way, John Miller reminds us that a confession of faith is an act of life and not the result of a discussion between theologians. Or, as Bonhoeffer said, christology is possible only in the humble silence of the worshiping community for whom the possibility of christology is not one of immanence but of transcendence, not a matter of scientific classification but an experience of existential confrontation, not a quest for the alchemy of incarnation but an encounter with the sovereignty of God.

But how can one work out the ontological structure of the WHO of Jesus (his being, essence, nature) apart from the HOW or WHAT of revelation? Classical christology sought to make the incomprehensibility of Jesus Christ as comprehensible as possible by decreeing as heresy what may NOT be said about him (as in Docetism, Ebionitism, Monophysitism and Nestorianism, Subordi-nationism and Modalism, etc., regarding the attributes, natures, states, modes, and persons within trinitarian economy). The limita-tion of objectifying thought lay in the fact that it could express itself only in self-contradictions, exhausting the resources of language to say how Jesus Christ is not. The Chalcedon formula in effect rejects the possibility of defining how God became man and has therefore not altogether inaptly been described as a confession of the bank-ruptcy of Greek patristic theology. The fundamental dilemma of negative christology was the Fathers' preoccupation with the Greek concept of *ousia*, or ontological definitions of nature and essence. Consequently, they thought of the natures of God and man in Jesus as a paradoxical interrelationship of two almost physical substantial entities. Instead of understanding incarnation in terms of moral, per-sonal, and spiritual dynamics, the mystery and wonder of Jesus' relation to God was reduced to an apologetic for supernatural gyno-genesis.

While every I-Thou relationship presupposes an ontology, everything depends on the strength and quality of the correlation between *Akt und Sein* in Jesus' and our *Selbstbewusstsein* (self-consciousness). But, as not even natural science (since Einstein) posits a static ontology as a basis for relativity, we need to learn to think theologically without constant recourse to *isness*. Heraclitus already proposed that the basic principle of life is not identity but change. Unfortunately, however, our language, and particularly our theological language, is dominated by the verb *to be* which implies an illusory static quality and identity. We need instead to express value and reality as dynamic relation and function. At least part of the christological problem is semantic in that our word *is* in statements, such as God *is* man in Jesus, carries too much ontological freight in comparison to words like *see* which are freely used metaphorically as in process vocabulary which enables one to overcome the problem of ontological objectification in christology by understanding incarnation as Jesus' whole relation to history.

Apart from these formal considerations, the quest for the real Jesus is essentially the quest for the relationship between the historical Jesus and the heavenly Christ, between history and faith, between the *didache* OF Jesus and the *kerygma* ABOUT Christ. Must christology begin with Jesus or with the *kerygma* of his community? Martin Kähler argued that the real Christ is the preached Christ on the assumptions that the Jesus of history cannot be recovered behind the *kerygma* and that the surviving personal effect is the essence of reality. Inspired by Kierkegaard and Kähler—Brunner, Barth, Bultmann, and Bonhoeffer sang in chorus that the absence of historical evidence constituted the unique strength of evangelical faith, the miraculous certainty of which would only be destroyed by proofs. They insisted that the liberal *Leben-Jesu-Forschung* was dogmatically and methodologically untenable and agreed that it was neither possible, necessary, meaningful, nor interesting to try to recover from behind the Easter faith a historical Jesus, since everything depends not on a past fact of history but on a present call to decision. For half a century the world of scholarship was stunned by the conviction that we must base our faith not on tenuous fluctuations of historical research, but on the subjective effects experienced through the proclamation of the *kerygma*—upon the absolute truths of reason over against the accidental facts of history. For Kähler and his whole following, the real Jesus is not the man of Nazareth but the Christ of faith experienced as a contemporary reality. This emphasis on experience as the starting point of christology goes back to Schleiermacher and continues on through Bonhoeffer, who anchored his dogmatic christology in the experience of the present Christ at the boundary of human existence, at the center of history including the hidden center of the state, and at the heart of nature. Essentially, the presence of Christ was conceived sacramentally. No recourse to historical categories was allowed in understanding the fact or manner of his presence. In answer to the question, What and Where is Jesus Christ, Lutheran theology invariably expounds the reality and form of his personal presence in terms of an ecclesiology of Word and Sacrament.

Post-Bultmannians like Bornkamm, Käsemann, Fuchs, and Ebeling insist that one cannot separate Jesus' self-understanding from anything else in his history and that we must discern the meaning of Jesus in his teaching, his actions, and his history, rather than by raising his messiahship into a system of dogma. James M. Robinson justifies the integrity of a New Quest on the grounds that the historical Jesus within the *kerygma* confronts one with essentially the same decision that the *kerygma* presents, though he has not adequately explained why the terminology in the shift from apocalyptic to union with Christ is so different if the *kerygma* is the same. The historical quest launched by Reimarus allegedly came to an end with the realization that Jesus was not a man of our time. The so-called New Quest resumed with the realization that the real Jesus did not stay in his time but passed beyond his time and still addresses us with his authoritative 'Follow thou me'. But the New Quest still raises the old problem: How is the Christ of faith related to the Jesus of history? What is the relation between the preaching of the Church and the teaching of Jesus, between subjective and objective evidence, between the inner and the outer word? Jeremias insists that every verse of the Gospels claims that the origin of Christianity lies not in the *kerygma*, not in the resurrection experiences of the disciples, not in the Christ-idea, but in the man who was crucified under Pontius Pilate, Jesus of Nazareth and his message (cf. *The Problem of the Historical Jesus,* 12). Pannenberg has shown that the doctrinal tradition cannot afford to ignore historical study of the historical reality of Jesus, because this history of Jesus carries its own meaning in itself and comes to us not as something external but as the logic inherent in Jesus' own activity and destiny. The basis and content of our faith lies in what happened in the past, quite apart from our present experiences, and faith has to do primarily with what Jesus was and secondarily with what Jesus is to us today. To prevent the Jesus tradition from deteriorating into superstition about Jesus, we need to go behind the christology of the Reformers and of Chalcedon to discern whether the language of the Church comes from Jesus and is consistent with Jesus. We need to discern how christological statements came about and what is their basis in Jesus' own historicity.

The method of christology is twofold: either from above or from below, beginning either with dogmatics or with history, either with a doctrine of the incarnation or with the *Sitz-im-Leben-Jesu.* Christology from above begins with the doctrine of the Trinity, which it presupposes, and then proceeds to explain how the second person of the Godhead assumed human nature. This method largely ignores the history in and through which the divinity of Jesus was manifest and recognized, particularly his relationship to the Judaism of his time, which is so essential to understanding the Jewish Messiah's self-understanding as Son of Man and Son of God. In dogmatic christology, the historical particularity of Jesus tends to become immaterial except for the fact of his death as atonement for sin. Even the fact of Jesus' death becomes a supplementary problem of explaining why Jesus, despite his divinity, had to die. Christology from above implies that we need only believe in Christ, not follow Jesus. That following Jesus is presumptuous and unnecessary is implicit in the logic of most atonement theories. That it is commonly held to be impracticable, inadvisable, and, in fact, impossible to do is evident from the history of interpretation of the Sermon on the Mount.

A christology from below discerns the meaning of Jesus in his life rather than in his death. Jesus died the way he died because he lived the way he lived. He did not live because he died. Therefore the significance of his death and the reasons for it must be sought within the context of his life, and not vice versa. The meaning of Jesus can not be dogmatically abstracted from the concrete reality of his historical existence. Jesus died "for us" in the very sense and very act of living "for us." His death was not a separate act apart from his life but the final act culminating the meaning of his life. Jesus lived by and died for what he believed. And a disciple of Jesus is one who believes what Jesus believed and therefore lives what he lived by and dies what he died for. That is why our prime concern is not what others believed about Jesus but what Jesus himself believed. That is also why holding to Jesus is so threatening once we acknowledge the christological implications of the fact that he was not a Christian but a Jew.

---

*"The Historical Jesus, the Anabaptist Vision and the Christianity of the Future."

UNDERSTANDING CHRISTIAN DISCIPLESHIP

I. DISCIPLESHIP IN THE NEW TESTAMENT
A. The Call to Discipleship

Our concept of Christian discipleship is derived from the historic fact that Jesus called disciples to follow him. Peter received the call "Follow me" on two separate occasions: once beside the sea of Gennesaret whereupon he left his nets and his craft (Mk. 1:17) and at the same place when the risen Lord confronted him again at his old trade (Jn. 21:22). The first call implied an external breach with his immediate environment. Peter left all and followed. Halfway between the two calls Peter confessed Christ as Lord. But it was not until after the second call, the call to the fellowship of martyrdom, that Peter realized to follow Jesus Christ is costly: it costs a man his life as it cost God the life of His Son.

"And as he (Jesus) passed on, he saw Levi the son of Alphaeus sitting at the tax office, and he said to him, 'Follow me'. And he rose and followed him" (Mk. 2:13-14). Levi's immediate response was more than a confession of faith in Jesus. His obedience testified to the absolute and unconditional authority of Jesus. Levi did not obey out of the consideration that he would then finally be doing something ultimately worthwhile; he obeyed simply because Jesus called him. The text displays no interest in the psychology of the decision; it records only his immediate break with the relative security of his old life and his exclusive attachment to the person of his Lord.

On their way to another village a man said to Jesus, "I will follow you wherever you go." Jesus warned him, "Foxes have holes, and the birds of the air have nests; but the Son of man has nowhere to lay his head" (Lk. 9:57, 58). This volunteer had good intentions, but, after he realized the implications of following Jesus, we hear no more of him. To another Jesus said, "Follow me." He replied, "Lord, let me first go and bury my father." To this would-be follower Christ said, "Leave the dead to bury their own dead; but as for you, go and proclaim the Kingdom of God" (Lk. 9:60). A third would-be volunteer said on his own initiative: "I will follow you, Lord; but let me first say farewell to those at my home." Jesus replied, "No one who puts his hand to the plow and looks back is fit for the Kingdom of God" (Lk. 9:62). To those who stipulated their own terms the Master had the last word. Discipleship implied unconditional obedience, not a program of their own to be arranged to suit themselves.

Jesus might have encouraged Levi in his tax office and Peter at his nets to pursue their trades diligently and honestly while enjoying religious experiences old and new. He might have been their present help in time of trouble. Instead, he wanted to be Lord of their lives. Considering this impossible in the old situation, he demanded the step of obedience that cut them off from the old situation and produced a new situation where real faith was possible. Only after being cut off from their previous existence could they learn the meaning of faith, and only then could they understand that obedience is the fruit of faith, though not chronologically distinct from it.

One day a rich young ruler came to Jesus to inquire about

ultimate good. Sensing the ruler's self-righteousness, Jesus referred him to the law of Moses, but then putting his desire for righteousness to the supreme test Jesus added: "Go, sell what you possess and give it to the poor . . . and come, follow me" (Mt. 19: 21). Jesus demanded discontinuity with the old life as a prerequisite to following him in the new life. But for this young man voluntary poverty was too great a price to pay. Because he had not understood the call, his practice of the commandments too was at fault.

The disciples knew how difficult it was to follow Jesus (i. e., to enter the Kingdom of heaven), but they believed in God's miracle. Jesus warned them that "the Son of man must suffer . . . be rejected . . . and be killed." Thereupon Peter reproached him. But Jesus rebuked Peter and said, "Get behind me, Satan! For you are not on the side of God but of men." Calling the multitude together with his disciples he said to them, "If any man would come after me, let him deny himself and take up his cross and follow me" (Mk. 8: 31-34). The law of Christ was the law of the Cross. Jesus' call to discipleship was an invitation to share his suffering and rejection without honor or dignity. To prevent Christ's suffering meant to prevent Christ from being Christ. And to tear the disciple from the Cross of his Lord meant to prevent the disciple from being a disciple.

When great multitudes accompanied Jesus, he turned and said to them, "If any one comes to me and does not hate his father and mother and wife and children and brothers and sisters, yea, and his own life also, he cannot be my disciple." Jesus did not call society at large; he called each one separately and demanded that each follow alone. In fact, it was Christ who made them individuals by calling them, for his call set up a barrier between the natural and the redemptive order. Christ demanded a breach, not only with the external immediacies of the world, but also with relationships of life that do not have their ground of being in him. The Mediator persisted between every I-Thou relationship of the disciple. Any immediacy in family or society (including those claiming Christian sanction) which bypassed the Mediator implied hatred of Christ.

In Mark 10:28-31 Jesus assured Peter that those who enter upon discipleship alone do not remain alone. In the society of Jesus they are compensated a hundredfold.

Finally, Jesus led the way to Jerusalem and to the Cross, and his disciples were overcome with fear and amazement at the road he called them to follow (Mk. 10:32), and so are we.

B. The Ethic of Discipleship

In the Sermon on the Mount Jesus called those blessed (Mt. 5:1-12) who left the crowd to become with him the poorest of the poor, the hungriest of the hungry, and the sorest of the afflicted. He called them blessed because they left everything to follow him to become mourners, to become meek, merciful, and pure in heart, and to become peacemakers. This visible community of the faithful Jesus compared to the salt of the earth, a city on a hill, and a lamp on a stand (Mt. 5:13-16). To them he proclaimed the new Kingdom righteousness, its perfection (Mt. 5:17f.), its application (Mt. 6), and its significance (Mt. 7).

Central to Jesus' new program of discipleship ethics was the emphasis on love, more specifically on love for the enemy: to do well to him who hates you, to bless him who curses you, to pray for him who insults you, insults by striking you, by taking your garment, and by making unwarranted demands; not to love as the sinners but as the Saviour (Lk. 6:27-46). The disciple must be entirely free of anger. For the angry word directed against the brother is a word of judgment, a word of murder seeking annihilation of his moral and material existence (Mt. 5:21-26). On the way of the Cross there is no place for revenge (Mt. 5:38-42), only for endurance of evil. But Jesus went further, demanding not only passive endurance of evil but active engagement in heartfelt love toward the evil person. This law of the Cross was an intolerable offense to natural man, for the notion of loving the enemy contradicted his idea of right and wrong.

Jesus did not instruct his disciples to marry, but he did sanctify the institution of marriage by affirming its indissolubility, liberating marriage from selfishness and consecrating it to the service of love, thereby condemning the unbelief so often latent in man's natural instincts (Mt. 5:27-32). He also demanded absolute truthfulness which far transcends earthly obligations, such as the legal oath (Mt. 5:33-37).

Jesus went on to say that the new righteousness of discipleship must be hidden from the disciple but not from the world (Mt. 6:1-4). He spoke of the disciple's inner life, of the power of his hidden prayer life (Mt. 6:5-8), of the secret of his devotion (Mt. 6:16-18), and of the simplicity of his carefreeness like birds of the air and lilies of the field (Mt. 6:19-29). Then he admonished the disciples never to judge unbelievers, as though discipleship afforded a point of vantage from which to attack others (Mt. 7:1-12), but to let the disciple's love be the condemnation of the sinner's sin.

Finally, the Master pointed out how extraordinarily narrow the path of discipleship really is, how hard it is to find, and how easy to miss (Mt. 7:13-23). To love the enemies of the truth they confessed and to believe Jesus' promise that those who follow should possess the earth while defenselessly facing their enemies, preferring to suffer injustice rather than commit it—this was indeed an extraordinarily narrow and unutterably hard way for the disciples. At times it seemed impossible, but then again they beheld Jesus going on before, step by step. Conscious of the great divide between them and the rest of the world they resolved to do the one thing pos-

sible, to do the impossible, and that without adding reflections of
their own, without asking questions, without posing objections, and
without offering to interpret the Master's words in a thousand different ways. And they resolved to do it immediately without hesitating
to see if others would follow their precepts. In so doing they became
disciples of the Lord Christ. (Cf. D. Bonhoeffer, *The Cost of Discipleship*, 29-176.)

II. INTERPRETING JESUS' ETHICS OF DISCIPLESHIP

How then are we to understand Jesus' call and teaching on
discipleship? While not taking his precepts literally would be evad-
ing the seriousness of his command, would doing so not reveal the
absurdity of the Christian position (e. g., plucking out the eye, etc.)
and thereby invalidate the commandment? Is it not true that—with
reference to poverty or riches, love or hate—what matters, in the last
analysis, is not what one does but one's faith in Jesus? But, on the
other hand, is it enough to combat the error of legalism by cultivating a spirit of inner detachment, by having as though one had not?
Does not this elimination of simple obedience on principle open the
door for a worse type of legalism, a wicked sophistry that perverts
the call to obedience into self-justification of worldliness? But must
we then respond exactly as did the first disciples as though we were
their immediate contemporaries?

These considerations bring us to the central problem, to the
paradox of the call of Jesus, whose inhuman demands devaluate the
very interests of family, of state, and of economics. Is Jesus' discipleship ethic of radical goodness then not ultimately irreconcilable
with the basic structures of life in this world? How can the call to
discipleship apply to all if, when followed by even a minority, it
would result in chaos for this world? Can God, who created the
world, desire that it perish through the radical teaching of His Son?
Throughout the ages the church has attempted somehow to recon-

cile the unconditionality of this Gospel with the conditionality of creatureliness.

The early Christians assumed a literal understanding of Jesus' teaching on discipleship as self-evident. With Paul, Peter, and John they understood themselves to be strangers and pilgrims in this evil and passing world but holding citizenship in another. Though not blind to the concept of good in the secular world nor completely indifferent to the responsibility of maintaining order in God's creation, this oppressed and persecuted Christian minority considered the world outside, generally speaking, as a crude and perverse generation rebellious against God and hopelessly enslaved in sin. Church (i. e., *Gemeinde*) and world became mutually exclusive. Christians regarded the world as evil and the nonbelievers came to despise and persecute the Christians as a strange and suspicious lot prejudiced against the state and refusing to participate responsibly in the life of society.

Realizing that outworn paganism, emperor worship, and dead mythology could no longer meet the need for a religious and political bond between the subjects of the Roman Empire, Constantine and his followers sought to renew the empire by Christianizing it. Theodosius succeeded in establishing the great divine society, catholic and cosmopolitan, the symbiosis of a world-state and a world-church where each depended on the other so that no area of life was excluded from the dominion of the one God. Pagan temples were destroyed and the worshipers not only barred from military and judicial offices but also threatened with the sword.

With the Treaty of Milan, the "salt had lost its savor." The church, having lost her eschatological vision and character, became conditioned to the realisms of this life. Her function now was to keep the doctrine pure while the state guaranteed the exclusiveness of the true faith by compulsory measures. The secularized church declared Jesus' discipleship ethic to be a counsel of perfection for a select few, not an unconditional command for all. He who could not reconcile his conscience with a compromise solution was advised to retreat out of the world into the monastery and there to live the Christian life uncompromisingly. The New Testament church-world dualism with its inherent tension between being *in* but not *of* the world was thus resolved in terms of a vocational ethic. What was impractical for the masses became the meritorious achievement of a few. In fact, the church considered it highly desirable that not everyone commit oneself to the ethic of Jesus, for only on the assumption of a double standard for clergy and laity could her existence and cultural function be guaranteed. To prevent schism, the church found room on its outer fringe for the monastic movement, a living protest against secularization. Since the protest was tolerated, it did not develop to its natural conclusion but served rather, on the assumption of the double standard, to justify the secularism it set out to condemn.

For Luther the double standard of Roman Catholic morals as exemplified by the doctrine of the Two Swords was a mock solution threatening the unity of Christian conscience. For Luther the call to discipleship implied leaving the cloister and returning to the world, not because the world was better, but because the cloister itself had become a subtle form of love for the world over against the self-deceit of the monastic retreat out of the world. Luther insisted the Christian must fulfill the demands of Jesus in the world within the vocation to which he had been called, that is, in which he had been born. But, since man needs protection for himself, his family, and his country, Luther exempted the powers of government from the requirement of conforming to the law of Christ. Though sensing a certain uneasiness about a Christian's participation in war, Luther, too, settled for the accepted doctrine of the "just war." As a member of the Kingdom of God, a Christian acts in accord with his conscience and the commands of Christ, but, as a citizen of the kingdom of this world, he acts in accord with the autonomous structure of pragmatic value judgments. "The hand that wields the sword of government is no longer the hand of man but of God, and not man but God hangs, racks on the wheel, executes, strangles and wars. . . . Not I beat and stab and kill (said Luther) but God and my Prince, whose servant my hand and my life are" (cf. Weimar ed. 30/2:174ff.). The Christian statesman was to offer the guarantee that even brute force stood in the service of love. Thus, the two conflicting ethical systems were interfused within the person so as to constitute a departmentalization within each individual. The norm for the vocational ethics of the Christian within civil service was not the law of Christ but the law of survival within a fallen creation. The hard sayings of Jesus were relegated to the sphere of personal ethics or to the category of the clerical vocation.

With Calvin the problem of discipleship ethics was of less account than with Luther. The contradiction between Jesus' ethic of radical love and the barbaric demands of Old Testament nationalism was resolved by founding the power structures of the "Christian" state of Geneva in the "Christian" law of the Old Testament and then tagging on New Testament sentiments about love as an afterthought of no practical account. Zwingli, Bullinger, and Oecolampad justified Christian participation in armed conflict by simply referring to the heroic acts of Gideon, Barak, Samson, Jephthah, and other blood tales in the Book of Judges. The theocratic structure of Calvinism lent itself much more readily to the endorsement of "Holy War" than did the personal dichotomy of Lutheranism. Assuming the intact symbiosis of church and state within the *corpus christianum*, the Reformers could not reasonably expect the only partially Christian society to practice the Christian ethic. Given a sinful world and the impracticability of the way of absolute love, secular approximations to the ideal of "relative justice" were given priority over distinctly Christian principles. Classical Protestantism thus offered a reformulation of the problem, but no solution.

Realizing the impracticability of Jesus' perfectionist ethic amid the relativities of society and the ambiguities of politics, the heirs of the Reformation heritage still by and large assume a double standard of morality in some form or other. Some hold that Christ did not insist on literal external obedience which torments our conscience by a legalism worse than that of Moses but that Christ, being the end of the Law, appealed to the inner motive to challenge the disposition of the mind and the will. But his being the "end of the Law" cannot imply that he is the end of ethics. Surely his ethical imperatives are more than paradoxical expressions void of content and meaning. Often this emphasis on attitude over against structured obedience led to the assumption that one can express Christ's loving attitude even by actions which by all indications seem to contradict it.

Those who take the imperatives literally often relegate their application to a future ideal—as in Fundamentalism—rather than to the imperfect world here and now. But would not the hard sayings of Jesus, such as to love one's enemies, seem irrelevant in glory! One hardly gathers the impression from the Gospels that Christ intended those whom he had called to postpone their response that long.

Common in Protestantism is the view that one cannot derive any direct guidance from the New Testament regarding concrete life situations, that the Gospel of Jesus related to personal salvation but not to social issues, and that medical, social, and economic problems were completely beyond the horizon of his thought and concern. On the contrary, the Gospels reveal how deeply Jesus was involved in the ambiguities of politics with Pilate and the Sanhedrin in the nationalist Zealot movement and in the social unrest of the poor and dispossessed of Galilee. Jesus' teaching is, therefore, not irrelevant to these spheres but inextricably interwoven with the very stuff of our own historical situations even if the brief Gospel accounts of Jesus' teaching do not encompass the entire scope of problems facing man in modern society.

Often it is argued that Jesus' teaching is an interim ethic motivated by apocalyptic concern for world catastrophe and intended only for the brief interval preceding his almost immediately expected return. We would challenge the assumption that the length of the interim preceding the fulfillment of the last things of history really determines the earnestness and radicalness of Christ's demands. Furthermore, the New Testament Church's expectation of world catastrophe was perhaps as much a result of as a motive for the radicalness of apostolic preaching.

The contemporary existential mood interprets Jesus' teaching primarily from the standpoint of dialectic: that man in every concrete moment of his existence is confronted with radical decision. Here, not the content of Christ's commands but the experience of being-in-encounter is what really matters. While it is true that man is confronted with God's imperatives beyond that measure of response demanded by formulated commandments, this spiritualistic absence of concretizing discipleship in history paves the way for a "situation ethic" which no longer feels the need to be instructed and corrected by the Word. It is safe to assume that modern existentialist reflections were foreign to the mind of Christ and those whom he called.

Protestantism has largely limited the radicalness of Christ's demands to either the narrow circle of original disciples—a lineage later extended into the clergy—or a distinct era of the past. The call to discipleship applies either to a different time than now or in a different way than then. It was at this point that the Anabaptist dissent became focal.

III. THE ANABAPTIST RECOVERY OF THE DISCIPLESHIP VISION

It was the genius of Anabaptism to have recovered a vision for what it meant to be a disciple of Christ in the sixteenth century

and to follow through consistently the implications of single-minded
obedience for the concept of the Church, its structure, and its theology of love and nonresistance. Somehow, the Anabaptists were conscious of the living Christ teaching and commanding them through
the Word. They referred much to concrete situations in the life of
Jesus: his mercifulness to the pagan woman who had fallen in adultery, his refusal to judge in matters of inheritance, and his escape
when the multitudes sought to crown him. Here they believed to discover a pattern of footsteps to be followed. For conformity to this
pattern they were prepared to sacrifice not only their vocation and
security but their life. For them obedience to Christ literally took the
form of running after Christ, a response implying not merely the
right attitude or motivation, not merely the inner decision of faith,
but including external action, including the deed. This external
response to the claims of Christ was an inseparable part of the inner
decision of faith. Discipleship meant not only the inner freedom but
also the external commitment, not merely true faith (the "*fides
orthodoxa*"), but also true life. No merit was ascribed to knowledge
of the faith not transposed into commitment in life situations.

The Anabaptists' faith was existential faith in the sense that it
was related most directly to external realities. Frequently such
Anabaptist leaders as Hans Denck emphasized that Christ as a person could not be known except as one committed oneself to follow
him. *Nachfolge* under the Cross was the prerequisite to all knowledge of the truth because he was essentially the way of truth. Truth
then was for them both a person and a way rather than a formula.
From their mystic relation to this person, the living Christ, they
derived their norm for right action in history. Plotting this course of
right action in any given situation was therefore by no means left to
the discretion of the individual nor were the essential directives
derived from the situation itself but directly from the command of
God in Christ. Hans Hut maintained, "God hath forbidden us to do
what we deem good, but what He commands we are to do and heed

and not waver to the right nor to the left." It was the Holy Spirit who in any given situation wrought the consensus of faith within the community of faith as to what the will of God for that situation should be. "No one can arrive at the truth except he follow in the footsteps of Christ and his chosen ones in the school of all trial." Only the obedient follower believes, and, as Hans Hut put it, "he who desires not to follow the footsteps, to walk the way and to carry the Cross of Christ, he neither has nor knows the Son" (cf. Lydia Müller, *Glaubenszeugnisse*, 14, 15, 34).

In the actual life situations which Christ faced from day to day, situations determined by political and social factors, the Anabaptist believed he detected the essence of the humiliated Christ, of the real Christ. Progressively the Son of God had denied himself in the incarnation, in his passion, and in his death to become an obedient servant testifying to the sovereignty of the Father who guarantees the ultimate triumph of truth according to His will, order, and time. Since the servant is not greater than his Lord, the Anabaptists understood discipleship to imply a comparable way of renunciation and humiliation, a way of love and suffering. They agreed with the Reformers that one can be saved only by faith but added, "only through the mediation of love can faith aspire." They agreed with the Catholics that without works there is no salvation but added, only if this flows forth from the motivation of selfless Calvary love is the good work acceptable to God.

It would be an oversimplification to interpret the Anabaptist discipleship ethic as a human attempt at imitating Jesus. The disciple would then have to make his own way comparable to that of his Master and perhaps parallel to him. Still, to follow Jesus meant something more and other to them than that he vicariously walked the lonely road for all. They understood the disciple to be much more significantly involved in what the Master is doing, involved after the event but nevertheless involved step by step, observing and practicing what he sees as he participates in the life of his Master. The emphasis then is not on the fact that the disciple is doing something by himself but on the presence and grace of the Master who enables the disciple to participate significantly in his Master's life and work. Thus discipleship is the allegiance to the person of the Master while creatively participating in the Master's vocation. Where the disciple's ground of being is not in himself but in the Lord of history, the problem of ability or inability remains unknown, for God the Father enables the disciple through the power of His Holy Spirit to participate in the perfect obedience of His Son. In the Word and by the Spirit the Anabaptists discovered their ground of ultimate being as disciples to be participation in the redemptive work of their Lord.

IV. THE DYNAMICS OF DISCIPLESHIP

Lawrence Burkholder keenly observed that ever since the sixteenth century the Anabaptist vision of discipleship has been clearer in theory than in practice, clearer theologically than sociologically, clearer for the first generation than for its descendants, for conditions of poverty than for those of prosperity, and more likely for a small minority than for a majority (cf. Guy F. Hershberger, ed., *Recovery of the Anabaptist Vision*, 150).

The discipleship vision of the Anabaptists cannot be recovered by merely admiring or even imitating their piety but by rekindling the fire of the Spirit that inspired it. We cannot thrive on the faith of our forefathers; their faith must become our own. Any rekindling of the glow of their vision, any regeneration by the power of that same Spirit of Christ presupposes the same high level of commitment on our part, the same willingness to ask the radical existential questions all over again for the kind of world in which we live and to seek to comprehend at any price the ultimate dimensions of life.

To be a disciple implies, on the one hand, to transcend one's own life by losing it and to transcend the life of one's own people so completely as no longer to be bound by them, and, on the other hand, to be compelled in the depths of one's being by the imperatives of Christ to realize in history the religious ideal. The actual fruitfulness of the disciple's faith depends on the quality of the tension between the historic and the transcendent dimensions of life "in Christ" and on the manner in which this tension is resolved within the solidarity of Christian community.

A disciple is one who is under way. Like his Master he has no permanent resting place. On the one hand, his way is conditioned by the historic situation even as that of the incarnate Jesus of history. On the other hand, his way also transcends the values and achievements of history even as that of the resurrected Lord of history. Taking discipleship seriously, therefore, always implies reckoning with the inevitability of a radical dualism, not one structured between the two kingdoms as in Lutheranism, leaving unchallenged the illusion of a *corpus christianum*, not a dualism between Christian law and human weakness of the non-Christian citizen as in Calvin's Geneva, not a dualism between individual and social ethics (Niebuhr)—but one between the world of values associated with uncompromising obedience to Christ and between the world of unbelief. Christian discipleship means to resolve the dualism, tension, and paradox symbolized by Christ's Cross—not by a sanction of the world, not by a schizophrenic dichotomy justifying sin, not by isolation from the world, but by the obedience of faith that characterizes the community of faith amid a faithless world.

The disciple is a pilgrim between the earthly and heavenly Jerusalem. The dualism implied in his dual citizenship is, however, not one structured geographically or socially so as to require separate regions for saint and sinner (though it can be that too). For he who thinks he is only in the Kingdom often deceives himself, and he who tries to be in both realms suffers unbearable conflict (cf.

Richard Ullmann, *Between God and History*). The structure of obedience is not a changeless form, but a dynamic creation of faith,
hope, and love over against the persistence of unfaith, despair, and
hate. We might not often be able to distinguish in advance between a
situation in which faith is possible and one where it is not. The actual structure of faith decisions ventured in obedience to Christ comes
to view as a coherent pattern often only retrospectively as the distinct discipleship footprints of one to whom the reality of Christ
took precedence over the reality of living in this world.

Christian discipleship is not a pious escape from political
problems and responsibilities for the external order. It is not a pious
inwardness concerned only with personal salvation, but it is ultimate
commitment to incorporate Kingdom ethics into Kingdom theology
in a way often implying that one cannot be in the Church and in the
world in the same way and at the same time. Christian discipleship
does not imply avoidance of ethical tensions, conflicts, and offenses,
but it does imply resolving these by no lesser way than the way of
the Cross.

At times we may forget that the Kingdom of God is more like
a process than a camp and that those who claim to have priority in it
fall easily into presumptuous pretension of sanctity. Sometimes we
may tend to forget that the Church of Christ is universal, though not
invisible nor institutional, that it is above all a congregation and not
a segregation, that it is the process of gathering and sending, not a
clique or clan, that it is dynamic life, not static form, and that it
occurs in the world and for the world as a constantly creative
process much more by the grace and providence of God than by our
own doing or undoing. Sometimes we may not be willing to admit
that the only warranted segregation from the world is that initiated
by the world's rebellion and not that motivated by the Church's concern for self-preservation, that the Church's retreat from the world
ought always to be temporary, not permanent in character, always

motivated by a deeper concern for better service in the world. Sometimes we may lack the commitment to understand that retreat from the world or nonconformity to the world ought to be more on the level of stewardship of grace and of a continuum of ethical norms than in terms of physical and geographic asceticism and isolationism.

Where we confuse the law of the Cross with "a lower but true principle" (Penn), dilute the Gospel of the Cross to a universal panacea for the dilemmas of society, and fail to distinguish the suffering dimension of the community of the Cross, there we have forgotten that "when Christ calls a man, he bids him come and die. It may be a death like that of the first disciples who had to leave home and work to follow him or it may be a death like Luther's, who had to leave the monastery and go out into the world. But it is the same death every time—death in Jesus Christ, the death of the old man at his call" (Bonhoeffer, *ibid.*, 79).

Reprinted by permission of Faith and Life Press.

WHAT IT REALLY MEANS TO FOLLOW JESUS

The concept of discipleship first occurs in Jeremiah 2:2. "Thus says the Lord, I remember your devotion as a youth, your love as a bride, how you *followed* me in the wilderness, in a land not sown." While the people of the Old Testament did not understand their relationship to the transcendent Lord of Glory within the explicit context of discipleship, the prophets consistently proclaimed that to be God's people meant to participate in the perfections of God and to do the works of God: to plant the land of Canaan as God planted Eden, to clothe the naked as God clothed Adam, to visit the sick as God visited Abraham, to comfort the bereaved as God comforted Isaac, and to bury the dead as God buried Moses. To be God's people meant to be committed to a pattern of life in accord with the will of the Lord. The central idea in this pattern of life for God's people was conformity, not to their pagan environment, but to the image of God by following His way, as the soldier follows his captain, as the bride follows her bridegroom and the wife her husband, as the young prophet follows his master, and the student follows the rabbi riding on a donkey before him.[1] This is the image which the Gospels convey to us concerning Jesus. Throughout the land, vast multitudes from Galilee, Judea, and across the Jordan followed him here and there, now and then, to hear his astounding teaching and to witness his miraculous healing. And of these some committed themselves to follow him continually, relinquishing all ties and obligations to share his life and destiny in order to become his disciples. FOLLOW ME. That is the actual wording of the summons of Jesus, whose power and authority transformed ordinary men and women into saints and disciples. There is nowhere in the New Testament a reflection about this amazing phenomenon apart from the mere statement that it happened—a warning that we too had best not speculate about the possibilities of this miracle of God without committing ourselves to it. This is the spirit in which we wish to explore what is implied in the call to discipleship.

I. TO FOLLOW JESUS MEANS TO ACCEPT THE GRACE OF GOD

Jesus' call to follow is a particular kind of call, one in which God reveals and gives Himself to us in order that He may claim and sanctify us as His own witness in the world. As such, the "call" is therefore not a human "challenge" but essentially an expression of grace inseparable from the act of God in Christ and from our experience of salvation. It is because God has given Himself in this call to be our Saviour and leader that the nature of the call takes the form of a command. Essentially, the call has to do with the grace of God which is at the same time the command of God. But it is never command apart from grace; it is never imperative apart from indicative because it is never apart from Jesus Christ.

A command or call can only be issued to those who already belong to the commander. It is indeed this presupposition—that we truly belong, not to ourselves, but to Jesus Christ—which makes the call of Jesus Christ so imperative, so demanding. Jesus Christ is the basis of God's claim upon our lives, and it is in him and through him, through his personal call to follow, that this claim is revealed to us. Jesus Christ is the one in whom God's claim upon our lives is realized and fulfilled. Therefore, obedience to God always means obedience to Jesus Christ. To do the will of God is to obey Jesus' call TO FOLLOW. And to obey the call means to believe in Jesus Christ as Lord and to participate in his life as an apprentice in the vocation of the Master. We cannot hurry past Jesus Christ on our way to the ultimate good as if it were something beside, outside, or beyond him. To do so is to misunderstand the "good" as did the

Rich Young Ruler (Mk. 10:17f.), whose yoke became unutterably hard and whose burden unbearably heavy because he refused the grace of Jesus Christ and presumed to go on his own. No wonder the disciples responded with amazement, asking, "Who then can be saved?" But for him who trusts in the sufficiency of God's grace, His commandments are not grievous (I Jn. 5:3).

What makes this call so demanding is that it can be fulfilled only willingly or not at all. With this imperative of freedom, our total existence is at stake. Obedience to Christ's call can only be rendered in freedom or else it is not obedience. Jesus' call is not a word of tyranny or oppression but an invitation to freedom from the bondage and anxiety of our self-involvement, from the futility and vanity of our efforts to save ourselves by making our own way through the dark maze of life's ambiguities. The call to discipleship is not a call to a new form of legalism that goads our already wounded conscience but a proclamation of liberation from every burden and anxiety, from every oppression and torture that afflicts our conscience and casts a shadow of gloom over our life.

To follow Jesus is not something one might do on one's own initiative or at one's own convenience. A certain man, according to Luke 9:57, once made such an overture to Jesus, saying, "I will follow you wherever you go." Jesus quickly discouraged this would-be disciple with the reply, "Foxes have holes, and the birds of the air have nests; but the Son of man has nowhere to lay his head." This volunteer had noble intentions about redirecting the goal and purpose of his life, but we hear no more of him. Another offered himself as a volunteer upon the condition that he might first say farewell to his own household. To him, Jesus indicated that a limited readiness is no readiness at all. When the summons is issued, we can respond either immediately and totally or not at all. The call to discipleship is a call to unconditional obedience. It is not a program of our own arranged to suit ourselves. And he who once having put his hand to the plow looks back is not fit to be a disciple; he is not worthy of the call (Lk. 9:62).

The call to discipleship is not an invitation to confess one's faith in Jesus but a summons to take a first step in a new direction and to do so immediately without adding reflections of one's own, without asking questions, and without posing objections or alternatives. To obey the call means to take a first step forward, committing one's self to Jesus Christ and thereby hazarding one's old existence in self-denial and abandonment. It does not necessarily mean to do something big or brave but doing what has been proposed to us by Jesus Christ whether big or small, striking or insignificant. Nothing more or less than obedience is required. Apart from such obedience, faith is impossible. "Why call ye me Lord if ye do not the things which I say?" (Lk. 6:46).

To follow Jesus means to come to him and be liberated by him from everything in which we might otherwise put our trust, to be liberated from the confusing clutter and conflicting variety of life's attachments and activities, to realize the underlying direction, structure, and destiny of our new life under his Lordship. It means the loosening of all ties to the point of being able and willing to sever them at a moment's notice. It means "to have as though one had not" and to do as though one did not in the spirit of this implicit abandonment and detachment. It means to entrust our whole being to the one who has called us and freed us for this response. To follow Jesus means to become what we were meant to be.

II. TO FOLLOW JESUS MEANS TO BECOME AN INDIVID-
UAL FOR GOD

Jesus' call to discipleship makes one an individual. Whether one wishes or not, one cannot evade the compelling necessity of this decision. Christ calls each one individually, and each must follow alone. It is not a person's choice to become an individual but Christ's call that makes him one. One is terrified at the prospect of standing alone in the presence of the Lord and of becoming an individual for God. One may seek to evade the penetrating presence of the Lord by hiding behind an organization, behind material possessions, or social obligations. One may, in fact, volunteer to be indirectly involved in a general program of discipleship—anything to evade the eyes of the Lord fixed on oneself alone. But the call to follow Jesus is a very individual matter. It summons one to step out from the morphology of one's life and face up to the truth that one can have dealings with God only as an individual. Not until one can say "I," not until one has found oneself, can one say "Thou" to God. And, even when one does it in the context of community, doing it implies doing it as an individual alone before God. That was the case with the patriarchs and prophets to whom the Word of the Lord came. Abraham's call to go forth from Ur of the Chaldees (Gn. 12:1) implied an outward breach with his family and nation, and the call to sacrifice his only son on Moriah (Gn. 22:2) implied a hidden breach both within his own household and his own life. In this totality of his abandonment and commitment Abraham became an individual for God. It was in this individual way that those of the New Testament were confronted with the call that made them saints and disciples of Jesus Christ.

Only in becoming an individual before God is one open to the ultimate question of responsibility and truth. The crowd releases one from the capacity for repentance and weakens one's sense of responsibility. In our age, the integrity of the person (including the so-called Christian person) has become questionable through being collectivized by conflicting social and national forces that claim of one an unconditional allegiance properly belonging only to God. This collectivization marks the disintegration of one's faith both in God and in one's fellow being; it marks the paralysis of one's capacity for trust. By this emphasis on the individual we are not claiming that the individual is the truth, but we are reminding ourselves of the fact that when God reveals Himself He makes known His truth to a person.

And that is the reason for which a person exists. That is why the relation of an individual to God is always a unique relation, indeed, the primary and essential relation over against all other secondary and unessential relations. The decisive battles are not fought between groups but in the depths of the individual.[2] God's truth for us is inseparably bound up with our potentiality and responsibility for becoming a person for God in this world. And it is the content of God's self-revelation in Jesus that we can become a person only in Jesus Christ. That, in the final analysis, is what is meant by being a saint and a disciple.

To be an individual for God means to acknowledge Christ as the Mediator, not only between God and us, but between us and others, between us and reality, between the disciple and all other people or things. The disciple who has heard and understood Christ's call suddenly realizes that Christ is the Mediator who has redeemed him from all immediacies with this world, that all his innerworldly relations are founded upon the illusion of immediacy. Even the most intimate ties of one's life, one's kinship with father and mother, brother or sister, husband or wife, are ultimately real only in as far as they are mediated through Christ. There is no ultimately real way to other persons except through Christ in whom we and they first become real persons. Therefore, all relationships—including those claiming the sanction of Christian principles—that raise the claim of immediacy must be hated for the sake of Christ.[3]

The relationships as such are not being questioned as dubious or detrimental. One is not human apart from these relationships. But questioned is the compulsive intensity by which one may be bound and imprisoned by these most sacred relationships even as in other respects one may be bound by possessions or fame. Therefore, the call to freedom in Christ challenges the captivity of these relationships. "The excuse of the invited guest, 'I married a wife and therefore cannot come' (Lk. 14:20), is seen to be exactly on the same level as those of others who had bought land or oxen which claimed their prior interest. And, in the same connection, Jesus gives the remarkable reply to the man who was ready to be a disciple but first wanted to bury his father: 'Let the dead bury their dead, but go thou and preach the Kingdom of God' " (Lk. 9:59f.). "If any man come to me and hate not his father, and mother, and wife, and children, and brethren, and sisters, yea, and his own life also, he cannot be my disciple" (Lk. 14:26). "It is not the persons that are to be hated, for why should they be excluded from the command to love our neighbors? It is the hold which these persons have and by which they also are gripped. It is the concentration of neighborly love on these persons, which really means its denial. It is the indolent peace of a clannish warmth in relation to these persons, with its necessary implication of cold war against all others. The coming of the Kingdom of God means an end of the absolute of family no less than that of possession or fame."[4] On account of its fear of monasticism, Protestantism has largely ignored this radicalness of Christ's call.

To be an individual for God does not, however, mean to be worldlessly alone with God, working out one's own salvation by a self-conscious deliberate asceticism. The quality of a disciple's relationship to God is such that he, like Christ, is called to go through, not over or beyond, the world. The only way to follow Jesus is to follow him in the world. Therefore, the world must not be prematurely written off. Like his Master, the disciple is to go through the world that he might relate the world to God through his life. To be an individual for God has about it, on the one hand, the quality of personal strictness and detachment and, on the other hand, the freedom and commitment to share one's life with the unbelieving person in the unbelieving world so that he too may become a person open and ready for God. One cannot answer the claim of God upon one's life without answering with and for one's fellow being. To be unconditionally concerned with God means to be conditionally concerned with human beings as they are in God's fallen world. It is not for the next world that we are to be concerned but for this world God created, preserved, and atoned. To be an individual for God does not mean to be religious in a certain way but to be truly human without escaping into either the mass or the monastery.

III. TO FOLLOW JESUS MEANS TO BECOME THE PEOPLE OF GOD

Christian discipleship is not the terrifying loneliness of insular existentialism where no one knows the other and each is in a world alone. To follow Jesus is to be redeemed from the confines of a self-conscious, self-centered life to discover one's fellow being and through that one a whole new world of human relations within the society of Jesus. Jesus said there is no one who has left brothers or sisters or mother or father or children for my sake and for the Gospel who will not receive them back in this time (Mk. 10:29f.). It is through the discovery of Christ's own people that the individual comes to life and becomes a whole person in this broken world. It is through this company of the committed that the individual acquires in Christ a new identity, a new ground of being, a new sense of mission and destiny, and a new style of life.

God's people constitute a fellowship not of the human spirit but of the Holy Spirit. Their real life is born not of the will of man but of the will of God, a phenomenon not of nature but of grace in the freedom and calling of the Holy Spirit. Their ground of being is not the order of creation but that of redemption. Hence, the form of their life corresponds to no natural or civil order but to the form of Christ's own incarnate being and presence alone. The form of God's people is that of holy worldliness, for they are in the world for others as he was in the world for them.

God's people are known not by their "churchianity" but by their Christianity, not for their cultural sophistication but for their love.[5] "By this all men will know that you are my disciples, if you love one another" (Jn. 13:35). They differ from most people not because they go to church on Sunday but because they know why they are in the world on Monday. Their life together is Christian not because it takes place in "sanctuaries" but because it happens in His name. God's most peculiar people (including first-century Christians and sixteenth-century Anabaptists) feel most comfortable not in cathedrals but in house churches which consist not of bricks but persons. They prefer small groups to solemn assemblies, meetings that matter to those that do not, dialogue to monologue—because they believe in the priesthood of all believers. They prefer to talk *with* rather than about God and to pray *for* rather than over each other. And, when they meet, they expect to confront and to change each other in the freedom, spontaneity, and integrity of the Spirit. This is how they learn to take themselves and others seriously, to become open and honest, to understand and to accept, to give and to forgive, to bear and to forbear, to witness and to pray, to grow and to sacrifice, to trust and to obey, to love and to hope. It is through the quality and integrity of their life together that those who follow Jesus learn not just to know the truth and to do the truth but to be the truth, not only to work for the Kingdom but to live in the Kingdom.

God's people know that discipleship implies adjusting their style of living to the priorities of the Kingdom, so as not to miss the foundation of life. As citizens of two worlds, they know that the spiritual dimension of life cannot be separated from the physical and that the material is itself intended to be the means of grace. Consequently, God's people share the substance of their actual life with others, not as an act of compassion or obligation of charity but as an act of self-giving in which by the grace of God the sharing of goods becomes a sharing of brotherhood symbolized by the bread and wine of the Lord's Supper.[6] And those who take Jesus most seriously do not rationalize his teaching on "renunciation" (Lk. 14: 33) in terms of "stewardship" but forgo many things on account of the one thing needful (Lk. 10:41f.) lest they miss it as did the rich ruler (Lk. 18:18f.) or lose it as the rich fool (Lk. 12:20). Discipleship means participating in Christ's life by sharing our life for Christ's sake.

To be a disciple means to be concerned with much more than one's own salvation. The sectarian escape into a pietist conventicle is not the most Christian approach to the world in which Christ lived and for which he died. The call to Christian discipleship is not the call of a few choice spirits to a monastic retreat but an out and out "worldly" commitment on the part of all of God's people to do for God's sake what needs to be done in and for the world as a radical protest against the world. The people of God are not to be confused with that little band of refugees forever running away from the world and huddling together in heavily armed fortresses of nonconformity so as to save their souls and their inferiority complexes in the midst of hostile territory. A true disciple will not resent or fear the secularization of the monastery, for he will find his task in the temple of God's world of workers, citizens, and servants.

Christian discipleship means to partake of the reality of God within the reality of the world. In Christ we never experience the reality of the world apart from God (as do the secularists) nor do we experience the reality of God apart from the world (as claim some mystics). Discipleship means to live on the boundary between that which is worldly, profane, or natural and that which is divine, holy, or supernatural. Between God and history there is no other option. Where Christ and the world are conceived as mutually exclusive realms, he who claims to be in only one realm often deceives himself, and he who seeks to be in both suffers unbearable conflict. Essentially, therefore, the disciple's worldview is not that of a balanced dualism but of one reality in Jesus Christ in whom all things subsist. The cause of Christ is distinct from the world—the supernatural from the natural, revelation from reason—but always in such a way that being in Christ includes being in the world, that the supernatural includes the natural, that revelation includes reason. The ontological miracle of being is that God holds the world and man in His will by identifying it with His being-in-Christ. The epistemological mystery of being is that we know divine reality only in worldly reality, the supernatural only through the natural, revelation only as reason. Therefore, the Christian's worldliness ought not separate him from Christ nor ought his Christianity separate him from the world. To be a Christian means belonging wholly to Christ while standing wholly in the world, witnessing to and participating in the reality of Cross and Resurrection between nature and grace as a child of God.

Discipleship means to cultivate wholeness of being as that quality of holiness which integrates and sanctifies the whole of life and resists the disintegration of persons within a schizophrenic or casuistic dichotomy of sacred and secular spheres. To be whole persons in a broken world presupposes that we discern the nature of the tension between Christ and culture within the totality of our civilization. Only thus can we hope to avoid both pitfalls, that of confusing the Kingdom of God with the cultural process, on the one hand, and that of advocating a legalistic nonconformity on principle, on the other; instead, we shall commit ourselves as God's people to a truly redemptive strategy that communicates faith, hope, and love and preserves our own integrity as Christian persons.

An incarnationist theology invariably leads to engagement with our actual problems in the realm of industry and labor, science and art, politics and the press. Together with Moses, Jeremiah, and Jesus we are called of God to identify ourselves with the plight, desolation, and despair of the world's people to forge the worldly implications of the Gospel in the midst of social revolution lest we perpetuate an otherworldliness incapable of grappling with the forces that cripple the body and kill the soul.

This means, in general, that every area of life is the subject of Christian concern and, in particular, that the vocation to which we are called in Christ is the place where we are to work out our sanctification in the holy worldliness of Christian discipleship, bearing the marks of Jesus in our body and producing the fruit of his Spirit in the labor of his love.

IV. TO FOLLOW JESUS MEANS TO PARTICIPATE IN THE SUFFERING OF GOD

The grace of discipleship is costly. With it everything is at stake. It costs us our life as it cost God the life of His Son. Jesus' call to follow is an invitation to share suffering and rejection without dignity and honor and, in the final analysis, it is an invitation to the supreme fellowship of martyrdom. As much as we would like to evade this point, we cannot bypass the reality of Christ's Cross standing in the midst of history and casting its shadow across our life. Whatever is said about the implications of following Jesus will have to be said in the light of the symbol of that Cross.

Jesus informed his disciples that "the Son of man must suffer . . . " and ascribed Peter's concern to prevent this to the influence of Satan. Then he reminded those about him: "If any man would come after me, let him deny himself and take up his cross and follow me" (Mk. 8:34). The law of Christ is the law of the Cross. To prevent Christ's suffering meant to prevent Christ from being Christ. And to tear the disciple from the Cross of his Lord means to prevent the disciple from being a disciple. Suffering with Christ is not an accidental but an essential dimension of the specifically Christian life.

Our Anabaptist forefathers understood this better than we do today. Hans Hut maintained: "No one can arrive at the truth except he follow in the footsteps of Christ and his chosen ones in the school of all trial. . . . He who does not wish to walk in the footsteps of that way and carry the Cross of Christ, he does not have or know the Son."[7]

No religious group in Europe suffered so tragically and shed so much martyrs' blood in obedience to Christ. Literally thousands of Anabaptists were executed, hanged, burned alive, or otherwise martyred by Catholic and Protestant officials of the state and of the church because their outspoken pacifist ethic endangered the solidarity of Christian Europe at a time when it was harassed by imminent threats of invasion by the Turks. When interrogated, they always pointed to the unequivocal teaching of Jesus: "Love your enemies . . . and you will be sons of the Most High" (Lk. 6:26f.). Since "it is enough for the disciple to be like his teacher" (Mt. 10:25), they literally followed his footsteps, bore the marks of Jesus in their bodies, and believed themselves to "complete what remains of Christ's afflictions for the sake of his body, that is, the church" (Col. 1:24). Through their own suffering they discerned how in the mystery of salvation-history God redeems the world through suffering. In the light of Good Friday they understood Christianity to be not a success story but a religion of endurance and forbearance.

The preface to the *Martyr's Mirror* contains a remarkable ode to these "Knights of the Cross" which reads in part as follows: "From all ages most honor and glory has been given the great knights of war who have risked their lives on enemy territory and won great battles. There is for example the most eminent of Greek warriors, Ulysses, whose illustrious victories the great Homer devoted twenty-four books to praise. Quintus Curtius described the deeds of Alexander, the son of Philip of Macedonia, in ten books, how he conquered and enslaved Europe, Asia, India, and the lands of the East along the great World Ocean until finally he ended his life in Babylon. Plutarch wrote a great book to the honor and dedication of the most excellent warrior. Titus Livius described the Roman heroes and how honorably they fought for the Roman fatherland. Virgilius Maro and others praised Caesar Augustus as had been done and continues to be done in all lands throughout the world. But none of these, no matter how great, mighty, famous or victorious they might have been and irrespective with what honor and glory they might have been crowned, can be compared with the least of the martyrs who voluntarily suffered as a witness of Jesus Christ, . . . even as also the battles which they fought were infinitely more useful, and their victories, though wrought by the hand of God, infinitely more glorious and worthy."[8]

Those who proclaim only cheap grace and not the bitter Christ stand corrected by the witness of the Christian martyrs of all ages. The Gospel of Jesus Christ is not a mere emotional uplift but a proclamation of the realism of the Cross. The Cross is God's answer to the problem of evil and speaks for the fact that there is no such thing as holy war, only holy martyrdom. The Cross stands between natural and Christian existence. To bridge this transition means to experience something of its realism in one's own life. The Cross of Christ challenges the self-evidence of life and history and calls in question the integrity of those who claim to be members of the Kingdom of God and the kingdoms of this world at the same time and in the same way.

Jesus' teaching on the meaning of the Cross for human relations is painfully specific. According to Luke, the essence of Jesus' Sermon on the Mount is to love one's fellow being, not as the sinners who love only their friends, but as disciples who love their enemies also (Lk. 6:20ff.). This hard saying is an intolerable offense to our natural selves, for it violates our notion of justice. Even theologians sought to interpret the Master's words a hundred different ways to imply that either he did not mean what he said or we do not know what he meant. The Catholics limited what he said to monks and priests. Luther claimed Jesus meant what he said only for the sphere of one's personal life. Calvin found it altogether too unrealistic. Evangelicals argue as Augustine that they can love their enemies while killing them since what matters is not the body but the soul. The Scofield Reference Bible states (cf. p. 1,000) that the Sermon on the Mount is not intended for Christians, at least not until the millennium. Christians need not love their enemies until the millennium when there are not supposed to be any. One hardly gathers the impression from the Gospels that Jesus intended his disciples to put off their obedience that long![9] Others argue that what matters ultimately is not how we live but what we believe. It almost seems Jesus anticipated this response when he concluded his sermon, saying: "Why do you call me, 'Lord, Lord,' and do not what I tell you?" (Lk. 6:46), or again, "Not every one who says, 'Lord, Lord,' shall enter the Kingdom . . . but he who does the will of my Father" (Mt. 7:21). "Go therefore and make disciples . . . teaching them to observe all that I have commanded you" (Mt. 28:19f.).

To be a Christian means to be conscripted by Christ for the great revolution between the powers of good and evil that rage in this world which God created and for which Christ died. The very conflict within our own life is a part of this revolution, and unless we have resolved within ourselves this matter of personal and total allegiance we are not fit to be "soldiers of the Cross."

Can a Christian be a soldier? When Cromwell's men sought to persuade George Fox to take up arms for the Commonwealth against the king, he told them, "I live in the virtue of that life and power that took away the occasion of all wars."[10] Richard Ullmann, an exponent of Quaker thought and practice, once said: "Some actions may sometimes be right and at other times wrong" (e. g., the use of wine in the Eucharist or at the bar); "other actions like warfare or cannibalism can never be right in any conceivable situation because they destroy in themselves the structure of being, which is the ground of the true self-hood, and are therefore self-destructive."[11] What has war to do with religion? Mark Twain never did get the connection. His War Prayer depicts this dilemma: "O Lord our Father, our young patriots, idols of our hearts, go forth to battle—be Thou near them! With them, in spirit, we also go forth from the sweet peace of our beloved firesides to smite the foe. O Lord our God, help us to tear their soldiers to bloody shreds with our shells;

help us to cover their smiling fields with the pale forms of their patriot dead; help us to drown the thunder of the guns with the shrieks of their wounded, writhing in pain; help us to lay waste their humble homes with a hurricane of fire; help us to wring the hearts of their unoffending widows with unavailing grief; help us to turn them out roofless with their children to wander unfriended the wastes of their desolate land in rags and hunger and thirst, sports of the sun flames of summer and the icy winds of winter, broken in spirit, worn with travail, imploring Thee for the refuge of the grave and denied it—for our sakes who adore Thee, Lord, blast their hopes, blight their lives, protract their bitter pilgrimage, make heavy their steps, water their way with their tears, stain the white snow with the blood of their wounded feet! We ask it in the spirit of love, of Him Who is the Source of Love, and Who is the ever-faithful refuge and friend of all that are sore beset and seek His aid with humble and contrite hearts. Amen."[12] One example of this religious spirit is the soul-stirring prayer of the American Lutheran Chaplain who, on August 5, 1945, "blessed" the Hiroshima H-bomb (hence known in Japan as the "Christian Bomb") just prior to that fatal mission.[13] But there is already enough "christian" blasphemy in print. Besides, Major Eatherly's conscience is still burning—despite all psychotherapy.[14]

Why not be "realistic"? The Jews of Jesus' day were. They argued: "If we let him go on thus, everyone will believe in him, and the Romans will come and destroy both our holy place and our nation" (Jn. 11:48). Consequently, "they took counsel how to put him to death" (v. 53). But they did not reckon with the reality of the resurrection. Unbelievers still do not. Consequently, they cannot understand that survival at any price is not the chief end of life, nor do they comprehend why Christians are less concerned about their own survival than that of others. Because they did not understand (I Cor. 2:8), they crucified Jesus as a rebel, denounced Paul as an agitator (Acts 24:5), condemned the Anabaptists as traitors, and denounce Christian Pacifists as Communists. It is the only way unbelievers can make sense out of people who are in but not of this world. When one responds to Jesus, one becomes irresponsible to Caesar, and, when one is willing to suffer or even die for a right cause rather than live to fight for a wrong one, one becomes politically unreliable. The question is not whether the way of the Cross works for pagans but whether the unity of love and truth which it symbolizes holds for Christians in such a way that they can affirm life by transcending it, find it through losing it, and "walk cheerfully over the world answering that of God in every one."[15]

That is how a disciple becomes like his Master. Freed from the dominion and bondage of the "gods" of this world, the disciple triumphs in Christ over the uncommitted powers and forces that constitute the stuff of actual life and history. To follow Jesus is to know the fellowship of his suffering and the power of his resurrection and to live on the resurrection side of the Cross.

God is not dead but continues to live in the lives of His followers. The resurrected living Lord is present with us now, speaking to us through the witness of his Word and Spirit. The Spirit of God attests the power and glory of His presence in the obedience of the children of God. To do His will is to know His grace and truth.

Essentially, discipleship is not our decision for or against this or that course of action. Obviously it is that too. But essentially it is always a decision for or against Christ, and therefore our situation is really not so different from that of Levi the tax collector or Peter the fisherman. These men saw a rabbi and a healer and believed Christ. We perceive the witness of his Spirit through his Word and believe. What any one of any era makes of the call of Jesus depends on what Jesus is to that one. To acknowledge him as the Christ is to be overcome by his authority and power. To believe in him is to be transformed by him. Essentially, he does not meet us differently than he did those disciples then. The same Lord who called the prophets and apostles is calling us now. And, in recognizing who it is that calls, both they and we understand the content of that call: to trust God and love our neighbor.

The Bible is not a precise pattern of obedience for us to imitate but a witness to Jesus Christ, confronting individuals then as he confronts us now. We are not simply to imitate the experiences of Peter or Levi as the pattern of obedience for our own life. Instead, we are to listen to Jesus Christ in order to understand what it is that he has to tell us. Only from him can we learn what decisions and partings are in store for us. Only he who bids us follow knows the way and the journey's end. In answering his call we need not fear where he will lead us, for we know it will be a road of boundless mercy and joy. Because it is Jesus Christ whom we obey, we need not worry about the goal and result of that obedience.[16]

---

[1]Gerhard Kittel, ed., *Theologisches Wörterbuch zum Neuen Testament* (Stuttgart: Kohlhammer Verlag, 1933), I:210f.; *Die Religion in Geschichte und Gegenwart* (Tübingen: J. C. B. Mohr, 1960), IV:1286f.

[2]Cf. Martin Buber, "Die Frage an den Einzelnen," *Martin Buber Werke*, Schriften zur Philosophie, erster Band (München: Kösel Verlag, 1962), p. 215ff.

[3]Dietrich Bonhoeffer, *Nachfolge* (München: Chr. Kaiser Verlag, 1952), p. 47ff.

[4]Karl Barth, *Church Dogmatics* (Edinburgh: T & T Clark), IV/2:551f.

[5]Cf. John W. Miller, "The Renewal of the Church," *Concern* 12 (Scottdale, Feb. 1966):32f.

[6]Cf. my essay, "The Theological Rationale for Mutual Aid," *Report* VII, Nos. 3 & 4 (Akron, Pa., Winter 1965), p. 15ff.

[7]Lydia Müller, *Glaubenszeugnisse oberdeutscher Taufgesinnter,* Quellen und Forschungen zur Reformationsgeschichte, No. 20 (1938), pp. 14, 34.

[8]T. J. v. Braght, ed., *Der blutige Schauplatz, oder Märtyrer-Spiegel der Taufs-Gesinnten oder Wehrlosen Christen,* 1660 (Elkhart, Indiana, 1870), p. 10.

[9]On the history of interpretation cf. my booklet, *Christian Discipleship* (Newton: Faith and Life Press, 1964), p. 7f.

[10]John L. Nickalls, ed., *The Journal of George Fox* (Cambridge: University Press, 1952), p. 65.

[11]Richard K. Ullmann, *Between God and History* (London: George Allen & Unwin, 1959), p. 128.

[12]Quoted from *The Christian Century* LXXXIII, No. 34 (Chicago, Aug. 24, 1966), p. 1030.

[13]Cited in Helmut Gollwitzer, "Die Christen und die Atomwaffen," *Theologische Existenz Heute,* Heft 61 (München: Chr. Kaiser Verlag, 1957), p. 7.

[14]Cf. Claude Eatherly, *Burning Conscience*; the Case of the Hiroshima Pilot, told in his letters . . . , 1st Amer. ed. (New York: Monthly Review Press, 1962).

[15]Fox, *Journal*, p. 263.

[16]Bonhoeffer, *Nachfolge*, p. 149f.

RECOVERING THE ANABAPTIST MOVEMENT

I. THE QUEST FOR IDENTITY

Mennonites are spiritual pilgrims. For generations they have lived amid diverse cultures and nations without fully belonging. They conquered the frontiers of Russia and of North and South America but never joined the political establishments. They came as trusty pioneers and they remained as restless settlers. Mennonites— as Jews since the time of Abraham—have wandered over this world recalling their history and seeking their destiny. Instead of being satisfied with the fruits of honest labor and that security, leisure, and pleasure which affluence affords, they are forever in quest of their identity. Indeed, they are a peculiar people—all the more so in that they are neither fully conscious nor wholly unconscious of their *Daseinsberechtigung.* Try as they might, they can neither completely abandon the world to work out their own salvation nor fully conquer it for Christ. They are in the world but not of the world, and, inasmuch as they are for the world, it is not for them. They can identify with it only as they transcend it, but they cannot claim it as their own ground of being. They can affirm the world as the place where God speaks and acts, but they can be attached to the world and involved in the world only inasmuch as they are not bound by the world. The transcendence of their other-worldliness qualifies the historicity of their this-worldliness so that regardless of whether they appear to be plain people or fancy people they remain peculiar people. To understand this peculiar Mennonite self-understanding is to come to terms with its historical landmarks and its theological roots within the sociology of the Reformation and the consciousness of Jesus.

II. HISTORICAL LANDMARKS

Under the influence of the Swiss Reformer Ulrich Zwingli
(1484-1531), three young men of Zürich, Conrad Grebel (later to
be known as the founder of the Swiss Brethren), Felix Mantz, and
Georg Blaurock, along with Wilhelm Reublin and others were
awakened to faith and captivated by the Christian way of life they
discovered in the New Testament. In the hope of recovering the
true Church in accord with the Gospel, they demanded radical
reforms to abolish those established Christian practices (such as
infant baptism, the Catholic Mass, and the use of the sword) which
did not conform to the teaching of Jesus. Zwingli, who had inspired
this radical vision in his disciples, urged caution and moderation in
deference to the City Council of Zürich, which felt threatened by
the surrounding Catholic cantons. Thereupon, Grebel voiced dis-
pleasure with the reformation of Zwingli and of Martin Luther,
lamenting that it was all too little and too late. Grebel reprimanded
Luther for his compromising tactics and concessions, and Luther
indicated he was at a loss to know how to respond. Grebel com-
plained that the evangelical pastors drank the purest water and then
stirred much turbidity for their sheep so as to defend their own
interests with their scandal. The Grebel group was committed to
Christian obedience, not to political expediency, and what Zwingli
and Luther considered the better part of wisdom these young radi-
cals interpreted as betrayal of the Gospel.

In their impatience they sought to implement the house
church ideal Luther had popularized but never realized. On January
21, 1525, they met in the house of Felix Mantz to implore God to
enable them to act in accord with His will. Thereupon, Grebel baptized Blaurock, who, in turn, baptized the others. Thereafter,
"Anabaptism" became the shibboleth of this movement. The rift
with Zwingli was inevitable, not because he opposed believer's baptism, but because its implementation appeared proleptic, presumptu-

ous, and politically irresponsible.

On March 16, 1525, the Zürich City Council declared rebaptism a criminal offense punishable by exile, and soon Anabaptists were persecuted throughout the German Empire. But the suppressive measures employed against this movement furthered more than hindered its rapid expansion throughout and beyond Europe. Grebel testified in Schaffhausen and taught in St. Gall, where by Palm Sunday he won five hundred converts. Mantz baptized in Graubünden. Having been literally whipped out of Zürich, Blaurock went as apostle to the Tirol while Reublin left for Upper Germany where he baptized three hundred, including Hubmaier, whose disciple Jacob Gross founded the church at Strassburg. Hubmaier baptized many in Augsburg and Moravia, including Melchior Rinck, the apostle to Hessen and Thüringen, and also Hans Denck on August 22, 1526. That month, Denck baptized the colporteur Hans Hut, who in turn baptized one thousand others in Franconia, Swabia, and Austria. Meanwhile, Michael Sattler was active in Strassburg and the Upper Rhein while Melchior Hofmann introduced Anabaptism to East Friesland and the Netherlands. Hofmann baptized Obbe Philips, who in 1535 baptized Menno Simons under whose leadership the Mennonites spread throughout the Netherlands while Jacob Hutter organized his communities in Moravia and Pilgram Marbeck stabilized the movement in South Germany. The zeal and power of the Anabaptist vision had spread throughout Europe like a forest fire.

III. ANABAPTIST MARTYROLOGY

But Anabaptist history is martyr history. By the middle of 1526 Conrad Grebel succumbed to the plague. His father was beheaded in Zürich the following October. Felix Mantz was the first to be martyred by Protestants who, on January 5th, 1527, bound him hand and foot and drowned him in the Limmat River which flows through Zürich. Most of the Anabaptist participants in the so-called

Martyrs' Synod at Augsburg in 1527 were apprehended and subsequently executed. Michael Sattler, a former Benedictine monk from South Germany who inspired the Schleitheim Confession of faith, was tried and tormented with glowing fire tongs and grilled in the marketplace of Rottenburg on May 21, 1527. Eight days later his wife was drowned. Hans Hut burned to death in his prison cell in September, 1527. In November, Hans Denck died of the plague. On January 14, 1528, Leonhard Schiemer was executed in Rattenberg. The same fate befell Hans Schlaffer and Leonard Funck at Schwaz. On March 10th Balthasar Hubmaier was burned alive in Vienna, and his wife was drowned in the Donau River. May 11th, Hans Langenmantel was beheaded, and about the same time Johannes Brötli was burned at the stake. In 1529 Wolfgang Brandhuber and seventy other Anabaptists were executed in Linz. In September, Georg Blaurock was burned to death at Klausen in the Eschtal. Jacob Hutter, Jakob Zaunring, Offrus Griesinger and countless others suffered the same fate. Kirchmayr estimated that in 1531 in the Tirol and Görz counties alone there had been one thousand executions. According to *Die Älteste Chronik*, "*die Summe der Erwürgten*" by 1581 in that Hutterian community in Moravia was 2,169. Sebastian Franck recounted six hundred executions in Ensisheim and estimated the number of martyrs by 1530 at two thousand. The historian Ludwig Keller estimated the number of Anabaptists imprisoned, tortured, branded, exiled, and executed at about ten thousand by 1530, but the most severe persecution raged after that date and of this no records have survived.

Between 1525 and 1761 no less than 213 Imperial mandates were issued against the Anabaptists demanding their imprisonment and torture until they recanted, which, in most cases, meant until they expired. Some mandates allowed suspects to be beheaded if they recanted, otherwise, to be burned at the stake. Many edicts offered high rewards for identifying suspects and made attempts to shelter, feed, or employ them a criminal offense.

IV. THE MISUNDERSTANDING OF THE CHURCH

From its inception, the Anabaptist movement by its very existence as a voluntary community of believers threatened the theological and, in turn, political intactness of the *corpus christianum* into
which, since the time of Constantine the Great, all Europeans were
automatically inducted at birth by the ecclesiastic rite of infant baptism. Soon after birth, every infant was involuntarily baptized into
the church before it was old enough to know what was intended or
able to give its consent. With pedobaptism, everyone inherited the
Christian identity, irrespective of whether he believed it or not, and
retained this identity, irrespective of whether he lived it or not and
irrespective of whether he wanted it or not.

The Anabaptist dissent from this medieval misunderstanding
of the Church effected a radical breakthrough in consciousness
regarding what it really means to be a Christian. Within the emerging Anabaptist movement, believing in Christ meant following
Jesus and committing oneself to the Christian way of life without
reservation. This new consciousness implied a radically new understanding of the Church as a voluntary fellowship of believers committed to embodying in their faith and life the actual teaching of
Jesus, an awareness that was the fruit of a rediscovery of the Scriptures as the revelation of God's will for our lives. Along the road-
sides, in house meetings, at secret forest gatherings, and wherever
possible, the Bible was being read in the vernacular and applied in
preaching and mutual admonition. Prior to Luther's translation of
1522, eighteen German versions of Scripture were already in use
among the common folk, and here and there former humanist scholars, like Conrad Grebel and former priests like Felix Mantz and
Michael Sattler, interpreted and taught the Word from its Greek and
Hebrew originals. The 1527 Worms edition of Scripture came to be
known as the Anabaptist Bible. Within the emerging Free Church
consciousness, the priesthood of all believers implied that one could

no longer assume God's will to be identical with tradition and establishment. Thousands of court records reveal how much Anabaptists knew and quoted the Bible—especially the teaching of Jesus—as the norm for faith and life.

V. THE WAY OF PEACE

From its inception the Anabaptist movement was consistently committed to the way of peace exemplified by loving one's enemies and not resisting evil with evil in accord with Jesus' Sermon on the Mount. The evidence for the Anabaptist emphasis on nonviolence is overwhelming. Andreas Castelberger, co-founder of the Grebel group, preached that war is sin and that, before God, a soldier is a murderer. Hearing of Thomas Müntzer's intention to defend the Gospel with the sword, Grebel wrote to reprimand him, saying that true Christians neither use the sword nor go to war, for they have put away all killing. When a traveling goldsmith confirmed Müntzer's intentions, Grebel added a postscript of stern reproof.

At his trial, Felix Mantz testified that no Christian slaughters with the sword and that no Christian should judge, kill, or punish with the sword. Just before his public drowning, he wrote an ode to Christian love entitled, *"Bye Christum will ich bleiben,"* one stanza of which read in part: "Christus tut niemand zwingen in seiner Herrlichkeit . . . die Lieb in Christo reine verschonet hie den Feind."

The court record of Junghans Waldshuter, a Zürich weaver from the Grebel group, recounts his dialogue with a local minister over a glass of wine. The Pfarrer argued that a Christian government had the right to take life. Waldshuter replied that no Christian should kill. For this, Waldshuter was imprisoned.

Kessler, the chronicler of St. Gall, reported that, contrary to prevailing custom, the Anabaptists wore neither sword nor dagger, an observation confirmed by the mayors of Bern and Zürich as being the only certain way of detecting an Anabaptist.

The first Anabaptist confession, the *"Brüderliche Vereinigung"* of Schleitheim, 1527, devotes the longest article to the rejection of the sword as "eine Ordnung Gottes ausserhalb der Vollkommenheit Christi." In response, Zwingli published a rebuttal ridiculing their alleged "perfection" in which Zwingli argues: Murder does not always come by the sword; sometimes it is by a spear or a stone. Ought we then remove mountains and forests because weapons are made from them? One dies from the seed of a raisin, another from a goat's hair in a glass of milk, or from a bee sting. Should we therefore abolish grapes, goats, and bees? I do not understand their nonsense for refusing to bear arms. Instead, let everyone be faithful in his calling and note that Christians in particular are called to judge, for that, concludes Zwingli, is how God's Kingdom is built and united. Needless to say, this line of reasoning has not died out with Zwingli!

Soon after Schleitheim, Michael Sattler was burned at the stake in Rottenburg, partly because he said he would not resist an invasion even by the Turks. Sattler declared that the Turk is a Turk according to the flesh whereas those who claim to be Christian while martyring true believers are Turks according to the spirit. He was accused of having said that, if war were morally justifiable, he would rather side with the Turks than with the hypocrites! Since Archduke Ferdinand was encountering great difficulty soliciting volunteers for the Imperial army, Sattler's views were most unsettling. Sattler volunteered to publicly defend his convictions from the original languages of Scripture, but the clerk of the court retorted that the hangman would take up the disputation with him. Sattler's tongue was removed, then he was bound to a wagon and disemboweled with hot fire tongs en route to the marketplace and finally burned at the stake with a sack of gunpowder tied to his neck.

To obtain any adequate impression of the centrality of this so "heretical" doctrine of nonresistance in the life and death of these sixteenth-century Anabaptists, one must read the epistles, tracts, and confessions of Hans Hut, Leonhard Schiemer, Peter Riedemann, Jacob Hutter, Klaus Felbinger, Leonhard Dax, Ambrosius Spittelmayr, Pilgram Marbeck, Leopold Scharnschlager, Thomas von Imbroich, etc., not to mention many volumes of legal documentation from the court trials of Hans Marquart, Plathans von der Sorge, Curt Schenk, and countless others, mention of whom is made only with respect to their pacifism. But the picture is quite incomplete without taking into account the extent to which their nonviolence became the focus of interrogation at the extensive disputations held with Anabaptists at Aarau 1531, Zofingen 1532, Bern 1531 and 1538, Pfeddersheim 1557, Frankental 1571, Worms 1577, Emden 1578, and Leeuwarden 1596, most of which were in continuous session for weeks—not to mention numerous less dramatic encounters. The overwhelming evidence indicates almost without exception that the Swiss Brethren, the Moravian Anabaptists and those of Upper Germany were convinced pacifists as were the followers of Menno Simons in Holland, a fact which Zwingli, Bullinger, Capito, Bucer, Luther, and other leading Reformers themselves invariably admitted and which was equally evident to the mayors, judges, and hangmen of many a European court.

VI. CHURCH AND STATE

How can one explain the Reformers' collaboration in the mass extermination of these pacifist Anabaptists? Protestants generally excuse the Reformers' intolerance on grounds of their ignorance (in somehow confusing pacifists with rebels), thereby underestimating their intelligence, while Mennonites usually ascribe it to the Reformers' malevolence, thereby underrating their integrity. The root of the conflict lies deeper and within the sociological rather than the personal sphere. In the interest of defending the intactness of the socio-political order, the Reformers rationalized the necessity of exercising the most harsh conceivable measures against these pacifists lest in time of national crisis the common citizen lose faith in the baptized body politic and ideological confusion lead to political anarchy and national disaster. On account of their refusal to become "responsible" citizens, Heinrich Bullinger warned the Swiss Republic not to tolerate the Anabaptists lest the nation suffer shame, embarrassment, and defeat in battle. The Anabaptists' refusal to bear arms or to swear the loyalty oath constituted an intolerable security risk. Bullinger was keen enough to foresee that, once a people's faith in '*Kriegsdienst als Gottesdienst*' is shattered, one can no more anticipate of them a brilliant military performance than one can expect milk from a dead cow. This political shrewdness was shared by Lutheran theologians who at the Colloquy of Worms in 1557 condemned Anabaptist nonviolence "als gewisslich an sich selb Aufruhr und Zerstörung der Obrigkeit und ordentlich Regiment." Anabaptist pacifism constituted a threat to the security of the socio-economic-political status quo inasmuch as, if pressed to its ultimate conclusion, it amounts to a declaration of Christian freedom from the national necessity to survive.

In Anabaptist perspective, persecution of a community committed to the Way of the Cross by a society committed to the national ethos and the amenities of life seemed self-evident. Leonhard Schiemer reminded his persecuted congregation that Jesus himself was crucified for creating unrest among the people from Jerusalem to Galilee. And the Jewish rationale for Jesus' execution was: "If we let him go on thus, everyone will believe in him and the Romans will come and destroy both our place and our nation" (Jn. 11:48). The sixteenth-century Anabaptists concluded: "Als geet es auch allen Christen, dan der Jünger ist nit mer dan der Meister."

VII. ANABAPTIST DISCIPLESHIP

The key to Anabaptist faith and life is its identity with Christ and its imitation of Christ. The Anabaptists understood the life of Jesus as an example or precedent to be imitated or followed. Jesus patiently endured suffering, refused pagan power structures, and rejected all forms of violence. Therefore, said they, we must do likewise. Christ has shown us the WAY and it is the essence of Christianity to be a people of this WAY, that is, to follow in his steps. To teach us this WAY of Christ and to enable us to walk in it was seen to be the essential meaning and purpose of the Gospels. The City Council of Nürnberg advised its ministers in 1527 that the heresy of the Anabaptists consists, in the first instance, in their insistence that a Christian must walk in the footsteps of Christ and his apostles, do what they did, and leave what they left. From his prison cell, Felix Mantz wrote his brethren: "Christ never hated anyone and therefore his servants also do not hate anyone and follow after Christ on the right way, even as he walked before. They have this light of life before them and rejoice therein to walk."

According to the 1527 Anabaptist Schleitheim Confession, "if we run after him, we will not fall into darkness. . . ." Anabaptist obedience literally took the form of "running after" Jesus. Through the Gospels they became conscious of the living Christ teaching them and directing their lives in conformity to his own. The very acts and decisions of the historical Jesus became normative for their own lifestyle. In Jesus' mercy toward the woman caught in adultery, in his refusal to judge in matters of inheritance, and in his escape when the multitudes sought to crown him king they discovered a guide for their own living. In the actual historical and political situations in which Jesus' divine nature was manifest in service and in suffering, they found the meaning of their own renunciation and humiliation and of their own way of love and suffering. For conformity to this pattern and example, they were prepared to sacrifice their vocation, their security, and their life, for their identity with Christ and his Way of life constituted the whole meaning of their being.

In Anabaptism, discipleship meant not merely right faith (*fides orthodoxa*) but also true life. Obedience to Christ was more than an inner decision of faith: it implied the commitment of one's whole life to the Lordship of Christ. Hans Hut testified: "God has forbidden us to do what we deem good, but what he commands we are to do and keep and not waver to the right nor to the left." In the 1531 Bern disputation, Hans Pfistermeyer attested: "What I can find in Christ Jesus, in his teaching and life, that I will consider to be right, and what not, I will not accept."

The Anabaptist theology of discipleship is poignantly expressed in the words of Hans Denck: "Christus niemand vermag wahrlich zu erkennen, es sei denn, dass er ihm nachfolge mit dem Leben." The same motif recurs in Hans Hut who claimed that "no one can arrive at the truth except he follow in the footsteps of Christ and his chosen ones in the school of all trial. He who will not follow the footsteps, will not walk the WAY, nor carry the Cross, he neither has nor knows the Son."

Anabaptist faith was very existential in the sense that it expressed itself in total life commitment. It implied an epistemology of obedience inasmuch as God's will could be known only through concrete commitment. *Nachfolge* under the Cross was for them not a mere formula but the vital experience of living in the very presence of Christ. The hermeneutical principle of single-minded obedience to the living Word of God made the Gospels normative for their understanding of the Church as a committed fellowship of disciples and for their view of the Christian life as a service of love and nonresistance, a way of renunciation, humiliation, and reconciliation, the way of love that suffers evil but refuses to commit evil. The Anabaptists agreed with the Reformers that one can be saved only

by faith but added, "only through the mediation of love can faith
aspire." They agreed with the Catholics that without works there is
no salvation but added that good work is acceptable to God only
when motivated by selfless Calvary love.

Anabaptist discipleship is more than a merely human attempt
at following Jesus. It is, above all, a decisive allegiance to the person
of the Master and therefore effective participation as apprentice in
the Master's vocation. And, since the disciple's ground of being is
not in himself but in the Lord of history, the question of the disciple's ability or inability remains unknown, for God Himself, through
the power of His Spirit, enables the disciple to participate in the perfect obedience of His Son in the ministry of reconciliation and
redemption.

VIII. RECOVERING THE VISION

The Anabaptist vision cannot be recovered merely by admiring the commitment of those who embodied it nor even by perpetuating a semblance of their piety but only by rekindling the fire of the
Spirit that inspired it. We cannot thrive on the faith of our forefathers
unless their faith truly becomes our very own. Any rekindling of the
glow of their vision, any regeneration of the power that inspired
them demands the same level of personal commitment and spiritual
integrity on our part, the same willingness to ask the radical existential questions of faith and life all over again for the kind of world in
which we live today, the same openness to comprehend at any price
the ultimate dimensions of life, the same readiness for God.

It has been keenly observed that the Anabaptist vision is
clearer in theory than in practice, is more convincing theologically
than sociologically, is more appropriate for sixteenth-century
Anabaptists than for their twentieth-century descendants, that it
applies more directly to conditions of poverty than to those of pros-

perity and is more representative of small pilgrim-oriented minorities than of large established majorities. No one vision is adequate for all times and circumstances, but, where there is no vision, the people perish, for one cannot live by bread alone. The genius of that vision and the essence of that movement become the subject of diverse interpretation depending on the perspective and maturity brought to the task of historical research. It is enough to realize that the inner dynamics of Anabaptism were the living expression of the Spirit that inspired it. We can empirically describe the form of that sixteenth-century event, but we cannot capture its dynamic for our time nor determine its future course. The record of Anabaptist obedience may inspire future obedience, but neither that inspiration nor that obedience is inherited with the Mennonite label. Once the experiential reality of that vision is transformed into a terminal cultural symbol it has lost the inspiring influence of its spiritual intention. Perpetuating form without power is spiritually more harmful than hopeful and borders on hypocrisy. No wonder Mennonites who have failed to recover the Anabaptist vision for their own life and time seek to replace it with charismatic experience, evangelical fervor, or a service-oriented lifestyle. Though truth is flung into the heart by a thousand means, one should not sell one's birthright for a mess of pottage nor reject the inspiration that has informed our past without knowing what one is doing. Though God chooses to reveal Himself in different ways at different times, He does so with a consistency that characterized the witness of the prophets, apostles, and disciples of all ages.

There is no easy way into authenticity. Every generation must seek and find its own truth. But none can recover the larger meaning of being that was meant to inform our destiny without recovering the integrative principle that embodied the highest self-understanding of those who have gone before. Since all who follow the truth are guided by the same light refracted through the ages in a thousand different ways, the continuity of meaning cannot be built on historical ingratitude or ignorance. The Anabaptist heritage is a priceless historical legacy of the highest spiritual order. It would surely be a great pity for any Mennonite worthy of that name not to be captivated by its wonder and power or for an enlightened mind not to be inspired by its wisdom and truth.

The Anabaptist vision enabled transcendent spirits to rise high enough above that ocean of accepted truths constituting the thought currents of their time to recover within the Gospel the reality of the living Christ. That confrontation transformed their martyr witness into a burning and shining light which continues to illumine our own way.

NOTES ON JEWISH–CHRISTIAN DIALOGUE

DO JEWS AND CHRISTIANS WORSHIP THE SAME GOD?

DO JEWS AND CHRISTIANS CONSTITUTE ONE PEOPLE OF GOD?

Indeed, both Jews and Christians confess God's UNITY, but their respective confessions divide them at the very heart of their spiritual being.

Jews and Christians are united in God's SAMENESS but divided by their affirmation of His ONENESS.

Jews and Christians affirm the ontological uniqueness of God. Xenophanes said: ALL is one. Moses said: God is One, for only He is God.

This means that God is not the world and the world is not God. God and world are two, not one, and the relation between them is expressed by creation and redemption.

Creation is not a co-mixture of God and world, and incarnation is not an identification of God with the world as in Pantheism (nor is the world an emanation of God as in Gnosticism).

God alone is free and independent in His being. All other being is dependent being. All other existence is borrowed existence within the space and time God has created for us and granted to us.

All other being is called into being through the Word by which God created the world and reconciles it to Himself.

God alone is the ground of all being, of ultimate being, of true being. He alone is perfect and eternal in His being and His love.

Jews and Christians agree that God's unique being is the meaning of (all) being.

Throughout the ages, the Jewish-Christian proclamation of the Shema Israel (Hear O Israel, He our God, He [is] One) has effected the extinction of Olympus and Valhalla as it did the priests of Baal on Mt. Carmel.

Though Jews and Christians stand united in affirming God's ontological uniqueness, they are DIVIDED over the moral implications of that affirmation.

For Jews to proclaim that God is one means that none beside Him may be worshiped (I Kgs. 8:22f., Isa. 44:6, Hos. 13:4, Zec. 14:9, and Mal. 2:10).

Jesus confirmed the priority of the SHEMA for faith and life (Mk. 12:28f.), declaring that one shall worship and serve God alone (Mt. 4:10).

But his followers, beginning with Thomas, declared him Lord and God (Jn. 20:28). Christians claim that the abiding fullness of God became flesh in Jesus.

Jesus taught his disciples to pray, not to himself, but to God. Jesus was a Jew and prayed as a Jew. Christians, however, are divided from Jews by their prayers inasmuch as they pray TO or THROUGH Jesus rather than AS Jesus prayed.

For JEWS, Christian trinitarianism and incarnation compromise the absoluteness of God's uniqueness. Jews insist 1) that God is incorporeal, 2) that His existence is not like that of any living being (Maimonides), and 3) that the forms of God's self-manifestation are as indeterminable as is His nature.

From the central affirmation of faith the division extends to the nature of the Messiah and of the Divine Presence in the world.

Most Jews do not hold that Jesus WAS the Messiah, for in his time the power of Rome was not broken, the Davidic kingdom was not restored, and the scattered not returned. When the King comes, they expect his kingship to be visible.

Nevertheless, they respect Gamaliel's word to the Sanhedrin (Acts 5:39): "If this (Jesus) movement is of God you cannot overthrow it, lest perhaps you be found to fight against God."

"Without the Jewish Messiah, Judaism is defective; but, without the Christian Messiah, Christianity does not exist at all."

Since the Christian Messiah is the Jewish Messiah, Christians and Jews need to discover through each other their common hope.

At first the only difference between Christians and other Jews was that the Messianists proclaimed the Messiah had already come, while the others held that the Messiah was still to come—for how could the King come without his Kingdom!

Inasmuch as the Kingdom comes through Jesus' teaching, Jews as Christians are charmed but offended by his demands. For how can a nation triumph if it becomes pacifist? How can a state endure if it abolishes the oath? How can a culture prosper if its investors are condemned for being camels that cannot squeeze through the needle's eye of austerity? How can a people survive if its eunuchs are idolized?

Jews understood that following Jesus is too costly, while Christians, with the aid of their theology, have devised an amazing variety of explanations for why one could not or should not obey the commandments of Jesus. Within Christendom, the WAY of the Cross has become a THEOLOGY of the Cross. With transition from the existential to the epistemological plane, the command to FOLLOW JESUS has become an intellectual problem of BELIEVING (in) CHRIST.

What most Christians and Jews have in common is their rejection of Jesus' teaching. But the question remains: How does the INTEGRITY of JEWS who reject Jesus compare with the HYPOCRISY of CHRISTIANS who claim him as Lord but do not do what he says?

Jews also differ from Christians in their understanding of God's self-manifestion. Judaism lives by the unmediated Divine Presence encompassing all of life, nature, and history, while Christian piety perpetuates itself in sacramental presence mediated by Christ, Mary, saints, and priests.

Christians are confronted with the mystery that the covenant of Sinai lives on within the Jewish people. It would be far simpler theologically if the OLD COVENANT disappeared when the NEW ONE came into effect. As it is, there are two mutually exclusive People of the One God.

JEWISH-CHRISTIAN DIALOGUE

Existing Difficulties

1) Deliberate destruction of both the body and the spirit of

European Judaism in the HOLOCAUST is still very real in the Jewish mind.

2) The Vatican does not officially acknowledge the existence of Israel, and the World Council of Churches is accused of carrying on secular politics with Israel's enemies, that is, the PLO.

3) Jews see the Christian missionary attitude and aim as an extension of Christian imperialism (especially the intention of establishing in Israel a Jewish Church). Jews resent Christian attempts to convert them (the first Anglican bishop, Alexander, himself a Jewish convert, was sent in 1841 to Jerusalem to missionize Jews).

4) Dialogue often deteriorates into monologue, into the intellectual exercise of enduring another's opinion as the price for presenting one's own without any real mutual listening, introspection, internalization, or common prayer.

THEOLOGICAL dialogue, especially, appears to Jews as a contradiction in terms, since God (*Theos*) cannot really be described by *Logos*. They feel that silence is more conducive to growth in faith than is dialogue, as in the case of Job who, when he came to faith in God, became silent: "God takes speech away from the faithful" (Jb. 12:20). Confession of faith is essentially more than a theological discussion—it is meant to be an act of life.

INTER-JEWISH DIALOGUE ON THE MEANING OF FAITH

Between Religious and Nonreligious Jews

For secular Jews, the most common logical fallacy in thinking about God is the habit of hypostasis, that is, the assumption of a separate identifiable existence of anything and everything for which language has a name (whether gravity or God) and the investiture of its reality with personal attributes.

Modern secular Jews hold that, just as ancient peoples personified the natural powers of rain, sun, sea, earth, etc. to comprise a pantheon of gods, so early Judaism under Greek influence personified the generic concept of JHWH, ascribing to that ONE personal traits (power, wisdom, love, justice, sovereignty, etc.—all that now comprises the concept of God as eternal, omnipotent, omnipresent, omniscient, etc. and proclaims this personification as the object of prayer or praise) without realizing that such use of religious language implies other-worldly projection of language that has only inner-worldly meaning.

The secular Jew hopes to recover the intended meaning of religious God-talk as the quality of interhuman relationships that make life worthwhile in the deepest, most abiding sense.

They think of God functionally rather than ontologically, as quality rather than as entity, as that which enhances life rather than which exists supernaturally. For them, God is not a reservoir of magic power to be tapped at the boundary of human resources but is the dynamic interaction of life's creative forces and potentialities, that organic unity that gives meaning to life.

For the modern secular Jew, no metaphysical assumption beyond the affirmation that life is worthwhile is necessary. For him, this elemental awareness that life is meaningful is not the result of the religious proposition of God's existence out there somewhere but rather is the innate awareness of the creative potential in authentic human togetherness here and now. It is faith in the ethical quality of life—without metaphysics.

MY FEET STOOD WITHIN YOUR GATES
O JERUSALEM

Jerusalem is a very special place. Just living there expands the horizon of human comprehension. The very meaning of its name, *Yerushalayim*, combines the insight of "vision" (*yireh*) with the promise of "peace" (*shalom*). Its mystique is compounded by the paradox that, since the Stone Age, this citadel of peace has been the arena of war. It has been besieged, conquered, destroyed, rebuilt, and demolished over and over again. Yet, its spirit survives as the oriental sun refracts with dazzling brightness from its golden domes and as the fervent prayers of Jews, Christians, and Moslems re-echo within its ancient walls. Though many times reduced to ruins, those ancient stones, so enduring and strong as that tenacious ancient faith that inspired them, have survived the contempt of all ages.

According to Isaiah, Jerusalem "shall be a crown of beauty in the hand of the Lord," and in the words of the Talmud, "There is no beauty like the beauty of Jerusalem." Isaiah also foretold, "In the latter days" Torah shall go forth from Zion "and the Word of the Lord from Jerusalem." Today, endless streams of humanity from all parts of the earth are flowing day and night through her narrow ancient streets to behold this glowing radiance and to ponder this prophetic mystery. Jerusalem the Golden has become a charismatic city for all time. Its inhabitants speak eighty languages and represent over one hundred cultures. Jerusalem is still pregnant with the power of divine suggestion as though the eye of Jahwe were forever infusing her with the inspiration of His transcendent presence. It is here that waiting for God was born and that anticipation of everlasting peace came to light. Now more than ever Jerusalem embodies the prologue of redemption in its yearnings for a new beginning.

Singers and dancers alike say, "All my springs are in you" (Ps. 87:7).
In the silence of the night the strings of the lute quiver with the same
faith and hope for Jerusalem that inspired those familiar Psalms
which for millennia have permeated the surrounding hills. Great
moments of history have bound the hearts of God's people to
Jerusalem forever. Here, moments of divine revelation became
moments of self-realization. Now a new light has kindled her soul,
an inextinguishable inspiration, an illuminating presence like that of
the glowing bush. "The heart is aflame, and faith is not consumed"
(Heschel).

Nowhere have Israel's hopes and fears been expressed with
more pathos than at the Wailing Wall: that wall of frozen tears, silent
memories, and sealed hopes. "The old mother crying for us all.
Stubborn, loving, waiting for redemption"—as if here all history
were waiting for Godot! That unreachable tombstone for the nameless dead has itself become a Wall of Celebration where a new generation "chants in joy for the rock of our salvation" (Ps. 95:1). That
Wall, so impervious to the desecration of centuries-old garbage
heaped up to cover its face, is itself an unceasing witness "of mysterious majesty in the midst of scorn."

To stand within the gates of Jerusalem in momentary contem-
poraneity with David and Jesus is to realize that not only the joy but
also the burden of experiencing God in history rests upon all who
pass through those gates. Though God is allegedly on the side of the
poor, the inhabitants of those sacred slums are enduring the crippling effects of poverty without consolation. In the fearful eye, the
hate-filled heart, the divided personality, one detects everywhere the
appalling contradiction between promise and fulfillment. While
there is much prayer within the heart and life of these peoples, their
prayers fail to unite them in the divine Oneness which Jews, Christians, and Moslems so ardently profess. Here, as elsewhere, prayers
divide persons and eclipse God. No wonder Jesus wept over

Jerusalem, crying out to its people: "If only you knew what makes
for peace! For this still remains hid from your eyes!" (Lk. 19:41f.).
Within these same walls the acrimonious disputes over religion and
property still perpetuate unreconcilable animosities within the old
fraternities. Within the heart of this city the forces that crucified
Jesus are still operative.

Despite the darkness of the human condition, the eternal
flame is aglow within the heart of Everyman. Though the evidence
be so slight that only the eye of faith perceives it, that faith can overcome mountains of opposition to the Way of Love and can affirm
life even in the midst of death. Standing within the gates of
Jerusalem, one realizes that we are called to live within such contradiction for the sake of this world and its peace. "Pray for the peace
of Jerusalem! May they prosper who love you!" (Ps. 122:6).

There are those who claim God meets us in time rather than in
space, in faithful moments rather than in sacred places. However
that may be, as God endowed Jerusalem with the mystery of the
Shekinah, so He wills to pour holiness into all our moments and to
fill our common form with Divine Presence. Having been there
makes a difference.

THE MYSTERY AND MIRACLE OF THE BIBLE

There is something unique about the Bible, for when one reads it one somehow experiences the mystery and miracle of this book. Throughout the ages, the Church has recognized the Bible as holy, not because she was overwhelmingly impressed by its literary quality, but because she heard in its words the Word of God. Christians of all ages have come to this conclusion not by human logic but by inner conviction of the truth to which the Bible bears witness. For through the Bible we are confronted not merely by its authors but by God Himself.

THE WORD OF GOD AND THE WORD OF MAN IN THE BIBLE

When we speak of God's Word, we do not mean man's word about God, but a word God Himself speaks to man. Man as such is not able to speak God's Word. In his being man stands divided between creation and redemption, profanity and holiness, sin and grace, and this division cuts into his speech. Man's word is, therefore, by nature not about God as it ought to be, but about self.

While the Word of God is different than our word, it is not totally different, for whenever God speaks, He speaks in and through our language. Biblical authors spoke and wrote the Word of God in the language of their time. The origin of the Bible marks the fact that God's Word has become human word, and its nature reflects the manner in which the human word becomes God's Word. It would be false to argue that the Bible is either God's Word or man's word and, if the former, then every particle of it would be divine and, if the latter, none of it would be trustworthy. The uniqueness of the Bible is not that the human element is suppressed and the divine supersedes but that both elements are fused into an essential unity. While the divine element remains primary and decisive, the human element is indispensable both in its active and passive role. The Bible was not written by angels in heaven (as the Moslems claim for the Koran) but by people on earth. The Bible is the rule of faith and life for the Church because of its divine origin and its human nature.

In the Old Testament the Word of God came to the prophets and was proclaimed by them. But in the New Testament we are confronted by one who *is* the Word of God, by Jesus Christ, in whom *the Word became flesh* (Jn. 1:14). The Bible thus declares God's Word to us by proclaiming Jesus Christ who *is* the Word of God. He is the heart through which everything in the Bible unfolds and the criterion by which everything must be valued. The Bible mediates the Word of God to us to the extent that we comprehend the Son of God through it.

In a comprehensive way God creates and redeems through the incarnation of His Word. Through the Word He created the world and through the Word He reconciles it to Himself. Between creation and redemption God's Word became our word in the world so that our word might become God's Word in the Church. This is the power and mystery of God's dialogue with us in history.

REVELATION AND HISTORY

When God speaks and acts He does so in such a way that His history and our history become a common history. God's being with people in this historical way is what the Bible calls revelation. Revelation is as historical as the nation of Israel, as Cyrenius the governor of Syria, or as Pilate who was accorded a place in the Apostle's Creed. We cannot, therefore, ignore history as do those who claim an immediate God relationship that bypasses or circumvents history.

Every such effort to separate divine revelation from history obscures both the nature of God and our relationship with Him.*

While all history presupposes God's creative will, history as such does not however reflect God's redemptive will, for there is much within natural history that contradicts God's redemptive purpose even as there is much within nature that does not reflect God's glory. Divine revelation cannot, therefore, be identified with history as was the case in Idealism, where humanity at its best was regarded identical with the divine. To confuse humanity with deity, history with revelation, is to deny Christianity's basic fact, the act of God in Christ, by universalizing its uniqueness.

From the Christian perspective, the meaning of history is limited to those events within it which are a transparent medium of divine revelation. God is present and active within the historical process but by no means identical with it. The Bible authenticates the fact that God spoke and acted in history, and this indeed is the significance which it ascribes to history.

THE BIBLE AS WITNESS TO REVELATION

The Bible communicates the meaning of life and history by pointing not to itself but to Christ. The Bible is the witness of specific persons proclaiming Jesus Christ—prospectively in the Old Testament and retrospectively in the New Testament—as the hope of the world both now and forever.

Designating the Bible as witness of revelation implies considering as one its human distinctiveness from revelation and its divine unity with revelation. As a book, the Bible is not identical with revelation and yet it mediates revelation. Validating the Bible's historic-

---

*Cf. Gustav Aulén, *The Faith of the Christian Church*, p. 42f.

ity implies, however, that we must not confuse its "writtenness" with its holiness. What compels us to consider the Bible holy over against all other books is not the manner of its communication but rather the content of that communication. The uniqueness of the Bible lies not in its literary form but in the fact that at its decisive center it affirms the incarnation and resurrection of Jesus Christ. And what makes the Bible sacred to us is not the manner in which these claims have been communicated to us through oral and written tradition but the fact that we are compelled to acknowledge and submit to these claims.

The fact that the Word of the Lord came to prophets and that the apostles were eyewitnesses of the Christ-event does not mean that they therefore ceased to be human. That the biblical characters discerned the Word of God and saw His glory does not essentially mean that they themselves were caught up into the glory they witnessed. In contrast to the angels, these witnesses continued to be in history, and unlike Jesus Christ they never claimed for themselves divine nature. They retained their humanity as ordinary people precisely in their function as witnesses.

Validating the historicity of the Bible does not, however, allow us to minimize the divine element to which it testifies. We comprehend God's Word only in human language and God's acts only in history. These are human, not God's limitations. God chose to conform to them in revealing Himself and continues to do so in communicating His will. When God's Word came to man and became man's word, it did not thereby cease to be God's Word.

The validity of mankind's word is determined by the historic situation out of which it arises and to which it is addressed. But God's Word judges the human situation and transforms it into a redemptive situation.

By bearing witness of the revelation of God in the past

through the Bible, the inspiring Spirit of God prepares the hearts of people for present and future revelation. Thus, in attesting revelation and promising revelation the Bible becomes revelation.

Although it is not always meaningful or possible to distinguish form from content in revelation, it would not seem correct to say that the Bible *is* revelation for the simple reason that the book itself is not identical with the Spirit who inspired it. The Bible bears evidence of the "breath" or "inspiration" of God's Spirit in the obedience of prophets, evangelists, and apostles—and is an instrument of that Spirit effecting similar obedience in the lives of people today. Neither this inspiring "breath" of God nor the obedience of these persons is present before us because the Bible is before us. The presence of the Bible is not identical with the presence of the Spirit of Jesus, and the fact of obedience to that Spirit is not identical with the record of that fact. Because it is possible to hear the Gospel without obeying it, it is, therefore, possible to have the Bible without having the inspiration of the Spirit of which it testifies. Luther well said that to have the Scriptures without acknowledging Christ is to have no Scripture.

When God revealed Himself in His Son and continues to reveal Himself by His Spirit through the Bible, the Son and Spirit are identical with the subject and predicate of revelation in a way in which the Bible is not. God speaks through the Bible, but His Spirit is not in the Bible the same way as God was in Christ. The Bible creates the divine possibility of His presence, but the presence of the Lord does not lie in our power as the presence of the Bible does. Therefore, prayer to invoke His presence must always have the last word. We cannot force the miracle of revelation to happen, but we can accept the Bible witness that it has happened, trust its promise that it will happen, pray that it might happen, and commit ourselves to the fact that it does happen as we are willing to let it happen.

To ask whether revelation is objective or subjective is somewhat hypothetical in as far as God does not reveal Himself "out there" in the abstract but always to specific people at specific times in specific circumstances. There is little point in discussing whether the Bible *is* revelation in itself since revelation does not happen unless it happens to someone. But, when it happens, it is ultimately real. The Word of God is, in fact, the ground of all reality including our own and therefore both objective and subjective. Subjectively, the Bible is word and objectively it is of God. Various aspects of revelation can be identified, each characterized by this divine union of objective and subjective dimensions. God "revealed" Himself in Christ, He "inspired" the witnesses to witness and to pass on in oral and later written form what they experienced. His Spirit "illumines" this witness to those who hear the spoken Word and read the written Word. Whether in revelation, inspiration, or illumination, God reveals Himself both objectively and subjectively in the unity and variety of His Being as Father, Son, and Holy Spirit.

The written Word commends itself only to the heart that is confronted by the Living Word. Paul did not meet Christ in the Scriptures until he met Him on the Damascus road. In this respect, the Bible resembles a love letter the message of which cannot be discerned without perceiving the soul of its author. The letter conveys the soul that inspired it, but its inspiration is not identical with its form. The Spirit of God who inspired the Bible frees and compels one to believe not in the Church or its Bible but in Jesus Christ through both Church and Bible.

THE MEANING OF INSPIRATION

In II Timothy 3:16 Scripture is spoken of as *theopneustos*,*

---

*Cf. Eduard Schweizer, *Theologisches Wörterbuch zum Neuen Testament* VI:452f.; W. Philipp, *Religion in Geschichte und Gegenwart* 3, III:775f.

that is, God-breathed, translated "inspired by God." In the first instance, this is not a statement about the Scriptures in themselves nor about the process by which the spoken word was transcribed but about their divine origin. The text says that the Scriptures are of God and, therefore, profitable as the moral equipment of the person of God. The Scriptures are inspiring because they are inspired, but the inspiration is not an inherent characteristic of the Scriptures but of the breath or Spirit of God. The breath of God through the Word inspires obedience. But this text does not imply that God breathed into the manuscripts (as was said of Adam in Genesis 2:7 who thereby became a living soul). The Scriptures are produced by God's breath, but they neither contain it as a container nor do they perpetuate it as a living soul. The breath of God through (not into) the spoken and written Word produces obedience to the Lord of the Bible. And that, in the final analysis, is the inspiration of the Bible.

In II Peter 1:20-21 the Holy Spirit is referred to as both the real author (men spoke from God as they were moved by the Holy Spirit) and as the real interpreter of prophecy (v. 20). The inspiration of the Spirit to speak, write, or interpret does, however, not imply a violation of the genuine humanity of the prophets, evangelists, and apostles. The fact that the Holy Spirit was the real author does not mean that the actual authors did not fully exercise their humanity within the total context of that obedience in which they were involved both actively and passively. There is no reason to assume that the Spirit put "inspired" words into their mouths or even "inspired" thoughts into their minds or that He operated their mouths to speak by divine dictation (as a flute player uses his flute) any more than He activated their feet to walk by divine direction as an automaton. The moving of the Spirit does not imply a forced supernaturalism on the part of the witnesses and scribes. The miracle of the Christ-event was not in the minds of the witnesses who perceived nor in the hands of the scribes who wrote but in the Person of the Christ who occupied the cradle of Bethlehem and left the

empty tomb in Gethsemane. The people who witnessed and record-
ed that miracle were no more and no less divine than we who now
read that record. And we ought not claim for them what they did not
claim for themselves lest we substitute the false offense of a supernatural Bible for the real offense of a human Christ.

The concern to uprate the transcribing process reflects our
unwillingness to accept the mystery of the rule of God in the hearts
of people. When the Spirit of God moves or inspires persons to obedience, He does not thereby compel them to deny the freedom of
their humanity. Obedience is rendered in freedom or it is not obedience. Our comprehension of the supernatural is not uniquely Christian unless it includes both creation and incarnation. Our God is too
small if we cannot accept His Lordship within the natural order, and
He is too far away if we cannot discern His rule among individuals.
The miracle of the incarnation is that God chose to glorify Himself
in His humanity, and the miracle of the Christian life is that He continues to do so. Only when the Church loses the compelling witness
of the Spirit in its own life, will she feel threatened by historical criticism and seek the false security of humanly verifiable criteria to
prove the existence of that Spirit in the Bible.

The inspiration of the Bible does not rest in the infallibility of
its authors but in the power of the Spirit to communicate life in
Christ. What matters ultimately is not whether David destroyed
seven hundred Syrian chariots (II Sm. 10:18) or seven thousand
(I Chr. 19:18) or whether a particular census in Israel was commanded by God (II Sm. 24:1) or by Satan (I Chr. 21:1) but whether
the message of the Bible produces Christ. The Bible is more than
just another piece of writing by the very nature of its unique message, by the fact that the writers of the Old Testament look forward
to the Messiah and those of the New Testament declare Jesus as the
Christ. This testimony is the criterion by which we discern the inspiration of the spirits (I Jn. 4:1-3). And this is what distinguishes the

inspiration of the Bible from that of the creative artist.

The miracle of the Bible is not that infallible persons spoke inerrant words—that would be no miracle—but that the Word of God came to and through sinners. To refuse to accept this is to refuse to accept the comfort of the Bible and the promise of its relevance. Like the prophets, evangelists, and apostles we too are fallible human beings. If God could use them, He can and will speak His Word to and through us, effecting our participation in the witness of His Church throughout the ages. This is God's miracle and our hope.

The human nature of the Bible is in some sense analogous to the human nature of Christ. But we cannot press the analogy beyond the necessity of recognizing the reality of both a divine and a human dimension wherever God speaks and acts in history and people are "moved by the Spirit of God."

The very fact that God was incarnate in Christ and not in the Bible suggests that we ought not press the analogy to imply that the Bible is free from human error as Christ was free from sin. To do so is to fall into the error of Menno Simons who denied the "sinful" influence of Mary in the humanity of Jesus so as to establish the sinlessness of the Church. Apart from the sovereignty and freedom of God, there is nothing whatsoever about sinners saved by grace that validates or guarantees the miracle of God's grace. The trustworthiness of the Bible depends neither on its inerrancy nor on our ability rationally to distinguish between its divine and human dimensions and to define the nature of their interrelationship. God Himself establishes and authenticates the reality and truth of His self-revelation as we acknowledge the miracle of the Bible as the basis for our own Christian life. But, if we shake ourselves free from the message of the Bible and deny by our lives the inspiration of the Bible, our protestation that the Bible is the Word of God will not carry conviction. "To say 'Lord, Lord' is not enough. What matters is to do the will of God if we are to know His grace and truth—for that is the inspiration of the Bible."*

WHY THE CHURCH NEEDS THE BIBLE

The Church cannot bypass the Scriptures and go directly to God, because the Bible is God's Word for the Church. If the Church were already in Glory, she would not need the Bible, but, as long as she is in history, the Bible is indispensable to her life and mission. The ongoing life of the people of God depends on their obedience to the Word of God. The Church of Jesus Christ exists only there where a relationship of obedience to His Word exists. A relationship of obedience to the Lord of the Bible implies taking seriously the biblical record and witness of past obedience on the part of the prophets and apostles. But neither the Early Church in this record nor the record itself is to be absolutized, for it is the ongoing life of obedience that matters. Such obedience is repudiated when the Church is no longer governed by the Bible but becomes self-governing, when she no longer acknowledges the absolute authority of the Word of God distinct from and superior to her own relative authority under the Word.

The Church that professes to be the Body of Christ does not have her ground of being in herself but in her Lord. In as far as the Church is the Church she does not preach about herself but about her Lord, about the self-revelation of God in Christ and the meaning of His death and resurrection. The Church whose preaching is biblically oriented carries forth the tradition of her forbears' proclamation. When today's preachers preach the Gospel, they essentially preach about what Isaiah and Jeremiah—about what Peter, Paul, and John preached. This growing community of proclamation is what constitutes the Church's true apostolic succession of faith and loyal-

---

*Karl Barth, *Church Dogmatics* I/1:533-34 and sec. 19 in general.

ty to the great commission. It is a succession of obedience, not of the bishop's office.

True apostolic succession implies that the word of the antecessor is normative for that of the successor. But the actual witness of the prophets and apostles can retain its free and independent influence upon the Church only when it is fixed in writing. In the oral tradition, the Church is primarily in conversation with herself. The oral tradition cannot judge the Church because it is the Church. The Church does violence to the word of those prophets and apostles when it sets itself up as a standard whereby to judge their testimony. The Church cannot judge the Bible. The message of the Bible judges the Church, compelling her to accept the Bible as the basis for her own authority.

The Church that claims to embody in her own existence the source of authority tends to become a self-sufficient memorial society cultivating her own ideals and sentiments. Here, there is only conversation within herself but no dialogue with a higher principle outside of herself. The Church is called to obey not herself but her Lord and to find her directions for the structure of that obedience from the example of the obedience of the prophets and apostles who went before her. It is for this reason that the Church cannot live without the Bible. The Church does not have her life and authority apart from the Word, but through and under the Word. While the confession of the Church is important, it is of relative importance in relation to the confession of the biblical witnesses which it presupposes.

The evangelical decision is always a decision for the Scripture as the final source of appeal for all questions of faith and life. It is only on the basis of this decision for the Bible that reformation within the Church is possible. The moment the Church wants to be alone with herself and refuses to subject herself to the authority of the

Word, it ceases to be the Church. It may have all kinds of activity evolving and revolving within it, it may have action and reaction giving the appearance of some sort of life, but the real life of the Church does not consist of activities or relations but in encounter with the sacred Word. Where such encounter is lacking, whatever else goes on within the Church may be considered more a sign of decay than of life. Conversations conducted in the absence of the Lord are no longer conducted in the Church, for she has ceased to exist when the dialogue between God and humanity through the Bible is reduced to a monologue within the organization.

The Church cannot live without the Bible because apart from the community of the Living Word of God the creature knows only the solidarity of misery and death. The Church that is governed by the Word of God is governed by the authority of Jesus Christ, and, because it is His authority, she obeys; she does not have to worry about the goal and result of that obedience.*

---

*Cf. Karl Barth, *Ibid.*, sec. 20.

FROM HOMER TO JASPERS

The basic issues and most profound questions of human life and destiny demand—beyond the art of theological articulation—awareness of the whole perspective of human self-understanding in literary history. Our understanding is enlarged and our commitment deepened as we discern, in the wisdom of the poets and philosophers of all time, that independence of conscience and authentic moral will which together constitute the hope of history and the light of the world.

This essay intends to sample the diversity and thus establish the implicit continuity of moral deliberation in the great classics of Western thought in which we are confronted with the general history of self-understanding: the aspirations, capabilities, fears, and limitations in the antithesis of good and evil. One of the objects of this survey is to elucidate the premise that the human conflict of conscience from Homer to Jaspers is essentially a conflict between inner awareness of the truth and outer compulsion of the social order which ever threatens to bend moral conviction to the expedient.

I.   The *Odyssey* of Homer (900 B. C.) is a Greek epic poem narrating in twenty-four books what Ulysses, once King of Ithaca (now sole surviving legendary Greek hero of the fall of Troy, 1184 B. C.), endured for offending the sea-god Neptune and the sun-god Hyperion. After losing all his men, this "son of wrath" drifted aimlessly about the Mediterranean for ten years, suffering countless bizarre adventures in Ogygia, Phaeacia, Ismarus, Sicily, Aeolis, Aeaea, and Hades before returning home to Ithaca to slay his conspirators, reestablish his authority, and bring peace to his kingdom. When finally the men of Ithaca refuse to let the blood feud die, Athena herself calls out from heaven: "Be reconciled and let bloodshed cease. . . . Make an end of war and conflict and fear the wrath of Zeus who sees all things."

According to Homer, god is responsible for the good and the bad. God weaves the thread of fate that constitutes man's destiny. In disguise he visits the cities of men to watch their doings, and he gives victory in battle to whom he wills. Indeed, there is little in the affairs of men of which it cannot be said: the hand of god is in it. That is the meaning of the many omens, portents, prophecies, incantations, revelations, manifestations, incarnations, and propitiations by which man hopes to discern god's will and appease god's wrath and so to raise his own level of consciousness—as do the disembodied spirits of Hades when they drink of the blood sacrifices. Athena's counsel is for man to enjoy in silence the gifts which the gods may give him. Beyond that, Homeric man stands perplexed at the riddle of the meaning of his being, for he is caught between the knowledge and fear of the gods by the terrible mystery of god's capricious will. Perhaps that is why Plato thought Homer had a deleterious effect upon the morals and religion of the young.

The cartography of the Odyssey is the pilgrimage of Homeric man on the quest to understand and transcend himself. Whether contemporary morals, politics, and religion differ significantly from Homer's characters three thousand years ago remains an open question.

II.   It was Aeschylus (525-456 B. C.) the tragic poet who preoccupied himself with reasons why anger of the slaughtered never sleeps. The theme of his last great work, the Oresteian trilogy, is the moral dilemma of *Orestes* whom the Delphic oracle at Apollo's bidding persuades to avenge his father's murder. In so doing, he himself is caught in the spider's web of fated evil, not knowing which to

fear more, the gods or men. *The Libation Bearers* lament the perpetuation of the vicious cycle as those who try to wash the blood from
their hands to cure the mad disease but become ever more implicat-
ed in blood guilt. Sent by the mother's dead spirit, the Furies drive
Orestes from the land. He wavers at the edge of madness. Finally, in
Eumenides, refuge and absolution for his crime are found in the
temple of Pallas Athena. By the intervention of Athena, he is acquit-
ted of his guilt and freed from the wrath of the Furies.

Aeschylus tried to show that the Furies do not exist indepen-
dently of consciousness and that the only hope of redemption from
the doomed cycle of the institution of revenge must come from a
reach beyond man's grasp.

The growth of moral awareness produced the compelling
insight that only the initiative of a god can bring law to lawless people. Only to the extent that one understands the entire order can one
understand oneself within the drama of divine and human justice.
Orestes is purged of the guilt, pollution, and madness of the vicious
perpetuation of clannish blood morality to seek the meaning of
being within a new and wider order in which the terrestrial and
celestial complement each other. Retribution is not the only way to
deal with wrong. But the way of expiation and reconciliation presupposes the ordered control of primitive passions by an enlightened
reason which inspires the institution of objective justice within the
larger *polis*. This control of mind over passion accords with divine
intention and is the condition for man's self-understanding of his
fate and guilt which opens him to the more noble possibilities of the
politeia, founded on justice rather than revenge.

III.   The moral tension between the will of the gods and the
ways of men finds its tragic climax in Sophocles' (496-406 B. C.)
Antigone, who, in obeying her conscience, buries her brother in defi-
ance of the decree of Creon her father, the proud and stubborn King

of Thebes. She owed a greater debt to the dead than to the living, for she believed the laws of the gods are higher than the laws of men. She won her integrity at the cost of her mortality. She realized that all strength is weakness against the immortal unrecorded laws of god and that what matters is not the fact of one's death but its reason. Eventually, the seeds of his own corruption overwhelm King Creon with the realization that he himself, who sought to epitomize in law and order the good of the city, stands condemned before the highest court as the very one who precipitated its ruin. The chorus interprets historical events for those who foresee the truth along with Teiresias the blind seer to the effect that the meaning and hope of being even at the very edge of fate lie in one's moral wisdom to discern and obey the will and voice of god.

Again, in *Oedipus Rex* the prophet reproaches the king for unconsciously being the cause of the city's corruption and pollution. Oedipus attempts to keep the state from going down in the storm but is overwhelmed by the dread of knowing the truth without finding in himself the resource to fulfill it. Having experienced the depth of calamity in his own life and household, this wandering, tormented, blinded, exiled king in a state of utter desperation and despair eventually stumbles onto sacred ground at Colonus, where he faces his own guilt and through divine mediation experiences a sense of salvation and expiation in death.

IV. The subject of Sophocles' dramatic tragedies was not unrelated to the actual tragedy that had meanwhile brought to the brink of disaster the institutions and values of the ancient world through the destructive violence of the Peloponnesian War (431-404 B. C.). Neither Athens nor Sparta had sufficient cause for war. No one seemed to want it, but neither did they take the initiative to prevent it. Its actual causes will always be subject to debate. While Athens was spreading democracy, its allies were looking to Sparta for liberation. There was breakdown in communication. There were feelings of jealousy and hatred and incidents of intrigue, and so it was generally agreed that all-out war was inevitable. Early in this ancient world war, Thucydides (460-400 B. C.) was appointed general to guard Athenian interests in Thrace. But, since the Spartans overran the town he hoped to defend, Thucydides was relieved of his command and exiled for twenty years, most of which he spent gathering materials to write *The History of the Peloponnesian War* in eight books. When the war ended and the history was finished, Thucydides returned to Athens under a general amnesty only to be assassinated soon thereafter.

From Thucydides we learn all the logistical data, all the political science, and all the military rhetoric that go into the making of a great world war. Each side persuasively defends its self-respect and self-interest with honor and by the most persuasive rhetoric of its most eloquent generals. They remind us that, because happiness depends on freedom which depends on security which in turn depends on justice, therefore, honor that is prepared to risk defense of justice is all that abides. Consequently, in order to defend peace with honor, war is inevitable. It is a very old argument, but from Thucydides one does not gain the impression that there was sufficient religious or philosophic self-transcendence manifest in Greek civilization to break the fatalistic inevitability of this preemptive rationalization of total violence.

V.   Then there was Aristophanes (448-380 B. C.), who appeared to see through both the comedy and tragedy of the Great War, both its causes and effects. In forty to sixty plays, he sought to communicate what he observed and discerned. He was an elusive poet whose mocking irony baffled his audiences and perplexed his readers. They could not decide whether to take him seriously as a great moralist and patriot or to see in his fantastic disguise primarily the comedy to provoke cathartic laughter. To nurture the delicate balance of this ambiguity, Aristophanes often combined with transcendent fantasy the lower comedy of social farce which bit satirically into his political commentary as he attacked both generals and popular morality without fear or favor. His play entitled *Birds* serves as a sample of his art.

In it two elderly Athenians flee the city's corruption for the realm of the birds with the hope of building Utopia in the air, a kingdom where important human relations claim first priority and where people do not waste their lives haggling over lawsuits or inventing war strategies. Since none of the cities of Hellas qualifies for the quality of such life, they collaborate with the birds of the air in a grand scheme: to build a bird state between gods and humans and levy toll on both. The gods must pay tribute if the smoke of human sacrifice is to reach them, and the people make payment if their crops are not to be devoured. The vast bird empire of Nephelococcygia develops fantastically, and the chorus leader sums up its new philosophy for the benefit of the human race: "Ye men who are dimly existing below, who perish and fade as a leaf, pale, woebegone, shadowlike, spiritless folk, life feeble and wingless and brief, frail castings in clay, who are gone in a day like a dream full of sorrow and sighing. Come, listen with care to the birds of the air, the ageless, the deathless, who, flying in the joy and the freshness of ether, are wont to muse upon wisdom undying." In effect, says the poet, it is the birds and not people who are given to things transcendent and who explore and apply the first principles of the world. No temples are needed and no one need go to Delphi anymore, for, unlike the gods, the birds will not be remote and inaccessible but near at hand. "We shall not withdraw ourselves to the highest clouds like Zeus, but shall be among you and give to you and your children health, wealth, life, peace, and happiness." Eventually, the new bird pantheon disintegrates in the fantasy of its own complexity. On the wings of his imagination, this tragic poet sought through words to give wings to the mind for soaring to heaven, there to seek what one cannot find on earth.

VI.   During those critical years of the war, Socrates, who claimed to be appointed by God as a stinging gadfly for the good of Athens, spent his time cross-examining all who had a reputation for knowledge, particularly politicians. As a result, he aroused against himself enormous hostility of a particularly bitter and persistent kind. Eventually in 399 B. C., he was indicted for "corrupting the minds of the young" by not acknowledging the idols of the state. In effect, he was prosecuted for challenging the premise that the wars of human beings are fated by the dreadful hatred and battles of the gods and for implying, instead, that people bring upon themselves their own calamities contrary to better knowledge.

In his *Apology*, Socrates formally addresses the court of Athens: "Gentlemen, I am your very grateful and devoted servant, but I owe a greater allegiance to God than to you; and, so long as I draw breath and have my faculties, I shall never stop practicing philosophy and exhorting you and elucidating the truth for everyone that I meet. . . . This, I do assure you, is what my God commands; and it is my belief that no greater good has ever befallen you in this city than my service to my God; for I spend all my time going about trying to persuade you, young and old, to make your first and chief concern not for your bodies nor for your possessions but for the highest welfare of your souls, proclaiming as I go [that] wealth does not bring goodness, but goodness brings wealth and every other blessing, both to the individual and to the state. . . . I am not going to alter my conduct, not even if I die a hundred deaths."

Socrates went on to explain that he was "subject to a divine or supernatural experience" which began in his early childhood—"a sort of voice which comes to me" and always dissuaded him from doing wrong, wherefore, "if I had tried long ago to engage in politics, I should long ago have lost my life, without doing any good either to you or to myself. Please do not be offended if I tell you the truth. No man on earth who conscientiously opposes either you or any other organized democracy and flatly prevents a great many wrongs and illegalities from taking place in the state to which he belongs can possibly escape with his life. The true champion of justice, if he intends to survive for even a short time, must necessarily confine himself to private life and leave politics alone."

Socrates predicted: "When I leave this court I shall go away condemned by you to death, but they will go away convicted by Truth herself of depravity and wickedness. And they shall accept their sentence even as I accept mine." Thereupon, Socrates was charged with "impiety," and, as predicted, the jury pronounced the death sentence. Crito tried in vain to persuade his friend to escape this consequence. Socrates admitted that "there are and always will be few people who think like this" and that consequently those who do not will always feel contempt for those who do. But Socrates could not compromise his hypothesis "that it is never right to do a wrong or return a wrong or defend one's self against injury by retaliation."

With *Euthyphro*, the priest, Socrates had previously explored the true meaning and essential nature of piety as intrinsic holiness of life, not just in relation to God but also in relation to others. He concluded that holiness has to do with right action defined as "that aspect of righteousness concerning our therapeutic relation to God." Finally, he sought to discern to what end one is to serve God and what it is that God requires of us, but his questions remained unanswered.

VII.   The quest for the meaning of the good for the individual and for the state is pursued by Aristotle (384-322 B. C.) in treatises on *Ethics* and *Politics* respectively. The object of both is to discern humanity's highest good and to provide the knowledge enabling one to act in accord not with passion but reason. We are told that to identify the good with pleasure is too carnal, to define it as honor is too superficial, and to think of it as virtue is too incomplete. Nor is it sufficient that the good be good in itself; it must be good for something. In contrast to the 'supernaturalism' of Socrates and the idealism of Plato, the question concerning the good becomes for Aristotle an empirical and, in turn, political science. The nature of happiness is deduced from the rational function of human being, and the concept of virtue is derived not from the perfections of the gods but from intelligent contemplation and responsible action. The moral and intellectual virtues are held to be neither from nature nor contrary to nature. By nature, humankind has the potential of becoming virtuous, but the actual virtue of a person is the state of character manifest in the integrity of action. Aristotle's empirical and functional approach to ethics finds its *telos* in the constitution of the state, for human being is by nature a political being who realizes full natural potential only in the exercise of civic virtue as a responsible citizen. The shift from Socrates to Aristotle has to do with *ontologisches Wirklichkeitsbewusstsein*: the compelling voice of God has become the self-realizing law of nature.

VIII. Fifteen hundred years later, the heritage of Aristotle becomes the intellectual structure of Europe through Thomas Aquinas (1225-1274), the great medieval synthesizer of Greek thought and Christian faith who sought to integrate the conclusions of natural reason within the framework of supernatural truth. His *Treatise on Law* exemplifies the logic by which eternal law and natural law are correlated within the expediency of human law in such a way that a citizen is bound in conscience by the claim of the common good as defined by the authority of a given ruler because "it is not permissible for everyone to expound what is useful and what is not useful to the state." The question raised by Aquinas as to whether there can be law without force is answered by the supposition that wars are waged in quest of a more perfect peace of which the decisive element is the work of justice in removing obstacles to that peace.

IX.   How the means of nature can be rationalized to justify the end of man is exemplified in that treatise on the political science of despotism fittingly entitled *The Ruler*, which Nicolo Machiavelli (1469-1527) dedicated to His Magnificence Lorenzo de Medici. This astute and masterful analysis of *Realpolitik* represents the modern divorce of politics from ethics. When it is assumed that the successful politician should be concerned with having a good reputation but not with being virtuous, that he must employ force and deceit, prefer to be feared than to being loved, master the art of duplicity and the use of propaganda to gain and hold popular approval, and rationalize that that war is just which he deems necessary, then we have before us a shattering commentary on the contemporary scene documenting the modern departure from Aristotle's understanding of politics as a scientific means to an ethical end.

X.   Through the dramatic poetry of William Shakespeare (1564-1616), the moral degradation and corruption of the ruling nobility become the subject of universal entertainment in the theater and literature of the Western world. *Hamlet* "the prince," who at the behest of his father's ghost is persuaded to avenge his "most foul, strange, and unnatural murder," wins universal appeal as his own moral tragedy epitomizes the hopes, fears, frustrations, and despair of all mankind. Disintegration of character is disclosed in Shakespeare's poetic eloquence and compelling drama as the inevitable consequence of conflict between the call of duty and the claim of morality. We come to accept on the authority of experience that "to be honest as the world goes, is to be one man picked out of ten thousand" and to identify with Hamlet's rationale: "I must be cruel, only to be kind. Thus bad begins and worse is left behind." We are captivated and intrigued by Hamlet's deliberation: "Whether 'tis nobler in the mind to suffer the slings and arrows of outrageous fortune or to take arms against a sea of troubles." But, had he not overcome his moral ambivalence and natural repugnance to commit murder to revenge murder, the "play" could not go on.

In *King Lear* we "see how this world goes" through the eyes of a ruler who brought degradation, madness, and ruin upon himself through his lust for power, his wounded pride, his unresolved conscience, his decay of virtue, and eventually his total erosion of character. When Shakespeare's tragic heroes in whom nature stands "on the very verge of her confine . . . speak what they feel," the audience identifies with them in the realization that they may never "see so much nor live so long."

The change from honor and happiness to degradation and ruin likewise constitutes the character development of *Macbeth*, and, with astute psychoanalysis of his motivational drives in particular, Shakespeare elucidates a lust for power implemented by deceit of the vilest sort. Again, the apparitions and predictions of witches confuse and overrule the moral conscience to accept that "fair is foul and foul is fair." And, since "all our yesterdays have lighted fools the way to dusty death," the verdict of history appears to be that "life's but a walking shadow, a poor player that struts and frets his hour upon the stage and then is heard no more: it is the tale told by an idiot, full of sound and fury, signifying nothing." The only consistent conclusion to the matter—unless "conscience doth make cowards of us all"—is the observation that " 'tis safer to be that which we destroy than by destruction dwell in doubtful joy." It is, in other words, "better to be with the dead . . . than on the torture of the mind to lie in restless ecstacy." Is it any wonder that in most of Shakespeare's sensuous and bloody plays most of the leading characters murder one another? The morality of tragedy as entertainment is, to say the least, not obvious.

XI.   In the *Leviathan* (1651) of Thomas Hobbes (1588-1679) we have an influential English treatise on the liabilities of the human condition by a student of political affairs who was born prematurely for fear of an invasion by the Spanish Armada. Hobbes concludes that the natural condition of humanity is war, a state in which force and fraud are the two cardinal virtues. To covenant with God is considered impossible if so doing conflicts with the right of nature to exercise one's own power in one's own interest. Hobbes' philosophy of natural right and law establishes self-interest as the only viable basis of social contract and fails to transcend those contracts by which one is bound through mutual fear, distrust, and threat. Without a common power to fear, the state of citizens is thought to degenerate into a condition making "the life of man solitary, poor, nasty, brutish, and short." Hobbes' version of the good for humanity contrasts sharply with religious interpretations and aspirations. His understanding of the condition and meaning of human being derives from a political and physical philosophy which limits ethics to modern materialist and behaviorist determinations.

XII.   In the satire of Jonathan Swift (1667-1745) we have a compelling appeal to human reason that is at once desperate and hilarious. His famous and entertaining *Gulliver's Travels* is an imaginative attempt to put into larger perspective the strange phenomenon of the human race as it might appear to creatures smaller or larger, better or worse than ourselves, however painful and humiliating that exercise in self-realization might be. Essentially, Swift's satire is directed at the folly of the human race as manifest in its basic political and clerical institutions, laws, and social conventions. Swift compels one to consider the extent to which the hope of one's self-transcendence lies in the madness that inspires such cynicism.

XIII.   Toward the end of the eighteenth century, Immanuel Kant (1724-1804) applied his logical mind to *The Science of Right* (1785) and the problem of *Perpetual Peace* (1795). He held the state of nature to be a nonjuridical condition in which justice does not prevail in contrast to the civil, juridical state where distributive justice obtains. In contrast to the political philosophy of his predecessors, Thomas Hobbes (1588-1679), John Locke (1632-1704), and Rousseau (1712-1778) who offer utilitarian reasons why people should enter into social contract for their own good, Kant the moralist appeals to what is intrinsically right, arguing that people ought to pass into the juridical state simply because it is wrong to live in the lawless state of nature. This immanent moral imperative to do what is right derives from the pure and practical logic that "there ought to be no war, neither between me and you in the condition of nature, nor between us as members of states." "War is an evil inasmuch as it produces more wicked men than it takes away." If war is to be, it should be declared not by the ruler, who in any event is himself least affected by it, but by the people who have to fight it, endure it, pay for it, and repair its damages. But to pay persons to kill or be killed entails misusing them as a tool in the hand of the state which violates the fundamental rights of mankind.

Kant understands morality to be practical and allows no implicit conflict between politics and ethics. Since everyone does not will what is required for perpetual peace, a uniting cause must override a variety of particular volitions to effect through them a common will. This is accomplished not by coercion but by appeal to reason which holds that "the rights of man must be held sacred, however much sacrifice it may cost the ruling power. One cannot compromise here and seek the middle course of pragmatic conditional law between the morally right and the expedient. All politics must bend its knee before the right."

For Kant, "the universal and lasting establishment of peace constitutes not only a part but the whole final purpose and end of the science of right as viewed within the limits of reason." And he is optimistic about the universalizability of the conditions of perpetual peace as the implicit logic of the Golden Rule in its negative form.

XIV. The realization of that juridical condition of justice and peace in accord with the necessities of nature and the design of Providence is allegedly what *The Declaration of Independence* of 1776 truly advocates. "When, in the course of human events, it becomes nec-essary for one people to dissolve the political bands which have con-nected them with another, and to assume, among the powers of the earth, the separate and equal station to which the law of nature and of nature's God entitle them, a decent respect of the opinions of mankind requires that they should declare the causes which impel them to the separation"—thus reads the first sentence establishing under God in the new world the liberty and veracity of the Ameri-can way of life. The Declaration continues: "We hold these truths to be self-evident: that all men are created equal; that they are endowed by their Creator with certain unalienable rights; that among these are life, liberty, and the pursuit of happiness. That to secure these rights governments are instituted among men, deriving their just powers from the consent of the governed. That, whenever any form of government becomes destructive of these ends, it is the right of the people to alter or to abolish it and to institute new gov-ernment, laying its foundation on such principles and organizing its powers in such form as to them shall seem most likely to effect their safety and happiness. . . . But when a long chain of abuses and usurpations, pursuing invariably the same object, evinces a design to reduce them under absolute despotism, it is their right, it is their duty, to throw off such government, and to provide new guards for their own security."

Then follows a narration of the King of Britain's "history of repeated injuries and usurpations all having in direct object the establishment of an absolute tyranny over these states." Therefore, it is declared that "a prince, whose character is thus marked by every act which may define a tyrant, is unfit to be the ruler of a free peo-ple." Furthermore, since the British 'brethren' "too have been deaf to the voice of justice and consanguinity" it is necessary also to "hold them, as we do the rest of mankind, enemies in war, in peace friends." The Declaration concludes: "Appealing to the Supreme Judge of the world for the rectitude of our intentions [we] solemnly publish and declare that these United Colonies are, and of right ought to be, free and independent states. . . . And for the support of this declaration, with the firm reliance on the protection of Divine Providence, we mutually pledge to each other our lives, our fortunes, and our sacred honor."

Linguistic analysis of the text of this historic document raises innumerable questions. The authors frequently use the term "right," identify with it, and rest their case upon it. Mention is made of "unalienable rights," of the need "to secure these rights," of "the right" of a people "to alter or to abolish" governments in order "to right themselves" and prevent "invasions of the rights of the people," because the Colonies "of right ought to be free" and therefore proceed to do what "independent states may of right do." What indeed do the authors mean by the term "right"? Are these "rights" natural or supernatural? Duties or gifts? Negative acts or positive values?

Frequent reference is made to deity. Do the arguments of the writers actually depend upon belief in God? It is claimed that "nature's God entitles" the Colonists to "separate and equal station," for "all men are created equal," "endowed by their *Creator* with certain unalienable rights," wherefore they "appeal to the *Supreme Judge* of the world" and support their declaration of independence "with a firm reliance on the protection of *Divine Providence*." Why appeal to *both* "the laws of nature *and* nature's God," the rights of man and the Providence of God? Did Congress expect "the Supreme Judge" to help? If so, how? Could the Colonists confidently claim "Divine Providence" in deposing the "Defender of the Faith"?

What determines "*when* in the course of human events *it* [i.e., rebellion] becomes necessary"? Is the implied necessity natural, juridical, or moral? Is the necessity self-evident? If so, why is it not also true for the King and British citizens? Or are they too dull to

comprehend the self-evident? Is the necessity self-determining? If
so, why appeal to the Supreme Judge to effect it? Who decides
whether the cause is "light or transcient"? By what criteria? How is
the right and rightfulness of political action established? Does the
consent of the governed make political power just?—even the
power of the British Sovereign exercising the "divine right of
kings"? Are all persons created equal? If so, should some be governed by others? Does belief in equality depend on belief in God? If
so, how? If not, why not? Finally, is the Declaration of Independence a moral document? Or simply a legal document? Both, or
neither?

XV.   In 1835 Alexandre de Tocqueville (1805-1859) published his
findings on the tendencies and instincts of *Democracy in America.*
He notes that Americans frequently err in their choice of administra-
tors who are inferior in capacity and morality. But they are so held to
their task of representing the peoples' interests that public officials
often achieve the good without intending it. Consequently, democracy does more for the people than any absolute government, although
it does fewer things well. Tocqueville observes American patriotism
to be a kind of civil religion which one believes without discussion: it
does not reason, but acts from the impulse of faith and sentiment and
is particularly irritable in its incapacity for self-critique.

     Tocqueville argues against centralization of power, for people
do not change their characters by uniting with one another, nor does
patience increase with strength. Human beings are not wise enough
to exercise much power and, when much authority is invested in
few, society is eventually enervated. He was alarmed not at the
excessive liberty that prevailed but by the inadequacy of security
against the tyranny of the majority which subdues creative dissen-
sion, silences all debate, and forces concession of all wills once an
irrevocable decision has been pronounced. The body is left free but
the soul is enslaved while "the majority lives in perpetual self-

applause." In feigning the approval of all, the despotism of the majority degrades the independent mind to the temper of a lackey. The "ardent, insatiable, incessant, invincible" American passion for equality by bending independent thinking to the interest of the many degrades, enervates, and stupifies men without tormenting them. American democracy is a leveler and the level is low. "Almost all extremes are softened or blunted," and "the sight of such universal uniformity saddens and chills one."

XVI. In 1859 in a discourse *On Liberty*, John Stuart Mill (1806-1873) explored the nature and limits of power which can be legitimately exercised by society over the individual. Having by the tender age of eight read all of Herodotus and six dialogues of Plato in Greek, Mill was fully cognizant of the tension between liberty and authority, a struggle which, as we have seen, constitutes a most conspicuous feature in the history of political and ethical thought since the time of ancient Greece. Mill defends the integrity and autonomy exemplified in the individuality of Socrates and Jesus and decries the tyranny of prevailing opinion and debilitating conformity that had come to characterize his own time. He observes that, "comparatively speaking, [all persons] now read the same things, listen to the same things, see the same things, go to the same places, have their hopes and fears directed to the same objects, have the same rights and liberties and the same means of asserting them. Great as are the differences of position which remain, they are nothing to those which have ceased. And the assimilation is still proceeding. All the political changes of the age promote it. . . . Every extension of education promotes it. . . . Improvement in the means of communication promotes it. . . . The increase of commerce and manufacturers promote it. . . . A more powerful agency than even all these, in bringing about a general similarity among mankind, is the complete establishment, in this and other free countries, of the ascendancy of public opinion in the state."

When governors were independent (as in early Greece, Rome, and England), liberty meant to restrict their otherwise absolute power by political and constitutional rights. However, now society itself is a tyrant and the individual needs protection against the tyranny of the prevailing public opinion or feeling enforced by custom without reason or examination. "Precisely because the tyranny of opinion is such as to make eccentricity a reproach, it is desirable, in order to break through that tyranny, that people should be eccentric. Eccentricity has always abounded when and where strength of character has abounded; and the amount of eccentricity in a society has generally been proportional to the amount of genius, mental vigor, and moral courage it contained. That so few now dare to be eccentric marks the chief danger of the time."

According to Mill the whole strength and value of human judgment depends on whether it can be set right when it is wrong. Rather than silence the dissenting voice on the presumption of its own infallibility, society must realize that all opposing opinions have the same intrinsic right to be heard. Socrates was put to death for impiety and immorality by those who knew him to be the most virtuous man of his day, and Jesus was misrepresented as the opposite of what he was. Peculiarly, the religious establishment, insisting on the depravity of man, has cramped and dwarfed the faculties, capacities, and susceptibilities of people in conformity to what it mistakenly assumed their Maker designed them to be. While the great writers of all ages have asserted freedom of conscience as an indefeasible right, in the minds of most religious persons, the duty of toleration is admitted with tacit reserve. But "he who lets the world, or his own portion of it, choose his plan of life for him, has no need of any other faculty than the ape-like one of imitation." "Originality is the one thing unoriginal minds cannot feel the use of. [So] the first service which originality has to render them is that of opening their eyes: which being once fully done, they would have a chance of being themselves original."

XVII. Henry David Thoreau (1817-1862), American poet-naturalist and nonconformist philosopher, resolved to think and live according to his own lights. Observing that "the mass of men lead lives of quiet desperation" he renounced everything inessential, reducing his necessaries from a thousand to three, and for two years lived in a cabin at Walden Pond to prove that life can be simple and enjoyable. Thoreau is, above all, renowned for his *Civil Disobedience*. When the state required Socrates to act against his conscience, he challenged its unjust presuppositions but felt duty-bound to endure its unjust consequences. Thoreau took a more radical stance, holding that it is not enough to disapprove or vote against injustice. Conscience compels one not only to oppose and disobey an unjust law but also to seek to hinder its enforcement. Thoreau's political philosophy is pithy and its expression is terse: "That government is best which governs least . . . which governs not at all; and when men are prepared for it, that will be the kind of government which they will have."

On the matter of civil disobedience, Thoreau asks: "Must a citizen ever for a moment, or in the least degree, resign his conscience to the legislator? Why has every man a conscience, then? I think that we should be men first, and subjects afterward. . . . The only obligation which I have a right to assume is to do at any time what I think right. . . . A common and natural result of an undue respect for law is that you may see a file of soldiers, colonel, captain, corporal, privates, powder-monkeys, and all marching in admirable order over hill and dale to the wars, against their wills, ay, against their common sense and consciences, which makes it very steep marching indeed, and produces a palpitation of the heart. They have no doubt that it is a damnable business in which they are concerned; they are all peaceably inclined. Now, what are they? Men at all? or small movable forts and magazines, at the service of some unscrupulous man in power? . . . The mass of men serve the state thus, not as men mainly, but as machines, with their bodies. They are the standing army, and the militia, jailors, constables, posse comitatus, etc. In most cases there is no free exercise whatever of the judgment or of the moral sense. . . . Others—as most legislators, politicians, lawyers, ministers, and officeholders—serve the state chiefly with their heads; and, as they rarely make any moral distinctions, they are as likely to serve the Devil, without *intending* it, as God. A very few, as heroes, patriots, martyrs, reformers in the great sense, and *men,* serve the state with their consciences also, and so necessarily resist it for the most part; and are commonly treated as enemies by it."

"How then does it become a man to behave toward this American government today? I answer, that he cannot without disgrace be associated with it." As for the democratic process, "All voting is a sort of gaming, like checkers or backgammon, with a slight moral tinge to it, a playing with right and wrong, with moral questions; and betting naturally accompanies it. . . . A wise man will not leave the right to the mercy of chance, nor wish it to prevail through the power of the majority."

On the matter of political responsibility, Thoreau counsels: "If the injustice is part of the necessary friction of the machine of government, let it go, let it go: perchance it will wear smooth, . . . but if it is of such a nature that it requires you to be the agent of injustice to another, then, I say, break the law. Let your life be a counter friction to stop the machine. . . . A man has not everything to do, but something; and because he cannot do everything, it is not necessary that he should do *something* wrong." "If a plant cannot live according to its nature, it dies; and so a man."

Thoreau was convinced "there will never be a really free and enlightened state until the state comes to recognize the individual as a higher and independent power, from which all its own power and authority are derived, and treats him accordingly." He imagined and hoped for such a state but confessed not as yet having seen it.

XVIII. Herman Melville (1819-1891) brought back to the awareness of his time the one thing it lacked: a tragic sense of life. As Dostoevski, he plumbed the depth of human experience and religious insight in his final masterpiece, *Billy Budd*, the story of the world, the spirit, and the Devil.

Each of Melville's characters has a platonic form. Captain Edward Vere, known as The Honorable "Starry Vere," is a man of superior order: humane, reserved, free from cant, intellectual, resolute, and "intrepid to the verge of temerity though never judiciously so." Billy Budd, a young sailor impressed from the vessel *Rights of Man* to serve on the crew of the English merchantship H. M. S. *Indomitable*, is the jewel or cynosure of them all by virtue of his natural alacrity, celerity, and unvitiated simple-minded unself-conscious innocence of the complexities of life, "a sort of upright barbarian," lacking intuitive knowledge of the bad. Then there is Claggart, Master-at-arms, with his suspicious past, soft humid ways, and obsequious intelligence. He is the evil agent of discipline of the most degrading sort for whom it is as natural to hate goodness as for Billy to personify it. Claggart's evil is causeless—like the venom of a snake—it is simply there, and "the monomania in the man . . . like a subterranean fire, eats its way deeper and deeper in him."

Through confederates, talebearers and spies, Claggart tries to bribe Billy into mutiny. When this fails, Claggart somehow gets Billy into a compromising position before he is sufficiently awake to withdraw. Thinking he has Billy in his power, Claggart accuses him before Captain Vere of attempting treachery. Captain Vere is not impressed; the tale looks too thin. Nevertheless, for the sake of form and discipline, he summons Billy to his cabin to confront Claggart. Confronted with the horrifying accusation, Billy stammers, is unable to speak, then in desperation strikes Claggart a lightning blow. To the amazement of all, the perjurer has been struck dead—by an angel of God; yet, in this world even angels must hang. Vere is caught by the nature of his position: as ship's commander he is committed to execute the Articles of War. So he acts against his fatherly instincts and, as an instrument of an institution, sentences Billy to hang. Thus ends Billy Budd, "a story not unwarranted by what happens in this incongruous world of ours—innocence and infirmity, spiritual depravity and fair respite." In the dynamics of human institutions, evil has a place as well as good. Vere is contemptuous of Claggart but cannot do without him; he loves yet hangs Billy, accepting and executing the universal "Articles of War" upon which our civilizations are built and by which they are maintained. Melville could not resolve this tragedy so accepted it in resignation, and, as his own end approached, cried out with Billy Budd: "God bless Captain Vere!"

Drawing back the veil of Victorian conventions, Melville disclosed the nakedness of life and death, love and hate, good and evil in the dark night outside dimly lit only by ancient stars in whose oblique illumination "Billy Budd" becomes universally autobiographical. The premature death of a handsome sailor is Melville's version of Adam who never intended disobedience and never foresaw the loss of Paradise—and of Jesus who by a juggling of circumstances necessarily hangs for all. Captain Vere is Jehovah in the drama of dutifully and grimly administering the terms of the Mutiny Act (according to the religion of Anselm and Calvin). Behind the certainties of dogma lurk the mystery of iniquity and tragedy of life itself: that one cannot survive against one's conscience. "Sailors" necessarily, habitually, and unconsciously distrust one another "in proportion to the fairness of their appearance." In matters of patriotism, the heart is ruled out and so is private conscience. He who swears allegiance to a king ceases to be a morally free and responsible agent. Patriotism is the last refuge of a scoundrel. And it is no comfort in the perpetual Calvary of the spirit to find a thief nailed on either side.

XIX. What Friedrich Wilhelm Nietzsche (1844-1900) had to say in
The Joyful Science, The Twilight of the Idols, and *The Antichrist*
speaks here for itself. It needs to be heard, before it is interpreted.

GOD IS DEAD

"Have you not heard of that madman who lit a lantern in the
bright morning hours, ran to the marketplace, and cried incessantly:
'I seek God! I seek God!'—As many of those who did not believe
in God were standing around just then, he provoked much laughter.
Has he got lost? asked one. Did he lose his way like a child? asked
another. Or is he hiding? Is he afraid of us? Has he gone on a voy-
age? Emigrated?—Thus they yelled and laughed.

"The madman jumped into their midst and pierced them with
his eyes. 'Whither is God?' he cried; 'I will tell you. *We have killed
him*—you and I. All of us are his murderers. But how did we do
this? How could we drink up the sea? Who gave us the sponge to
wipe away the entire horizon? What were we doing when we
unchained this earth from its sun? Whither is it moving now?
Whither are we moving? Away from all suns? Are we not plunging
continually? Backward, sideward, forward, in all directions? Is there
still any up or down? Are we not straying as through an infinite
nothing? Do we not feel the breath of empty space? Has it not
become colder? Is not night continually closing in on us? Do we not
need to light lanterns in the morning? Do we hear nothing as yet of
the noise of the grave-diggers who are burying God? Do we smell
nothing as yet of the divine decomposition? Gods, too, decompose.
God is dead. God remains dead. And we have killed him.

" 'How shall we comfort ourselves, the murderers of all murderers? What was holiest and mightiest of all that the world has yet
owned has bled to death under our knives: who will wipe this blood
off us? What water is there for us to clean ourselves? What festivals

of atonement, what sacred games shall we have to invent? Is not the greatness of this deed too great for us? Must we ourselves not become gods simply to appear worthy of it? There has never been a greater deed; and whoever is born after us—for the sake of this deed he will belong to a higher history than all history hitherto.'

"Here the madman fell silent and looked again at his listeners; and they, too, were silent and stared at him in astonishment. At last he threw his lantern on the ground, and it broke into pieces and went out. 'I have come too early,' he said then; 'my time is not yet. This tremendous event is still on its way, still wandering; it has not yet reached the ears of men. Lightning and thunder require time; the light of the stars requires time; deeds, though done, still require time to be seen and heard. This deed is still more distant from them than the most distant stars—*and yet they have done it themselves.*'

"It has been related further that on the same day the madman forced his way into several churches and there struck up his *requiem aeternam deo.* Led out and called to account, he is said always to have replied nothing but: 'What after all are these churches now if they are not the tombs and sepulchers of God?' " (*Fröhliche Wissenschaft,* 125).

"Nietzsche prophetically envisages himself as a madman: to have lost God means madness; and when mankind will discover that it has lost God, universal madness will break out. This apocalyptic sense of dreadful things to come hangs heavily over Nietzsche's thinking like a thundercloud.

"We have destroyed our own faith in God. There remains only the void. We are falling. Our dignity is gone. Our values are lost. Who is to say what is up and what is down? It has become colder, and night is closing in. . . . Sometimes prophecy seems to consist in man's ability to experience his own wretched fate so

deeply that it becomes an allegory of something larger. It is in this
sense that one can compare Nietzsche with the ancient prophets. He
felt the agony, the suffering, and the misery of a godless world so
intensely, at a time when others were yet blind to its tremendous
consequence, that he was able to experience in advance, as it were,
the fate of a coming generation."

Walter Kaufmann understands this as Nietzsche's "attempt at
a diagnosis of contemporary civilization, not a metaphysical speculation of ultimate reality" (Kaufmann, *Nietzsche*, 81-82, 84).

CRITIQUE OF CHRISTIANITY

"Christianity is still at any moment possible. . . . It is not
bound to any of those disgraceful dogmas with which it has been
identified; it does not require the belief in a personal God, nor of sin,
nor of immortality, nor of redemption, nor of faith; it has altogether
no need of metaphysics, much less asceticism, much less a 'natural
science.' . . . Whoever now says, 'I will not be a soldier,' 'I have no
interests in the courts,' 'I do not claim the services of the police,' 'I
will do nothing that disturbs my inner peace even if I must suffer for
it,'—nothing will maintain that peace more than suffering—he
would be Christian. Original Christianity is abolition of the state: it
forbids the oath, military service, tribunals, self-defense, or the
defense of any ground for distinction between compatriots and foreigners, similarly, any distinction in the social order. This is the
example of Christ: He resists not the evildoer; he does not defend
himself; he, moreover, turns the other cheek; he forbids that his disciples defend him. Christians have never practiced those precepts
which Jesus prescribed for them, and that disgraceful talk of 'justification through faith' claims primary and singular importance only
because the Church had neither the courage nor the will to embrace
the way of life Jesus demanded. Of what benefit is all academic
training, all criticism and hermeneutic, when such a contradiction in

biblical interpretation as the Church maintains does not make it red with shame? I consider everything which I have seen as Christianity a suspicious duplicity of words, a real cowardliness before all powers that happen to rule. . . . Christians [who advocate] general military duty, parliamentary voting rights, newspaper mentality—and throughout all speak of 'Sin', 'Redemption', 'Otherworldliness', and 'death on the Cross'—how can one endure such business?"

Nietzsche's epigram reads:
"In truth there was only one Christian, and he died on the Cross."

XX. Sigmund Freud (1856-1939) applied his psychoanalysis to a psychogenetic interpretation of religion and ethics. In *Totem and Taboo* (1913) this takes the form of a cosmic Oedipus complex, accounting for "original sin" and the Christian atonement dogma and ritual to expiate it. His *Future of an Illusion* (1927) is no less critical, and, in his final work, *Moses and Monotheism* (1939), these insights are applied to the origin of Judaism.

In *Civilization and its Discontents* (1929) Freud analyzes the "oceanic feeling" of an indissoluble bond, that sense of oneness with the external world which his friend Rolland claimed to be the source of all religious energy but which Freud had not discovered in himself. He explains the origin of this oceanic feeling as symptomatic of an arrested development in which infantile helplessness and the need for a father's protection is permanently sustained by projection into a heavenly providence. Its connection with religion then provides consolation in terms of a "oneness with the universe," an illusion effectively serving the function of a narcotic to disclaim the danger which the ego recognizes as threatening from without. "The religions of humanity must be classified as mass delusions of this kind. Needless to say, no one who shares a delusion recognizes it as such." Freud recognizes that religion is better able than science or art to offer psychological bolstering by a *Weltanschauung* that answers all questions of meaning and being. Nevertheless, he prefers science to religion: the truth about the actual world to a fantasy of an illusory one. And yet, Freud concedes that life is too hard, bringing too many pains, disappointments, and impossible tasks, to survive without palliative measures in the form of either deflections to make light of miseries and substitutions to diminish them or intoxications to compound them.

According to Freud, the "disturbing factor" constituting the discontent of Christian civilization is the Golden Rule. "Nothing else runs so strongly counter to the original nature of man." Man is so unhappy because such restraints are imposed upon his sexuality and aggressive instinct. The origin of the Christian superego lies in the renunciation of this erotic instinct, and the origin of all guilt is the Oedipus complex, the morbid tension between the ego and the superego which demands love of one's neighbor. But, since this ethical command provides too little happiness and is too hard, Freud concludes that one must, for therapeutic reasons, oppose the Christian superego by lowering its demands. For, if the demand exceeds the resources, a revolt or neurosis develops, resulting in even deeper unhappiness. Freud concludes that many paths lead to happiness but none is certain to take one there, "nor can religion keep her promises either." For, in the end, all that is left the faithful in their suffering is unconditional submission to the inscrutable will of God as a last remaining consolation and source of happiness. "And if man is willing to come to this, he could probably have arrived by a shorter road."

XXI. In conclusion, there is the *Way to Wisdom* by Karl Jaspers (1883-1969) for whom "the unconditional imperative comes as the command of my authentic self to my empirical existence." Conditional imperatives, says Jaspers, make me dependent on something outside me, but the unconditional imperatives have their source in myself, in my comprehensive consciousness of God which resists mediation and is not laid down in articles of faith. "The individual, always in his own historicity, stands rather in an immediate relation to God that requires no intermediary." Faith in mediated authority outside myself which I must obey because someone else has willed it or because "it is written" obviates my need to inquire for myself. As Socrates and Jesus, individuals must win authentic being as the foundation of their decisions.

"The unconditional is hidden, only in extreme situations does it by silent decision determine a man's road; it is never positively demonstrable, though it always sustains life through existence and can be definitely elucidated." The content of the unconditional imperative becomes clear as my decision for the good against the evil. Evil is unrestrained surrender to passions and sexual impulses, to the pleasure and happiness of the world, to empirical existence as such. Good is the life of one who subordinates the happiness of this world to the morally admissible. Good is the unconditional will to love, the will to reality. Evil is the will to destruction, torture, cruelty, annihilation, and nihilism. "Love impels to being, hate to nonbeing." A person can only want one or the other: inclination or duty, perversion or purity of motive, hate or love. All indecision is itself evil. One becomes oneself when one decides which way one is going and acts accordingly. Morally the decision to act in accord with love is based on reflective thought, ethically it represents a rebirth of good will, and metaphysically it constitutes awareness of true being, for the foundation of unconditional love is identical with the will to authentic reality.

THE NATURE AND TASK OF THEOLOGY

In our post-Christian era the relevance of theological education is no longer obvious, neither to the seminarian commencing his
studies nor to the churches financing the schools. We wish, therefore, to examine the nature and task of theology 1) as a function of
the Church, 2) as a medium of dialogue with the secular mind, and
3) as an academic discipline in its own right.

Theology is awesome and fascinating. It is a lofty and difficult art both on account of the scope of its purpose and the nature of
its subject matter. In its scope theology is unlimited. It "must deal
with the entire range of human concerns and attempt to determine
their relevance for ultimate concern."[1] In the words of Helmut
Thielicke, theology "reflects" upon the last things; "it asks wherein
lies the truth of our temporal and eternal destiny. And the arc of this
question reaches from the morning of the creation of the world to
the evening of the world at the last judgment; it reaches from the
least, the prayer for daily bread, to the greatest, the prayer for the
coming of the Kingdom." And, as for its subject matter, "it presupposes scientific and religious study of Bible texts, it ponders the
thought of the Church over two thousand years, it comes to terms
with philosophy and art, it broods over contemporary problems, and
it inquires who man is with whom it currently has to deal and in
what abysses he lives." [2]

THE DIDACTIC FUNCTION OF THEOLOGY
WITHIN THE CONFESSING CHURCH

In contrast to philosophy or the sciences, the enterprise of theology is legitimate only within the sphere of the Church. Theology is a function of the Church. The fact, possibility, and necessity of theology presuppose the existence of the Church. Those who study theology do so as members of the Church in the consciousness that they have a commission from the Church and a service to render to the Church.[3]

And yet, it is precisely from within the Church that objections are raised challenging the validity and necessity of theology. The believer who has encountered the simple Gospel only as the direct and personal speech of Jesus and his apostles is appalled and repelled by the immense apparatus of theological concepts. Although he accepts technical terminology in medicine and the sciences, he distrusts it when the Gospel is concerned. The ordinary layperson is inclined to see in the exegetical, historical, and systematic analyses of theology little more than a mere mass of subtle distinctions and arid definitions that thwart the freshness and directness of the Christian experience.[4] Consequently, he fears theology as a dubious application of the scientific method to an analysis of that which is holy. The misinformed layperson tends to regard theology as a speculative activity threatening the supernatural character of revelation. Since he regards the content of religious faith as supernaturally imparted, he concludes that it is not subject to rational criticism. Consequently, he looks upon the motive of theology with suspicion and denounces its practice as a threat to the faith and as evidence of pride and anxiety. It is sufficient for him that the Word of God be approached in simple faith without the support of intellectual crutches, without pride in the wisdom of this world. This prejudice against the academic discipline of theology often reflects a deficient undersanding of both the task of theology and the nature of

Christian convictions. Above all, it reflects an unconscious fear lest the articles of belief fail to withstand the test of critical examination[5] and lest one's personal faith fail to survive analysis and scrutiny.

Paradoxically, this protest against the rational character of theology is almost exclusively leveled against contemporary attempts to understand the meaning of revelation while past interpretations of the same order are accepted with uncritical loyalty as if untouched by human hands.

Advocates of Christian morality and personal devotion sometimes reject a large part of the discipline of theology in the interests of good works or missionary zeal. What is not functionally related to the activist program of the Church is written off as irrelevant if not distractive. Here the antitheological bias is not unrelated to the secular, typically American idolization of the activist. "So long as the engines puff and the wheels roll, all is well."[6]

The history of the Church bears witness that she ought not neglect the safeguard, purification, and stabilization that theology affords her witness. The Church needs theology to prevent her religious devotion from deteriorating into superstition.[7] The first task of theology within the Church pertains to this corrective function of critically examining her testimony to ascertain whether it agrees with her ground of being in Christ.

From its inception the Christian community has been a teaching body. Our Lord himself was a teacher who instructed his disciples to carry on his teaching ministry. And, in the succeeding generations, Christians devoted themselves to the apostles' teaching and fellowship (Acts 2:42). Perhaps it is more than accidental that teaching is mentioned first as one of the outstanding functions expressing the life of the Early Church.

The challenge of theology is indeed the challenge of the Church to fulfill her commission, to instruct, to witness and to proclaim and, in so doing, to answer the question: "*What* do we really have to teach, to testify, to proclaim?" This is the question regarding the *source* of the Word, the answer to which we must find for ourselves over and over again in the discipline of exegesis. Along with it there is the question: "*How* are we to proclaim?"—which takes us into the field of practical theology. And halfway between stands the discipline of dogmatics seeking to answer the question: "*What* are we to think and to say on the basis of what has been thought and said before?"[8] Biblical theology concerns the basis of the testimony (whether it proceeds from Christ); historical theology concerns its development, practical theology its application (whether it leads to him); and systematic theology its content (whether it is in agreement with him).[9]

Theology is a confession of faith, not a mere literary apostolic residuum. Theology is an existential, not a mechanical undertaking. Therefore it is not enough for the Church to recopy the truths of revelation from the dusty manuscripts of her history unless these become the basis of her own confession. Theology is the living confession of the living Church. Its content is not only historic but also existential. It concerns itself not only with the confession of the prophets and apostles, but with what, on the basis of their confession, we ourselves ought to confess.

Since the present confession or lack of confession is, to a great extent, determined by the history of confession, this history calls for evaluation. The Church knows herself only when she knows her history. She must know her history because Christ himself was present and active in and through that history. And to comprehend Christ is to comprehend his work, not only at the beginning of that history of which the New Testament testifies, but throughout the continuing process of the whole work of Christ in the history of the life of Christ in the Body of Christ, his Church. The present form of that life is a development of all that has gone before. And it is only by conscious acquaintance with our past that we are both bound to it and freed from it in the hope of becoming responsible ourselves in history.[10] It is the function of theology to give account of this history, but not to seek to repeat or reenact it. Theology ought rather in its reflection and discussion to bear the character of a living procession acknowledging the Lord of history as He unfolds it for us.

Theology is a scientific, analytical investigation into the nature and ground of the Christian faith, a reflection on the reality of the faith, not from without, but from within. Reflecting from a point of reference outside of the Church would fall into the domain of comparative religions, not theology. While this too could be a profitable venture, it is doubtful whether the genius of Christianity could thus be truly comprehended. The fact that the point of reference is within, rather than without the Church, does not make the method of inquiry less scientific. Whether in theology, comparative religions, philosophy, or the sciences, every investigation claiming to be more than merely descriptive presupposes some point of reference, some criterion of value on the basis of which to venture judgments of value. If the point of reference is not that of Christian presuppositions, it may be that of another religion or that of historical relativism, and so on. The presupposition of faith in Jesus Christ makes the study of theology no less respectable academically than do the presuppositions of any other discipline.[11]

The essential differences between the method of theology and that of other disciplines is that theology occurs within the context of the faith of the Church in Jesus as the Christ. Apart from this, theology confesses its humaneness and imperfection in solidarity with all genuine search for truth. But theology does not itself invent the criterion for its inquiry. The criterion of faith in Jesus as the Christ by which theology investigates the evidence of revelation and by which she discerns the true content of her heritage is not her own creation but a gift to her. While the appropriation of the truth of faith presupposes the commitment of the believer, the human part, though necessary, is essentially a secondary consideration. Faith is a gift of God, not a creation of human being, and therefore theology is never something the Church actually possesses in the sense of its being at her disposal. In the last analysis, it is neither possible nor desirable to make human securities out of the certainty of God.

In all this, theology is a gloriously positive and constructive enterprise within the Church. It is not structured around the contradiction of reason, but is oriented to the word of revelation. Theology does not begin with man's doubt in the hope of reasoning to God's existence. Rather than meddling in questions concerning the possibility of faith, the primary function of theology is to give a clear witness to the reality of faith. Theology is more concerned with the comprehension of the divine message than with the contradiction of man's reason outside the Church. The best way to meet this contradiction head-on is by the living witness of the Church, not by getting on the same ground with unbelief on the assumption that only then is dialogue possible.[12] The primary reality is faith as the glorious gift of God, not unfaith as the rebellion of the human heart. Therefore, the primary task of theology is not to educate the unbeliever by elaborating on the nature of his unbelief but rather to take seriously the need and fact of his forgiveness. Theology is not something to be talked about outside the Church but something to be worked at within the Church, not for the purpose of building a defensive Chinese wall around the Church but for the effect of challenging her members to a living confession within her. The adversary of the faith is not only at work without but also within the Church. The real problem of theology is not so much the clash between Christianity within and paganism outside the Church, but the conflict between types of faith within the Church, a conflict that saps the life of the Church, a conflict between types almost identical in form but not in content. The problem of so-called heresy within the Church is that forms of unfaith and disobedience claim to be the Church and threaten to become the Church—it may be the heresy of false doctrine, it may be the heresy of false life.

The entire history of the Church is characterized by this ongoing dialogue within herself. We think of the struggle of the Early Church against the production of "substitute" Gospels and the introduction of alien meanings into the canonical texts. Here, concern to keep the *kerygma* from being absorbed by the *Zeitgeist* called for the corrective function of theology within the Church. In fact, the entire Pauline corpus could be viewed as a dialogue within the Church between Hebrew-Christian and pagan Greek presuppositions. The Church Fathers also, especially during the third to fifth centuries, sought to preserve the heritage of faith from every wind of doctrine. Out of this struggle for the pure message of the Bible against perversions within the Church there came to be a Protestant Reformation theology. And it was out of the existential encounter of our own forefathers with magisterial Protestantism that the Anabaptist vision was crystallized in the concern not to compromise the truth of the Gospel to political considerations.

THE CHALLENGE TO THEOLOGY FROM THE SECULAR WORLD

While theology is essentially a function of the community of faith, it cannot afford to ignore the challenge of the secular mind. When the Church becomes indifferent to the intellectual climate in which it speaks, it tends to become hopelessly remote and irrelevant. And when she remains aloof to the intellectual struggle that takes place outside, she loses her ability to respond to the challenge of the secular world.[13] The Church's dialogue can not be reduced to a monologue within herself where communication with lower levels of faith and commitment has broken down to the extent that there is no one to convince because no one is listening. This happens when the Church, inbred in her own dogmatic intellectualism, no longer has any interests in common with the world. The vocation of theology becomes alive when the Church discovers her pioneering task in relation to the world as well as to her members. Living theology is the product of the Church's engagement with the living problems of people in the world as it is, the world of industry and labor, of science and art, of politics and the press. It is not enough for the Church to waltz around her own problems and let the rest of the world go by.

The task of theology is to translate the Gospel into every new language and civilization, to transmit the theological theme on a wave length that can be picked up in every new day and circumstance, to translate the Bible into the language and thought categories of the day in order that God's message may be appropriated in human language. To make biblical thought intelligible to the contemporary person the Church must wrestle with the mind of her day and be in dialogue with contemporary ideologies that pose as substitutes for the Christian faith. How else will the Church discern the nature of the opposition between biblical and modern thought? How else will the Church distinguish the wrong "offense" of being unintelligible from the genuine offense of the Cross?[14] The least that can be expected of theology is that it be meaningful: that it meaningfully communicate the meanings of the Gospel. The more demanding test is that of truthfulness. And, while the two are not identical, they are definitely interrelated. For no proposition contends to be true unless it possesses meaning, while its meaningfulness depends on the sense in which it purports to be true.[15]

Theology communicates meaning largely by employing symbols, such as the metaphors of language. In doing so, it changes the context of symbolic references by replacing metaphoric expressions of a bygone age that have long since lost their cognitive content with contemporary symbols that better convey the meanings suggested by the original metaphor. It does so in the concern to increase the cognitive content of the communication. It is not the function of theology to free the Gospel from symbols by replacing symbolic language with literal language, but rather to determine which modes of expression are adequate to the challenge of making sense out of the content of the Gospel in terms of contemporary frames of meaning.

It has been the tendency of fundamentalism to cling tenaciously to particular modes of symbolic expression without considering whether the quaint and outdated vocabulary of a previous age still effectively serves to elicit any meaningful response. How can the Gospel be proclaimed intelligently to the modern person as long as the traditional forms of expressing the Gospel remain unintelligible to him?[16] The whole purpose of speaking from a situation of the past is to make contact with a situation in the present. To communicate the Gospel for and within a situation is something else than throwing the message at the situation as one throws a stone! To address a situation presupposes rapport with the situation. "In order to answer a question one must have something in common with the person who asks it."[17] It is not enough simply to repeat biblical passages without using the conceptual tools of the contemporary period as did the different biblical writers when they spoke from within their own conceptual situations. Kerygmatic or missionary theology will avoid perpetuating a static tradition or emphasizing a mechanical use of the Bible. Instead, it will seek to interpret eternal truth for the changing demands of the human situation with prophetic and transforming power. The challenge of theology is to resolve this tension between the freedom of the *kerygma* and its orthodox fixation by uniting the message with the situation, by correlating the questions implied in the situation with the answers implied in the message without deriving the answers from the questions and without elaborating on the answers before relating them to the questions.

When theology fails to take seriously the challenge of the secular mind and speaks out *ex cathedra* on questions of cosmology or anthropology without reference to the contemporary situation, the "queen of the sciences" is promptly dethroned in the popular mind and relegated to realms beyond at the cost of denying the heritage of our faith any significant relevance for life in this world.[18]

THE CRITICAL TASK OF THEOLOGY

The function of theology is not identical with its usefulness as far as the Church herself is concerned. While the ultimate purpose of theology is service, theology should not be determined by considerations of its immediate usefulness within or by the Church. Theology is a free science. While the ground of its being is within the life of the Church, theology will not be enslaved or dictated by the Church. It must be free in its search and research, determined solely by its subject, not by its constituency. Theology will serve the Church best when it is not obliged to sell its birthright to the Church. If the function of theology is to enable the Church to reflect on the ground of her being, that implies the freedom to call in question the form of her being.

In order to fulfill its critical function within the Church, theology must be free to ask critical questions. At times its best service to the Church may consist in being a disturber of the peace within the Church, threatening the security and tranquillity of her organized life. It was the courage to ask critical questions that gave rise to the Reformation and in turn to the Anabaptist vision. This prophetic critical freedom of theology to question the form and life of the Church is legitimate only as a function of the Church, exercised by persons bound in heart and soul to the common cause of the Church. When these bonds with the Church are broken, critical theology ceases to be theology. In its critical function, theology exemplifies the bondage of freedom in Christ.

Every serious student of theology experiences within something of this tension between the bondage of faith and the freedom of search. In this dialectic between faith and critical inquiry, theology shares in the tension between life and thought, immediacy and reflection, a tension that characterizes self-conscious existence. Critical thought and reflection challenge the drama of life which they presuppose for the purpose of clarifying its ground of being and directing it along a higher plane.[19]

There is yet another, a deeply personal dimension of the critical challenge of theology. This relates to the fact that academic reflection on the reality of faith is not identical with the act of faith itself. The logical aspect of the thinking process, in theology as in any other science, is by its very nature objective and impersonal. Theoretically, it is therefore possible to come to logically correct conclusions in theology, as in any other discipline, without committing oneself to them. The problem is that our intellectual comprehension may exceed our spiritual experience and maturity. While the student of theology understands the logic of the system of truth like a learned mathematical formula, he may not yet fully comprehend the depth of its meaning other than conceptually. The gap between intellectualization and experience of the faith can lead, especially in the intellectually gifted student, to an illegitimate identification with a system of rational truth as a substitute for the growing commitment of personal faith. The spiritual conscience of the layperson is keen to detect this tendency towards an inner dichotomy between the intellectual comprehension of truth and the personal life of faith. Where the pursuit of theology does not simultaneously become a primary experience of personal faith and growing commitment, it leads to what Thielicke refers to as the worst and most widespread ministerial disease, the tendency to read the Bible in the third person as an object of exegetical endeavor with the intent of using it in a sermon for others rather than as a personal word from God for one's self.[20]

The tension between claiming to possess the truth and being committed to search for it may lead to the perplexity of inner uncertainty. The doubt that characterizes the student of theology may, however, not only be legitimate and harmless but a necessary and fruitful stage in the process of finding roots and gaining wings. There is truth in the claim that "education has commenced for any man when there begins the breaking up of his certainties, the shattering of his façades of safety, the crumbling of his walls of imagined security."[21] A certain openness to change at the cost of breaking with one's old securities marks the fact that the process of theological existence has begun. Karl Barth reminds us that "nothing in theology is self-evident. Nothing can be had for nothing. Everything must be worked through, in order to acquire validity."[22] If we were still in paradise or already in glory, our theology would not require such frankness and labor. As it is, theology between Easter and the Second Coming of Christ is a very human enterprise. And he who commits himself to answer the question about truth must be prepared to let it cost him a little sweat,[23] for the labor of theology is itself a means of grace.

Finally, he who undertakes the enterprise of theology ought diligently to cultivate his personal relationship to God and neighbor, lest, while developing a correct theology, he turn out to be a bad Christian. He who is not driven to pray frequently and urgently is scarcely fit for the task. Sacred theology can transpire only in an atmosphere of prayer. Whether it is sacred or not will depend not so much on the degree of its formal orthodoxy as upon the commitment of the hearts and minds that further it. The labor of theology is itself a prayer. And when it happens it is indeed a free and happy performance (Jn. 8:32).

Reprinted with permission from the *Journal of Church and Society*, Vol. 1, No. 2, 35-44.

[1]E. Ashby Johnson, *The Crucial Task of Theology* (Richmond, 1958), p. 149.

[2]Helmut Thielicke, *A Little Exercise for Young Theologians* (Grand Rapids, 1959), p. 27.

[3]Emil Brunner, *The Christian Doctrine of God* (Philadelphia), p. 8.

[4]Cf. *Ibid.*, p. 4.

[5]Cf. Johnson, p. 28.

[6]Martin Marty, Introduction to *A Little Exercise* . . . , xiii.

[7]Brunner, p. 34.

[8]Cf. Karl Barth, *Dogmatics in Outline* (New York: Harper Torchbook, 1959), p. 12.

[9]Cf. Karl Barth, *Kirchliche Dogmatik* (Zollikon-Zürich, 1955) I/1, p. 3.

[10]Cf. Paul Althaus, *Die christliche Wahrheit* (Gütersloh, 1958), p. 9.

[11]*Ibid.*, pp. 5-6.

[12]Cf. Barth, *KD* I/1, p. 28.

[13]Cf. Johnson, pp. 49-51.

[14]Cf. Brunner, pp. 83-84.

[15]Johnson, p. 161.

[16]Keith R. Bridston, *Theological Training in the Modern World* (Geneva, 1954), p. 25.

[17]Paul Tillich, *Systematic Theology*, Vol. I, p. 6.

[18]*Ibid.*, p. 8.

[19]Cf. Althaus, p. 14.

[20]Thielicke, p. 33.

[21]John D. Maguire, "Rediscovering the Aims of Education," *The Christian Scholar*, XLVI/2, p. 101.

[22]Karl Barth, *Evangelical Theology: An Introduction* (Chicago, N. Y., 1963), p. 122.

[23]*Ibid.*

THE QUESTION OF NATURAL THEOLOGY

I. KNOWLEDGE OF GOD

1) Knowledge of God is not a human but a divine possibility. We know God when we are confronted by Him through the Word in the Church. To assume a general, universal knowability of God *a priori* presupposes a stance outside the knowledge of God from which vantage point God's truth, worth, and competence can be temporarily suspended until proven. This general human possibility presumes the ontological and epistemological priority of the inquirer who plays the role of God, as in the case of Anselm who prayed God might help him in his logic so that he in turn might verify God's existence, or Descartes who assumed his own reality as the self-evident basis upon which to establish the reality of God. Since the reality of God is sufficient in itself, therefore, knowledge of God's reality cannot be evaluated in terms of possibility from a criterion outside of itself. Knowledge of God is not a human possibility but a divine reality, it is not the possibility of the creature but the reality of the Creator (as Son and Spirit) to whom our relation is one not of precedence, but of subsequence.

2) Knowledge of God is knowledge as faith (*Gotteserkenntnis ist Glaubenserkenntnis*). Knowledge of faith is similar to other knowledge in that it has an object, but it is unlike other knowledge in that its object is the living Lord of the knowing person, "his Creator from whom he comes even before he knows Him; his reconciler, who through Jesus Christ in the Holy Ghost makes knowledge of Himself possible; his Redeemer who is Himself the future truth of

all present knowledge of Himself" (Karl Barth, *Church Dogmatics*, II/1:21). The act of faith is an act of knowledge as acknowledgment (*Kennen heisst erkennen und anerkennen*). Faith is not irrational or antirational but rational in the proper sense of being illuminated by the wisdom of God in Christ to comprehend the meaning of our being as we "realize" our election and calling. Knowledge is a part of faith because there is no division in this matter of trust.

3) Knowledge of God is objective, that is, it is bound to the Word of God, not to our *Selbstbewusstsein*. Knowledge of faith is unique because God's objectivity is unique. He is primarily objective to Himself and secondarily to us in His self-revelation (i. e., ontology and economy of the Trinity). Knowledge of God is not oneness with God and therefore not a subjective phenomenon either in God or man. Not that we can have God as we have other objects, but that in faith He becomes *gegenständlich* (or real) *im gegenüber* (over against us). God is not our knowledge of God nor our experience of God.

Knowledge of God is also subjective because everything proceeds from Him. He gives us the categories in which we know what we know. He is both the object and the subject of our knowledge. His Spirit and ours are co-witnesses. This is the good conscience (*suneidēsis*), the wisdom of Christ in which *en Christo* one lives the meaning of one's life.

4) Knowledge of God is personal. It does not exist "out there" apart from the I-Thou relation. It is not knowledge of an idea. The intellectual cannot be isolated from the personal. (The fool denies God in his "heart," Ps. 14:1). To know God means to meet God personally and to be completely filled and determined by Him. We know Him by talking with rather than about Him. To know Him is to trust Him for the whole of living and dying. Knowledge of God never happens on neutral ground, never on our own terms.

5) Knowledge of God is grace of God. To know God is to comprehend His grace. That is the meaning of Christmas, Easter, Pentecost, and Parousia. The meaning of creation, incarnation, re-creation, and consummation is covenant: Our history is intended to be His *Heilsgeschichte* and His election is intended to include our redemption in Christ. To this knowledge the characters of the Bible were not compelled but invited, not challenged but awakened. Grace is not man's act but God's gift. We know this gift not as one's opinion but as God's decision *ephapax*, which establishes our relationship to Him, not our conception of Him.

Knowledge of God presupposes revelation of God.

II. REVELATION OF GOD

1) Revelation of God is being of God. In knowing WHO God is we know HOW His being is His revelation. That God reveals Himself means that Father, Son, and Spirit are subject, object, and predicate of His self-revelation in the unity and diversity of the three modes of His triune self. God exists neither in only one mode of His being nor in only one sphere of His action but through the whole of creation, incarnation, and re-creation. No knowledge of God has as its object only one dimension of His being or acting. Either we know God entirely or not at all. Denial of the Trinity means denial of the self-revelation of God in Christ through the Spirit.

2) Revelation of God is incarnation of God. In emptying and unveiling Himself, God in Christ moves into history as the object of human contemplation and experience in such a way that He assumes His own double as Son of Mary while simultaneously retaining His eternal being as Father in heaven. To know Christ is to know God. Not to know the Son is not to know the Father.

3) Revelation of God is inspiration of God. Spirit of God means

breath, movement, and power of God enabling one to participate in God's word and work. From the perspective of the Old Testament, a living person (or soul) is one into whom God the Creator breathed His eternal breath (Gn. 2:7). From the perspective of the New Testament, a real Christian is one in whom Christ the Redeemer breathed his Holy Spirit (Jn. 20:22). The first act is a divine creative act in which human being participates as object. The second act is a divine redemptive act in which human being participates as subject. When we say Holy Spirit, we have to do with the subjective dimension of the divine in our own life. We are confronted in the Bible with the reality of the Holy Spirit in all relations between God and man and man and man whether in creation, incarnation, or re-creation.

4) Revelation of God is mystery of God. The mystery is that we cannot distinguish its content from its form. When God appeared to Moses in the burning bush, to Abraham as an angel, and to Israel through prophets, there was a sense in which God was identical with His revelation, yet not quite. For God was not that bush, angel, or prophet as He is the Son and as He is the Spirit.

5) Revelation of God is miracle of God. The miracle is that God chose to glorify Himself in humanity (His and ours) and that in so doing He does not cease to be God, and humanity and *Geschichte* do not cease to be human and historical.

III. IMAGE OF GOD

1) Genesis 1:26f. describes the mystery of human origin not from below, but from above: "God said: 'Let us make man in our image, after our likeness.' . . . So God created man in his own image, in the image of God he created male and female. . . ." The *imago Dei* marks one as God's possession, for one's life may not be taken (Gn. 9:6). Requesting a penny, Jesus asked: "Whose is this image and superscription?" (Mk. 12:16). Upon the Pharisee's reply

Jesus added: "Render . . . to God the things that are God's," implying that the image in man is not Caesar's (as on the penny) but God's to whom man therefore owes undivided allegiance.

2) Throughout the Old Testament, *imago Dei* is associated with *gloria Dei* (*kabodh*), the self-revealing sum of all divine perfections characterizing God's presence (e. g., on Sinai, in the cloud, and temple, etc.). Throughout the New Testament, *imago Dei* describes the dignity and Sonship of Christ "who is the image of the invisible God" (Col. 1:15) and man "made in the likeness of God" (Jas. 3:9), "renewed after the image (Col. 3:10), "predestined to be conformed to the image of His Son" (Rom. 8:29), and "changed into his likeness from one degree of glory to another" (II Cor. 3:18).

3) Irenaeus, a second-century student of Polycarp (who conversed with many who had seen Christ), distinguished (in Gn. 1:26) between IMAGE (Hebrew-*Zelem*, Greek-*eikon*, Latin-*imago*, German-*Ebenbildlichkeit*) and LIKENESS (Hebrew-*demuth*, Greek-*homoiosis*, Latin-*similitudo*, German-*Ähnlichkeit*), concluding that in the Fall man lost only the divine LIKENESS (or supernatural element) but retained the divine IMAGE (or natural element) consisting in reason and freedom. This ingenious solution afforded a metaphysical distinction between normal people who retained the NATURAL divine IMAGE and abnormal people (saints) who recovered also the SUPERNATURAL DIVINE LIKENESS.

4) Challenging this distinction on the grounds that the Hebrew terms were synonymous, Luther concluded that the Fall affected not only man's SUPERnature (divine likeness) but his REAL nature (divine image) leaving him UNnatural, INhuman, totally corrupted by "original" sin, without freedom, knowledge of God, or capacity for righteousness. But, since even fallen man differed from the animals, Luther conceded that a relic of the *imago* was somehow salvaged. This connection between *humanum* and *imago* allowed for a "*tunkel*

Fünklein" in the conscience of Turks and pagans on the basis of which they could be held to account for not living up to the *lex naturae*. But the Enlightenment proved Luther had conceded too much.

5) Both the Catholic separation of image and likeness and the Protestant depreciation of the *humanum* in the relic concept reflect the scholastic-hellenistic misinterpretation of the Hebrew concepts as substantive rather than relational, defining man's lostness as quasi-physical corruption rather than personal contradiction.

6) Brunner defined the universal *imago Dei* as the Gospel's FORMAL *Anknüpfungspunkt* consisting in everyone's potential *Wortmächtigkeit* (capacity to discern God's Word) and *Wortempfänglichkeit* (capacity to receive God's Word), maintaining a) that God is still evident (*offenbar*) in His work of creation and b) that the distinctively human element in a person is theologically significant (*Man in Revolt*, 527), thus guaranteeing one *Wortmächtigkeit* ('verbicompetence') but not necessarily *Offenbarungsmächtigkeit* (capacity for revelation). Brunner distinguished GENERAL revelation IN nature (which is there objectively and is subjectively discernible by natural reason) from SPECIAL revelation in history discernible only in faith. Since natural man comprehends the Law (second table) but not the Law Giver, he is responsible not to the Gospel but for *lex naturae*. "God is greatly concerned that man, even as sinner, shall not be overwhelmed" (*MiR*, 541).

7) Barth claims that the emphasis in Genesis 1:27 is not upon some REFLECTION in man or nature but upon the ARCHETYPE itself: "Let US make man in OUR image." The text means that our ground and possibility lie not in nature but in God. God-likeness is not a quality or attribute of humankind. One is what one is not because of one's reason, responsibility, or freedom, but because God wills one as His counterpart. *Imago Dei* means I-Thou covenant relationship between God and person and "consists" in existential dialogue within

the "humanity of God" which has its prototype in the Trinity. There is no *analogia entis*, no common "ground of being" (R. C. and Tillich), only *analogia fidei* to express our noetic dependence on Him and *analogia relationis* to express our ontological dependence on Him.

8) The Reformers falsely associated *imago Dei* with an original state prior to the Fall. But there is no prior, no mention in the Bible of actual history in Eden preceding the Fall. The first thing we know about man as such is his fallenness. Since the *imago* never was man's possession, it continues to be God's work and gift, for the prototype, God Himself, is not destroyed by man's fallenness. Man's revolt cannot annul God's *Anspruch* (claim) and therefore the *imago Dei* is never "lost."

9) The I-Thou relationship is fulfilled in Jesus Christ who IS the *eikon* and *doxa theou* (I Cor. 11:7) through his Bride, the Church. The christological equation is the basis for the anthropological equation via the ecclesiological equation (and not the other way around).

10) To discern who REAL man is we must look to Christ, not to Adam. Since Jesus Christ IS the revealing Word of God, "he is the source of our knowledge of the human nature God has made" (III/2:47). There is no other valid approach to REAL humanity except via Jesus in whom the relation to God and humanity is perfectly actualized. "Jesus is man as God willed and created Him. What constitutes true human nature in us depends on what it is in Him" (50). Only in Jesus is the real existence of the creature revealed.

11) A phenomenology of man as such would not be an anthropology of REAL man, only of fallen man, who of himself knows neither his sin nor his creatureliness and cannot distinguish between what he was meant to be and what he is. An understanding of what it means to be truly human is derived not via Naturalism, Idealism, or Existentialism, but via Jesus Christ. For all their empiri-

cal conclusions, secular anthropologies fail to take account of the fact that noetically and ontically man is never without God.

12) That Jesus was sinless "implies a different status but not a different constitution of His nature from ours" (53). What is unique about Jesus is the presence of God in him as the real substance of his total life and work. Jesus is the creature who exists for God, for His glory, freedom, and love. "He is not a man for nothing, nor for Himself. He is a man in order that the work of God may take place in Him" (70). God's purpose is Jesus' purpose because he derives from God, is in God, and for God.

13) Real existence is determined not by nature but by the Word of God, an existence in togetherness with Jesus which means existence which rests upon God's election of man in Christ and therefore existence in true righteousness and holiness.

QUESTIONS

1) How is pre-Christian humanity related to Christ?

Christ is eternal. Election ln Christ precedes creation (Eph. 1:4). Pagans are not held responsible for what they do not know. It is hypothetical to question the mystery of divine election.

2) What about the Old Testament *imago Dei?*

The Old Testament points to Christ. The *logos* of Old Testament theophany IS the Christ of the New Testament event. Why go backwards before Christ to define it? There is only one God and Christ IS the revelation of the Father.

3)   Should we define human being phenomenologically as "Man in Revolt" (Brunner) or theologically as "Man in Christ" (Barth)?

Both agree that the *imago Dei* is not someTHING but the God-man relation. Brunner concedes that "Jesus Christ, as the perfect Word of God, is the *ratio cognoscendi* of the creaturely nature of man" (*Scottish Journal of Theology*, June 1951, 132), but, in so doing, he separates epistemology from ontology. Barth insists that God cannot be known formally, partially, naturally, or neutrally, for to know God is to be *en Christo*.

IV. WHAT ABOUT NATURAL THEOLOGY?

1) Theology begins with God, not man. To take a point of departure other than revelation, apart from grace and faith, is a perversion of theology. It is the constant temptation of the Church to civilize the *skandalon* of the *kerygma*, to compromise and domesticate the Gospel so as to make it innocuous, respectable, and relevant, by sanctioning man's unreadiness for knowledge of God on God's terms. It confers on man an independent word, an independent ground of being to contest the sovereignty of Christ. Natural theology is the natural rebellion of the natural man who is clever enough to feel he can conduct his case against the Lordship of Christ better with some sort of religious foundation. Natural theology is the voice of the respectable theologian in the respectable church justifying his enmity to grace.

2) There is no common ground between faith and unbelief and no natural way from philosophy to theology. The church that claims to be the Church should be so precisely in her witness. The greatest service Christians can do unbelievers is not to make them better unbelievers, but to introduce them to Christ (not nature), that is, to address them from a position of faith, not unfaith. Decisions of faith are not made on neutral or natural ground but in encounter with the living God.

3) Natural theology has no basis in Scripture: Witness that "the heavens declare the glory of God" (Ps. 19:1) originates not in

the clouds but in the people of Israel who worshiped not nature but God (cf. especially vv . 5-10).

In Romans 1:19, 20 Paul is not speaking about heathen as such and in general but about those Gentiles who are now confronted with his gospel of the resurrection of Jesus Christ. "What can be known about God is [now] plain to them." It is in the light of Golgotha (not in nature) that they are without excuse. He is simply describing natural man as an unwilling witness who "ever since the creation of the world" rebels against his Maker. Paul is not speaking about the possibility of a natural theology which, as a substitute for the Gospel, the pagans might catechize out of their own oracles. Paul is not making any positive statements about the possibilities of these heathen on their own. He is simply saying that, in the light of the resurrection, they can now justify themselves as little as can the Jews, since the only hope for both Jews and Gentiles is not nature but Jesus Christ. Precisely on this point Paul is most dogmatic, claiming that his gospel "is not man's gospel" but that it "came through a revelation of Jesus Christ" (Gal. 1:11f.). In the same breath Paul pronounced anathema on anyone proclaiming a different gospel than salvation in Christ by grace through faith.

The reference in Romans 2:14, 15 to "Gentiles who have not the law [but] do by nature what the law requires" refers to Gentile CHRISTIANS who in fulfillment of Jeremiah 31:31 have the Spirit of Christ in their hearts.

In Acts 17:22-31, where Paul commends the Athenians for worshiping at an altar of an unknown god, Paul was not proclaiming a natural theology but the resurrection of Jesus Christ so that they too might know the only true God, their Creator and Redeemer, whom they knew not.

WHAT MEN LIVE BY

The purpose of this paper is to explore the relation between faith and life, between Christian renewal and social responsibility. Stated in classical terms, it is an inquiry into the ethical implications of theology or, conversely, into the theological basis for ethics together with some indication as to how this affects Christian social action.

RENEWAL AND SOCIAL RESPONSIBILITY

The Christ-event is the only uniquely new event since creation, and the Bible is the only authentic record of this event. All renewal in *Heilsgeschichte* is inspired by this event through the reality of the Holy Spirit in the life of the Church. As one hears and receives the *kerygma* one is transformed or renewed by it. The nature of this renewal characterizes one's being in Christ in the world.

Renewal is the creative presence and dynamic ministry of the Spirit of God in the life of faith. The church that fears that the faith once delivered to the saints might be lost or adulterated fails to realize that the Gospel she seeks to preserve is itself the message of renewal and that the life of the Church does not consist in her antiquity but in her holiness. Only as the Church relies wholly on the Spirit will she overcome the temptation of institutional inertia that thwarts the creative wellsprings of the Spirit and will she become God's instrument of renewal in the world.

Before exploring uniquely Christian dimensions of social responsibility for the person in Christ renewed by his Spirit, it is fitting first to orient ourselves to concepts of responsibility from within the secular context.

MODERN MAN AND RELIGIOUS VALUES

Modern man is skeptical about the validity and relevance of Christian values. He tends to see all religions as by-products of history and culture. This contemporary indifference to ultimate values has its roots in the naturalism of Darwin, the historical materialism of Marx, and the naturalistic psychology of Freud who together have convinced modern man that the origin of moral values is to be found not in divine revelation but in the force of custom and superstition, in the wish-fulfillment fantasies of a disguised egoism, and in the conflicting social habits that make for guilt complexes.

The modern moral skeptic who has been thoroughly indoctrinated with historical relativism fails to realize that every person who acts and makes decisions does so on the basis of a scale of values. No one who is free to act can evade the moral question, WHAT OUGHT I TO DO? The moment human consciousness exists, one is faced with the ethical question of being socially responsible. No one can avoid setting up a functional order of priority to determine one's conduct in a given situation. The attitude of moral skepticism and relativism is therefore a sophisticated form of self-deception, a flight from the reality of an inevitable choice between a lower or higher level of responsibility determined by a lower or higher set of values. In the last analysis, it is the inevitable choice between God or an idol.

DEFINITION OF MORALITY BETWEEN INTENTION AND RESULT

The degree to which an action is ethical depends not so much on its result as on its motive. The action itself (whether preparing soup for a hungry person or drafting an IBM missile) is predominently technical though motivated by a variety of conscious and semiconscious motives. No action as such is Christian though some kinds of action are never Christian (e. g., war or cannibalism). While no action could be considered moral whose intended result were not moral, the actual result may not correspond to the intention. Good intentions may produce evil effects while evil intentions may, by the providence of God, have good effects. Ethics is therefore primarily concerned with the reason for preferring one line of conduct over another. And it is possible—at least in a hypothetical way—to plot comparative levels of value on the basis of which decisions are made.

LEVELS OF RESPONSIBILITY WITHIN
THE SECULAR CONTEXT

For the infant and for the primitive person who have not yet developed to the level of a reflective agent and for the extreme cynic who has already disintegrated below the level of humanity, the context of decision is immediacy with nature.

The first stage of human responsibility beyond hedonistic immediacy is conformity to custom, to an established pattern of group behavior not immediately determined by the utilitarian concern for survival. Behavior determined by custom is still impersonal and "irresponsible" to the extent that the collective deprives the individual of total responsibility, allowing him to become only partially an ethical person by ascribing to him only partial responsibility. It is this depersonalization of the self within the collective that constitutes the moral limitation of natural community over against Christian community which by nature of its togetherness in Christ is never less moral (Niebuhr) than the individual.

The average contemporary person, irrespective of what echelon of society he represents, applies his intelligence primarily to the perpetuation and well-being of his material existence. Though in exceptional cases human quest for the Infinite expresses itself in heroism or despotism, it seldom transcends crude utilitarianism. When it does—as in the case of the genius who cultivates the aesthetic for its own sake or who identifies with science or art— that one seeks the reason for being in the furtherance and enjoyment of the culture process. But, in despair of finding ultimate meaning for personal life, the genius tends to escape into either mysticism or idealism.

A human being, however, becomes a person not by the nature of creative artistic potential but by the quality of self-determination in freedom and responsibility. A consciousness of personal responsibility presupposes a divine imperative, not one imposed from without but one acknowledged from within. One becomes a responsible being at the point where one realizes that the meaning of one's being can be found neither in nature nor culture, neither in fate nor adventure but alone in the will of God. The persistent tendency to substitute a naturalistic or rationalistic basis for the religious roots of morality is what distinguishes the secular from the Christian understanding of responsibility. Secular morality rejects the transcendent revelation of the Christian faith and seeks the source of the moral imperative in nature or in man rather than in God.*

In naturalistic ethics the good is that which furthers personal well-being. Consideration for and adaptation to the group is advocated only as a means towards the end of self-interest and personal happiness. While its hedonism is rarely presented in so crude a form (as in Epicurus), the social altruism of naturalistic ethics (whether in Hobbes, Adam Smith or J. S. Mill) is but a guise for its underlying egoism. The naturalistic premise essentially limits moral responsibility to that which has promise of being expedient for one's self.

---

*Cf. Emil Brunner, "Die Stufen des immanent-sittlichen Selbstbewusstseins," Kap. 2 in *Das Gebot und die Ordnungen* (Zürich, 1939).

Here, there is no place for a feeling of obligation transcending self-interest. Consequently, naturalistic ethics is caught in the contradiction of trying to derive a sense of genuine social responsibility from self-interest.

In contrast to Naturalism, Idealism advocates duty for duty's sake (Plato, Kant) irrespective of pain or pleasure. For Kant, the moral imperative was universally valid for all people in all situations. Because of its universality, Kant held the locus of the imperative to be human reason rather than divine revelation. But, by making universality a criterion of the good, he transferred the idea of the good from the realm of obligation to that of existence, thereby denying the sense of duty he intended to foster and, in the last analysis, identifying moral law with natural law.

These examples suffice to indicate that in philosophical ethics there is no way of deriving the imperative of moral obligation from the indicative of natural inclination. While secular morality claims to have a standard of values, it fails to convince on rational grounds why a higher value is preferable to a lower one when it does not make for pleasure (Epicurus) or self-realization (Aristotle) or is not a compelling conviction within (Kant). Therefore, philosophical ethics is at best descriptive but not normative, for it fails to give a nonreligious argument for morality.

Perhaps the moral consciousness of Kant silently presupposed the Christian heritage of revelation. But one cannot have both reason and revelation as first principles since a human being cannot be both the one commanded and the one issuing the command. Man cannot be ultimately responsible to himself nor feel guilty for disobeying himself. Apart from an acknowledgment of divine revelation, there is no adequate answer to the nature of responsible being.

Questions of value and responsibility nevertheless occur out-

side the Church, because these questions are inseparable from the
meaning of human existence. But their occurrence is not identical
with their validity. In fact, man's quest for naturalistic and rationalistic answers may be an expression of his rebellion against God for
not giving man an answer apart from giving Himself. God's answer
in Christ is both too cheap and too costly for natural man who rebels
against God's judgment and grace.

THE THEOLOGICAL AND CHRISTOLOGICAL BASIS FOR ETHICS

For the Christian, the ultimate good is not immanent in man
but is based on the nature and will of God, His self-revelation, and
His covenant. The aim of ethical reflection is therefore not: How
can I be good or do good so that through my action the world might
become good, but rather the totally different question: What is the
will of God? This is so because not self and the world but God is the
ultimate reality, and the Christian concern is to witness to this reality
even at the cost of appearing other than good. The Christian begins
with the reality of God and accepts the reality of the world and self
"in faith" as derived from the Creator. One knows that God's will
embraces reality as a whole, including the reality of mankind together with all motives and purposes, fellow beings, and the entire creation. Everything is held in being by Him.

Essentially, the Christian understanding of God's will is christological; it is rooted in the unity of divine and human reality in the
incarnation. In fact, concepts of reality that do not focus in Jesus
Christ are speculative abstractions. The reality of Jesus Christ is the
resolution of all conflict between the ideal and the actual. The conflict between the OUGHT and the IS is resolved in Christ, who is
what he ought to be and in whom we become what we were meant to
be. Christ is the basis of God's claim on us and the content of His
command to us, not as an ideal for us to imitate but as the new reality

He creates in us. Christ is the subject and the content of the good. He alone is and does the good in his life and work through our life and work. To be and do good is to love him, to participate in him, to believe in him. In biblical thought the good, like the holy, is not substantial but relational. God alone is holy and good, and the holiness and goodness of human being consists in the (ontological and epistemological) reality of belonging to Him, a reality expressed in the reciprocity of love (I Jn. 4.19: We love Him because He first loved us).

How is the Christian's being in Christ related to his being in society? The message of the Bible is that God reveals Himself as Lord who reigns over His people. This is the ground of being of Israel in the Old Testament and of the Church in the New Testament. God's will is a will that creates community. That is why He creates man. That is why man is truly man only in loving and serving God and his fellow beings.

While the theological basis for community is implied in creation, it is most clearly revealed in the incarnation. God wills man because He willed the God-man. Because God in Christ shared with man His history and destiny, being in Christ implies sharing our life with our fellow being.

But the incarnation implied a Cross where *agape* was revealed distinct from *eros*. Normally, *eros* and *agape* are intermingled in life. *Agape* distinct from *eros* is possible only at the point of self-surrender inspired by divine surrender. As man comprehends the meaning of the Cross, he ceases to accuse his neighbor and, by acknowledging his own guilt, becomes to him a brother. The Word of the Cross is a Word of forgiveness that overcomes both conceit and despair and constitutes the foundation of new being. By freeing man from himself to become a brother to his neighbor the suffering servant motif of *Heilsgeschichte* constitutes the theological and christological basis for Christian social action.

In Christ we partake of the reality of God within the reality of the world. In Christ we never experience the reality of the world apart from God (as do the secularists) nor do we experience the reality of God apart from the world (as claim some mystics). The New Testament speaks about an ethical tension between that which is worldly, profane, natural, un-Christian and that which is divine, holy, supernatural, Christian. Misunderstanding the nature of this dualism, monasticism and pietism proclaimed the independence of the spiritual from the secular while Lutheranism and the social sciences proclaim the emancipation of the secular from the spiritual. Where Christ and the world are conceived as mutually exclusive realms, he, who claims to be in one realm only, often deceives himself, and he, who seeks to be in both, suffers unbearable conflict. The Christian doctrine of creation, incarnation, and reconciliation implies not a balanced dualism but one reality in Jesus Christ in whom all things subsist.

Yet, the cause of Christ is distinct from the world, the supernatural from the natural, revelation from reason, but always in such a way that being in Christ includes being in the world, that the supernatural includes the natural, that revelation includes reason. The ontological miracle of being is that God holds the world and man in His will by identifying it with His being-in-Christ. The epistemological mystery of being is that we know divine reality only in worldly reality, the supernatural only through the natural, revelation only as reason. Therefore, the Christian's worldliness ought not divide him from Christ nor ought his Christianity divide him from the world. For, to be a Christian means belonging wholly to Christ while standing wholly in the world, witnessing to and participating in the reality of "cross and resurrection" between nature and grace as a child of God.

AREAS OF CHRISTIAN CONCERN

Seen from this christological perspective, Christian social responsibility implies cultivating wholeness of being, which is a quality of holiness that integrates and sanctifies one's whole life, rather than sacrificing that wholeness within a schizophrenic or casuistic dichotomy of sacred and secular spheres. This presupposes discernment of the nature of the tension between Christ and culture within the totality of our civilization so that we neither confuse the Kingdom of God with the cultural process nor advocate a legalistic nonconformity on principle but commit the Church to a redemptive strategy expressing faith, hope, and love and bearing evidence of true community.

An incarnationist theology leads to engagement with the actual problems of people in the world of industry and labor, science and art, politics and the press. Together with Moses, Jeremiah, and Jesus, we are called of God to identify ourselves with the plight, desolation, and despair of the world's people, there to hammer out the implications of the *kerygma* in the midst of social revolution lest the faith we profess become hopelessly remote and irrelevant, lest we perpetuate an otherworldliness incapable of grappling redemptively with the forces that cripple the body and kill the soul.

This means, in general, that every area of life is the subject of Christian concern and, in particular, that the vocation to which we are called in Christ is the place where we are to work out our sanctification in the holy worldliness of Christian discipleship while bearing the marks of Jesus in our body and producing the fruit of his Spirit in the labor of his love.

THE STRUGGLE BETWEEN HAVING AND BEING

I. THE INEVITABILITY OF OUR INVOLVEMENT

Economic issues constitute the major portion of human concern whether on the local level of earning a living or on the international plane of economic competition between the power structures of Communism and Capitalism. Upon the currency which we carry in our pockets is engraved the aphorism "in God we trust." Whatever else that motto was meant to symbolize, it expresses the fact that between God and history we cannot very well escape being involved in economic affairs. The economic process supplies the goods and the bads of our earthy lives. It involves us in many of our most rewarding and most difficult human relationships. The economic order affects our family life, our religious life, and our cultural and political life, thereby placing its indelible stamp upon our personality.[1]

II. THE ETHICAL CHALLENGE: TO DISCERN THE RELEVANCE OF OUR CHRISTIAN FAITH FOR OUR ECONOMIC LIFE

The fact that we are by nature of our historicity inevitably involved in the divine potential and human sinfulness of the economic process confronts us with the necessity of discerning the ethical relevance of our Christian faith for our individual and corporate economic life. Accordingly, the purpose of this paper is to discern from the perspective and power of the Christian faith the place of economic values within the divine economy and the conditions whereby economic involvement becomes a means of redemption.

III. THE GOALS OF ECONOMIC LIFE

The purpose of economic activities and institutions is allegedly to meet our primary material needs, such as food, shelter, and clothing. The secular economist may in an optimistic mood define the goal of economic life as the distribution as widely as possible of the good things of life, a goal that assumes the test of effectiveness as a criterion of value. It remains for the Christian to define what the "good things" of life are and to what extent a definition of "practical" can serve as a moral criterion of responsible economic involvement.

From the Christian perspective, the economic process is not autonomous; it is neither an end in itself nor a revelation of God's will. Nor is economic efficiency the final norm or end of human existence.

Secular economists often assume acquisitive incentive as axiomatic. Despite the fact that Christian idealists often assume altruistic incentive where there is little more than enlightened self-interest, the Christian as a Christian cannot accept without qualification the validity of individual or group self-interest as a moral rationale for the economic venture.

The quest for biblical implications in the face of these problems is urgent. As long as we hold ethics to be a part of theology and claim that our life ought to reflect our faith, we are compelled by the sheer necessity of maintaining our integrity as Christian persons to relate our ethical values to our practical economic concerns.

IV. GOD AND/OR MAMMON

The voice of the Church has by no means always been unanimous on the relationship of God to Mammon. Up to the Reformation, the medieval monastics tolerated acquisition and spending only as necessary concessions to human frailty.[2] Within the Protestant

heritage, the Puritans, especially, never wearied of reminding themselves that wealth is a great danger the temptations of which never
end and the pursuit of which is not only senseless as compared with
the importance of the Kingdom of God but altogether morally sus-
pect.[3] "Nobody can inherit the Kingdom unless he is poor with
Christ" and, consequently, "a Christian should not have anything of
his own but should have all things in common with his brother"[4]—a
recurring theme within our own Anabaptist heritage, one that continues to challenge our capitalist complacency and to proclaim with
prophetic conviction that "there is only one way in which to deal
with this Mammon-god and that is by absolute renunciation (of
property rights), and there is only one way to renounce him and that
is by distribution to the poor."[5]

Here it is maintained that the demon Mammon is renounced
and the rule of God established only where Christians share life's
necessities from a common fund.

On the other side of the coin is evidence that it was not an
ascetic voice in the wilderness that made this country strong and free
but rather the ready acclimatization of neo-Calvinist piety to the spirit
of capitalist America whose outstanding churchmen convinced this
nation under God that "to secure wealth is an honorable ambition"[6]
and one of the great tests of a person's usefulness for the Kingdom.
God prospers the rich on account of their honesty and industry, and
we ought not sympathize with the poor whom God has punished for
their sins. Today's Christian businessmen express deep concern "that
so many people who love the Lord Jesus feel quite sincerely that they
should have no interest in money."[7] They argue that as Christians we
ought to be the most financially successful people on earth lest our
testimony for Jesus Christ suffer disrepute![8] Christ, they say, conquered the power of evil at Golgotha so that all who believe might
enjoy the bounteous fullness of the new life. Furthermore, Jesus'
parable of the nobleman who had his servants report on the invest-

ment of their talents is gospel proof that "the profit motive is an honest, legitimate, and scriptural motive" and that Christ supports free enterprise: the right for everyone to do with his own as he chooses.[9] If only Christians had the "mind of Christ" and "the wisdom of the Lord," they could conquer every form of poverty and enjoy material abundance in the fullness of their Christian inheritance.

The advocates of this position presume our affluent living standard to be the fruit and proof of our virtue on the assumption that godliness is profitable unto all things and that prosperity is a mark of divine favor as reward for virtue. This presumptuous attitude sometimes creates the not altogether unfounded impression that our wealth is proof of our vulgarity and unjust exploitation of others.

These conflicting interpretations within the Church impel us briefly to investigate the biblical foundations qualifying the Christian's intentions for economic involvement.

V. BIBLICAL FOUNDATIONS

In Paradise, God commanded Adam to "dress and keep" the garden (Gn. 2:15). Since the Fall, the nature and fruit of labor remain evidence of divine discipline and grace (Gn. 3:17-19). No one can evade the mandate to participate vocationally in the creation of things and values intended for the glorification of God. But the fact that the race of Cain has not fulfilled this mandate casts the darkest shadow over all human labor.[10] At Sinai, Israel was committed by the fourth commandment of the Decalogue to respect private property as a divine entrustment. Upon occupying the promised land of Canaan, Israel was warned not to be distracted by possessions or God might withdraw what is His own (Dt. 8:11f.). Israel's king was advised not to multiply his property lest his heart be turned from the Lord (Dt. 17:17). Woe was pronounced upon those who added house to house and field to field. To avoid the unjust accumulation of large private fortunes, the owner had to release his land and the creditor his money according to the law of the Sabbath. The prophets decried the economic corruption in urban life and regal politics and reminded Israel that all things belong to God (Is. 66:2) including the earth and its fullness (Ps. 24:1) and warned against trampling upon the poor (Am. 5:11). The prophets (especially Hosea) called for a restoration of the ideals of righteousness and economic order exemplified in Israel's seminomadic life in which she depended for her daily existence on God's manna and not on her accumulated reserves.

This motif of moral restoration was taken up by John the Baptist, the forerunner of Jesus of Nazareth who for our sake became poor that we by his poverty might become rich (II Cor. 8:9). The humble conditions of his birth in a stable, of his life as a son of a carpenter, and of his ministry as a wandering rabbi in Israel are signs of God's indifference to economic standards of value. Jesus warned us not to buy our physical advantages at too high a price (e. g., "What does it profit a man," Mk. 8:36; Parable of the Rich Fool, Lk. 12:20), implying that we might be called upon to die voluntarily both individually and collectively in order to preserve our Christian integrity. His "the first shall be last" is characteristic of his way of overturning the world's values.

The divine sympathy toward poverty expressed throughout both Testaments (as though God were always on the side of the poor to pronounce upon them His first blessing, Lk. 6:20) is indeed a striking phenomenon. It is reason enough to explore the economic relevance of biblical norms for our own day and to ask radical questions about the implications of Christ's voluntary poverty for the life and wealth of those who profess his Name.

VI. ECONOMICS AND THE KINGDOM OF GOD

There are those who maintain that Jesus did not concern himself with economic questions and that, consequently, the Church ought not do so either. It is true that neither in the teachings of Jesus nor elsewhere in the Bible do we find uniquely Christian answers to purely economic questions. The economic and social concerns of Jesus are all centered in concerns for the realization of the Kingdom of God. He denounced riches with considerable vehemence, claiming that "it is easier for a camel to go through the eye of a needle than for a rich man to enter the Kingdom of God." He did so on the premise that the meaning of one's life lies not in the abundance of one's possessions but in one's membership in the Kingdom. For his committed disciples, the Master advocated an attitude of passivity towards the adverse conditions of their economic existence in the implicit faith that God who cares for birds and lilies will in His own way also provide for His own. Essentially, this provision comes through the realization of the Kingdom or rule of God in the lives of people.

According to the teaching of Jesus, the Kingdom of God constitutes the meaning and destiny of being. It is the end toward which creation moves and the goal in which its fulfillment lies. The community of the Kingdom is realized not through a reform program of economic and social betterment but through the creation of a redemptive fellowship where gratitude for God's love issues in the service of love to one's neighbor. Whatever conflicts with the demands of that love is renounced by the presence and power of God. In the Kingdom fellowship, faith is not confined to ecclesiastical behavior but expressed in concrete human relationships which are in part economic. The chief end of mankind is realized through the integration of faith and life, work and worship in order to restore wholeness of being and to redeem the sacred dignity of one's vocation under God. Consequently, it is understandable that Jesus denounced those institutions which maximized ritual at the expense of personal righteousness and condemned those conventions which assigned status on the basis of wealth. Jesus spent the active years of his ministry inspiring individuals to a quality of discernment and a kind of living geared to the priorities of the Kingdom. And, wherever those who were overwhelmed by his teaching obeyed his precepts, they were transformed, and the Kingdom of God was realized within them and established among them.

VII. MARKS OF CHRISTIAN COMMUNITY

The amazing vitality of the small Christian fellowships scattered throughout the Mediterranean world lay not primarily in their unique teaching but in the quality of their community life, its common loyalties and ideals.[11] The type of living and the quality of human relations characterizing these fellowships met the total needs of the individual more adequately than other groups competing for allegiance.

1) Equality of status regardless of wealth, position, race, or class was the first principle characterizing their togetherness. Whether slave or free, rich or poor, Jew or Greek, all were equally in need of God's forgiveness. None was so good before God that he could dominate others and none too poor before men that he was not entitled to the resources of the common life. One cannot overestimate the impact of this appeal for personal honesty and integrity. To a society ossified by economic and class distinctions, the Christian community offered a unique quality of genuine human relations that seemed out of this world.

2) A second mark of authenticity was the quality of personal responsibility for each member and for the life of the group. While religious sects focusing on individual salvation through elaborate ritual or philosophical ideals eventually disintegrated and perished, the quality of interpersonal commitment characterizing the Christian community enabled it to survive and become the sole stabilizing and integrative power within the society of Imperial Rome at a time when its social, political, and intellectual foundations were crumbling.

3) A third ethical value that ranked high in the life of these fellowships was that of freedom. The commitment to prefer community welfare to personal gratification and the personal discipline to live sober, industrious, righteous, and holy lives are conceivable only on the voluntary principle. Freedom from the bondage of Jewish intellectual and moral legalisms gave rise to many a creative and dedicated Christian spirit.

VIII. CHRISTIAN INTENTION BETWEEN HAVING AND BEING

1) The Rationale for Christian Concern

All matters affecting the quality of human relations are matters of Christian concern. It is a misconception of the Gospel to assume that the spiritual and material dimensions of life are distinct and separate entities and that religion is primarily concerned with the spiritual. The material is the only medium through which the spiritual can be known or expressed. To ignore the material by leaving it to chance or charity is to abandon it to a materialism of the most subtle and worst kind.[12] The petition for daily bread in our Lord's prayer and the use of bread and wine in the Lord's Supper are symbolic of the importance of the material basis for the Christian life.[13] Seen from the perspective of creation and incarnation, Christian being (i. e., being in Christ) does not imply a denial of creatureliness but rather the redemptive resolution of its inordinateness.

2) The Motivation and Meaning of Material Aid

The Christian intention in sharing the substance of life is not merely to relieve primary material needs nor simply to fulfill the "obligation" of charity by an act of compassion but personally to participate in the communion of redemptive love. Mutual aid is a personal expression of the Christian intention of being 'inwardly' with others. Material aid acquires sacramental meaning when inspired by the intention of reaching that of God in our brother and neighbor by sharing with them not merely goods but brotherhood and thus proclaiming the immediacy of God. Material aid is not a mere symbol of friendship and brotherhood but a sacramental tool to lead ourselves and others to a greater awareness of the actual structure of Christian being. We share with one another not only that others might have a little more but that through our self-giving we might become together what we were meant to be.

The Christian understanding of material involvement as a means to a religious end leads to the paradoxical attitude of concern for the physical security and well-being of others over against a detached indifference to the material conditions upon which our own life depends. It is in the preservation and nurture of the lives of others that the Christian finds the fulfillment of his own and the redemption of all.[14]

3) Economic Welfare and Personal Salvation
High standards of living can constitute an obstacle to Christian faith by creating a false standard of success and a presumptuous sense of self-sufficiency. On the other hand, life can be so hard that it inhibits or crushes every creative initiative. Whether we think of the disastrous effects of housing conditions upon the morale of families residing in city slums or the crippling effect of unemployment upon those deprived of their place in community life as haunted outcasts, the sense of injustice that grows everywhere out of the stark contrasts between poverty and wealth may be the source of soul-destroying bitterness.[15]

The American ideal of plenty is part of the pursuit of happiness promised this nation under God in the Declaration of Independence. Though material abundance is unable to create this "happiness," every person needs a minimal livelihood for health and well-being for himself and his nearest and dearest. Even "the saintliness of the begging friar depends for its fulfillment on the material transaction."[16] We need to have and use material things in order to have the means of sharing. Economic involvement in the production and distribution of material things is, therefore, not merely a polite expression for sin but an honest admission that the investment of labor has been entrusted us as a means of grace. Like the husbandman who went away on a journey, the Creator entrusted us with the freedom of a certain independence to "work out" our salvation and sanctification by the reciprocity of giving and receiving in order that we might exercise our Christian calling as stewards of the grace of God.

4) Love and the Profit Motive

The distinctive element in Christian ethics is the primacy of self-giving love as the source and corrective for all attitudes and decisions in personal and social life. Capitalist economics praises the profit motive as the mainspring of progress and argues that some degree of inequality is good for the production incentive. Feeling the burden of this tension, we are tempted to rationalize our privileges on grounds such as family differences and professional requirements, and so forth. It is indeed rare to find a person who does not do so in his own interests. Jesus' words about the "needle's eye," about Dives, and about the rich fool keep haunting and warning us to mistrust the lure of wealth lest our Christian ideals be frustrated by selfish material involvement. A few resolve this tension between love and self-interest by reducing their standard of living to that of the least privileged group. But even then the moral value of voluntary poverty depends on the degree to which its advocates are freed of self-righteous illusions and to which they realize their own economic dependence upon those who have fewer scruples and less discipline with respect to life's necessities and appetites.

Self-interest represents both one's destructive and one's creative potential: one's capacity for dignity and misery, good and bad, glory and power. This is reflected in Jesus' appeal to the reward motif by his identifying ultimate self-interest with Kingdom interests. Self interest ought to be harnessed to identification with ultimate values rather than suppressed on principle.[17]

5) Primary and Secondary Community
Christian values emerge from small communities in which each member is a responsible person. Anonymous relationships between individuals do not make for responsibility. "Every person needs some type of community living if he is to develop responsible action, relationships in which he is answerable to others and in which his actions are checked by his fellow members."[18]

Every person in a pluralistic society is simultaneously a member of several communities within each of which he is responsible to God for the redemptive resolution of conflicting interests of individuals and groups. The words of Jesus, "If you love them that love you what credit is that to you?" (Lk. 6:32), express the obligation of the individual to the wider community beyond that of the family or ethnic group to which he is bound by nature and history. In fact, the health of the primary group depends in some measure on its capacity for genuine devotion to the welfare of those who are not peculiarly one's own. This capacity to identify with the ever widening community is subject to the resolution of self-love and altruism within the life of the primary group. Genuine Christian piety enables one to discern the relation of one's own life in Christ to that of all mankind. This ultimate perspective frees the self from the exclusive clannish alter-egoism of the narrower loyalties for service to and identification with the larger national and international community.

IX. IMPLICATIONS AND CONCERNS

1) How relevant are our ultimate beliefs? What nonprudential economic considerations and practices issue directly from our faith? How are the social service motives and practices of committed Christians different from those of enlightened humanists or naturalists?

2) How do we harmonize the prudential motif with the claims of love? Should we endorse conventional business ethics on the assumption that our motives are mixed and our vision is limited and consequently settle for a dual objective: in part spiritual and selfless, in part practical and prudential?

3) How can we resolve the religious tension between the desire to survive and enjoy the amenities of culture and still live in the integrity of the Christian spirit wholly committed to the ultimate claims of love and community?

4) What responsibility do we, who claim to transcend justice by our works of charity, have for strengthening the dikes against the sins of economic injustice on behalf of those who live by and under the law?

5) Is the theological rationale for Christian economic involvement to be sought in the order of creation or in the order of redemption? Ought we to aid our brother and neighbor with a view only to his and our salvation? Ought we to go about with a narrowly moral or religious yardstick to measure what is ultimately good for ourself and our neighbor or is it enough that all human invention and achievement in technology, science, and art create economic and aesthetic values compatible with the goodness of creation without contributing directly or consciously to mankind's salvation?

6) Since the criterion for material needs within our affluent society is somewhat indeterminable and there is neither a clearly definable limit for their satisfaction nor indeed a guarantee that economic means may not become ends in themselves, will a quantitative increase in comforts and securities proportionately further the spiritual values of life? Or will increasing preoccupation with our own material concerns distract us from investing more heavily in the larger mission to the moral and spiritual plight of mankind?

7) Christian fellowship generates concern for persons in their total relationship to reality, a concern that includes all the needs and possibilities of the development of each member. When the local congregation fails to concern itself with the whole person with the intent of resolving his economic and social needs including poverty, unemployment, crime, disease, and so on, by what validity does that congregation continue to be Christian?

---

[1]Cf. H. R. Bowen, "Ethics and Economics" quoted in E. C. Gardner, *Biblical Faith and Social Ethics* (New York: Harper, 1960), p. 271.

[2]Cf. *Religion in Geschichte und Gegenwart* I:365 for extensive bibliography.

[3]Cf. Max Weber, *The Protestant Ethic and the Spirit of Capitalism* (New York: Scribners, 1958), chap. 5 for bibliography.

[4]Ambrosius Spittelmayr, quoted by Herbert Klassen, *Mennonite Quarterly Review* XXXII (October 1958):259.

[5]John W. Miller, "Christian Ethics and Current Economic Problems," in Study Conference Report, *The Church and its Witness in Society* (Winnipeg, January 9-11, 1959), p. F-6.

[6]From Russell Conwell's popular sermon "Acres of Diamonds" delivered 6,000 times with a total earning of eight million dollars, according to M. W. Childs and D. Cater, *Ethics in a Business Society* (New York: Harper, 1954), p. 137.

[7]G. M. Bowman, *Here's How to Succeed with your Money* (Chicago: Moody Press, 1960), p. 10.

[8]*Ibid.*, p. 12.

[9]*Ibid.*, p. 30.

[10]D. Bonhoeffer, *Ethics* (New York: Macmillan, 1962), pp. 74-75.

[11]F. H. Knight and T. W. Merriam, *The Economic Order and Religion* (London, 1947), pp. 128-31, to which I owe the insights of this section.

[12]*Ibid.*, pp. 163-64.

[13]J. C. Bennet, "A Theological Conception of Goals for Economic Life" in *Goals for Economic Life*, ed. A. D. Ward (New York: Harper, 1953), p. 405.

[14]Cf. R. K. Ullmann, *Between God and History* (London: Allen & Unwin, 1959), pp. 185-192.

[15]Bennet, *op. cit.*, p. 418.

[16]Ullmann, *op. cit.*, p. 187 *et al.*

[17]Reinhold Niebuhr, "The Christian Faith and the Economic Life," ed. A. D. Ward, *op. cit.*, p. 445ff.

[18]Knight and Merriam *op. cit.*, p. 156.

THE CHRISTIAN VIEW OF MARRIAGE AND DIVORCE

THREE CONCEPTS OF MARRIAGE

Within the Christian tradition three prevailing attitudes toward marriage can be distinguished. The SACRAMENTAL view holds that marriage is designed for procreation and as a remedy for sin. This is the view of the Old Testament, of Roman Catholicism, and of those cultures in which parents make the marital selection. The classical text for this position is Genesis 1:28, "Be fruitful and multiply."

By contrast, the ROMANTIC view exalts erotic love, almost deifies woman, and idealizes romantic attachment. Isaac's love for Rebecca, Jacob's love for Rachel, and Solomon's Song of Songs are cited in support of the romantic motif.

The third type stresses COMPANIONABILITY based on a community of interests and ideals as the chief end of marriage. Partners committed to a common cause exercise discipline or dedicate themselves to continence within the marriage bond. This view finds support in Genesis 2:18, where God declared it not good that man should be alone and hence provided for him a helper as his counterpart. Deuteronomy 24:5, which decrees that a newly married man shall for one year be exempt from the army and from business to stay at home and cheer his bride, also supports this view. While all three motifs are rooted in the Christian tradition, they have not always been equally represented.[1]

OLD TESTAMENT MORALITY

In the Old Testament, matrimony was exalted and adultery penalized by stoning the offenders (cf. Lv. 20:10). The biographies of Jacob, Solomon, and Abraham indicate that prior to the Babylonian exile bigamy, polygamy, and concubinage were not uncommon in Israel. The example of the Patriarchs has always been an embarrassment to Christians. Some ascribe their aberrations to special pre-Christian dispensations for the purpose of populating the earth while others explain them in terms of progressive revelation. By the time of Christ, Judaism had become monogamous though the Mishnah allowed eighteen wives for a king and five for a commoner.

According to Deuteronomy 24:1-4, a husband could divorce his wife if he found some "indecency" in her. Since unchastity was handled by stoning, the alleged misdemeanor was something of less magnitude. The School of Hillel allowed a husband to divorce his wife if she spoiled his dinner, and Rabbi Akiba allowed it simply on the grounds that the husband had found a more pleasing prospect.

That the concessions of Moses lacked divine sanction is evident from the prophets who pronounced judgment upon husbands who broke covenant with their wives. According to Hosea, the marriage covenant exemplifies God's covenant with man. Since God persists in His faithfulness despite man's unfaithfulness, to be a man of God means to persist in covenant faithfulness despite the unfaithfulness of one's spouse. Malachi reminds unfaithful husbands that "the Lord was witness to the covenant between you and the wife of your youth, to whom you have been faithless though she is your companion and your wife by covenant" (2:14f.). Malachi rebukes these husbands, saying: "Take heed to yourselves and let none be faithless to the wife of his youth. 'For I hate divorce,' says the Lord. . . . You have wearied the Lord with your rationalizations, saying: 'Everyone who does evil is good in the sight of the Lord' " (2:17).

"Woe to those who call evil good and good evil" (Is. 5:20). "Woe to those who devise wickedness and work evil upon their beds" (Mi. 2:1).

JESUS AND PAUL ON ADULTERY AND DIVORCE

The decisive question for Christians is: What did Jesus teach? Did Jesus commend or condemn what Moses allowed? Did Jesus forbid divorce or did he allow it under certain circumstances?

One of the key texts to be considered is Matthew 5:27-32. The first statement (vv. 27-29) concerns *adultery*: "You heard that it was said (7th commandment), 'Do not commit adultery.' But I say to you whoever looks at a woman lustfully has already committed adultery with her in his heart. If your . . . eye causes you to sin pluck it out and throw it away. . . ."

The Torah forbade adultery of the body. Jesus forbade adultery of the mind or heart. Rather than commit adultery even of the eye, Jesus said it is better to sacrifice that eye than to bring the whole body into hell, for, when one makes his eye an instrument of impurity, one cannot see God with it. Jesus was saying that lust is impure because it is unbelief that leads into "hell" (vv. 29, 30) rather than into "life" (Mt. 18:8, 9) or "into the Kingdom of God" (Mk. 9:47). No sacrifice is too great, not even dismembering one's body, if it enables us to conquer a lust that cuts us off from Jesus, from life, from the Kingdom. This is no mandate for monkish asceticism as interpreted by those monastics who walked the streets blindfolded lest they behold a woman and be tempted to sin with their eye or mind. Jesus did not say that men should never see women, but that they should not see them as objects of sexual desire.

Behind Jesus' antithesis to the seventh commandment, a whole new world of positive human relations is inferred in which men and women in the new community of the Kingdom are no longer objects of lust and exploitation as in the world, but are "coheirs of the grace of life" (I Pt. 3:7). This free and sacred new relationship between men and women in Christ's Church is evident in their whole bearing and decorum. On the part of the woman, this is expressed in her dignity, sanctity, and simplicity and is reflected in the natural beauty of her holiness in keeping with her divine calling as coheir of the grace of life over against the curse of "hell" so evident in sinful exploitation of her personage.

Jesus' second statement (Mt. 5:31-32) concerns *divorce*: "It was said (Dt. 24:1-4), whoever divorces his wife let him give her a divorce certificate. But I say to you that every one who divorces his wife except on the ground of unchastity makes her an adulteress, and whoever marries a divorced woman commits adultery."[2]

The whole issue in a nutshell is this: Moses forbade adultery; Jesus forbade divorce. But does Jesus not make an exception in the case of adultery? The answer is NO. Jesus does not provide exceptions to the will of God.

In Judaism, the husband always initiated the divorce and the wife was always to blame on account of some "indecency." Contrary to this accepted legal custom, Jesus held the *husband* morally guilty, claiming that *he* "makes her an adulteress" by allowing her to remarry. When a husband divorces his wife, then not she but *he* is the really guilty one, says Jesus, except, of course, when she has committed adultery and therefore is indeed the guilty one. In that case, the husband does not first "make her an adulteress" by dismissing her because she already is one on her own account. But, even in that case, Jesus did not advise the husband to divorce her nor did he allow the elders to stone her as was the custom. (Cf. Jn. 7:53f., Lv. 20:10, Dt. 22:22.)

In this passage (Mt. 5:32), Jesus says that divorce and remarriage, though technically legal, in effect constitute adultery. And he who initiates this sin, namely the husband, is the first to blame, for in divorcing his wife he drives her into adultery (i. e., into breaking the existing marriage covenant by remarrying) unless she is already an adulteress by her own doing. According to Jesus, the adulterous act consists in breaking the marriage covenant, a sin which the husband initiates (by divorcing his wife) and which the wife commits (by marrying another). In Jewish practice, the husband had exploited the law to his own advantage by putting all the blame on his wife, whom he then divorced in order to legalize his own adultery by remarriage. Now Jesus (in accord with the prophets) calls the unfaithful husbands to account by saying that they, and not their wives, are the real culprits. That their wives were adulterous constituted the exception, in view of the impending death penalty. But, even in this exceptional case, Jesus does not say that the wife's unfaithfulness releases the husband from his marriage bond. Jesus never spoke of so-called "legitimate" reasons for divorce. He did not permit divorce under certain circumstances. Instead, he forbade it precisely for those circumstances under which the Jews allowed it.

THE CONTEXT OF THE MATTHEAN "EXCEPT" CLAUSE

All the parallel readings in the Gospel concur that, for Jesus, divorce and remarriage amounts to adultery despite the fact that it was legal. According to Luke 16:18 (which is probably the oldest version), Jesus explicitly accuses of adultery both the husband who divorces and remarries and the man who marries a divorcée. Mark 10:11-12 expands this formula to apply to the woman who divorces her husband and remarries, a situation corresponding to Roman law and custom in the non-Jewish territory of the young Gentile churches where not only the husband but also the wife could sue for divorce. But only Matthew has the "except" clause, both in 5:32 and again in 19:9. The first occurrence is in the context of the Sermon on the Mount which in Matthew's gospel constitutes an antithesis to the

moral laxness which Moses tolerated and the Pharisees endorsed. To
his disciples Jesus said: "Unless your righteousness exceeds that of
the scribes and Pharisees, you will never enter the Kingdom of
heaven" (5:20). Then follow the six antitheses (on Murder, Adultery,
Divorce, Swearing, Retaliation, and Love of Enemies, cf. vv. 21-48)
in which Jesus' high ethical precepts are contrasted with the Mosaic
tradition. To point out this contrast between the perfect will of God
to which Jesus bears witness and the status quo of Jewish morality,
each antithesis is introduced with: "You have heard that it was said
to men of old . . . but I say to you . . . ." Already from this context it
is evident that the "except" clause in Jesus' antithesis on divorce
cannot imply that he sanctioned divorce in case of unchastity on the
assumption that one infidelity justifies another! It is precisely this
ungodly attitude which Jesus condemns, urging his disciples to "be
perfect as your heavenly Father is perfect" (5:48).

In Matthew 19, the "except" clause occurs in a similar context. According to verse 3, the "Pharisees came up to him and tested
him by saying, 'Is it lawful to divorce one's wife for any cause?' " In
his reply Jesus referred to the order of creation by which it is evident
that "he who made them . . . male and female" intended that "the two
shall become one," not that the two should be divorced. To be even
more explicit Jesus added: "What therefore God has joined together,
let no man put asunder" (v. 6). But the Pharisees, still hoping to refute
Jesus by claiming Moses on their side, rebutted, "Why then did
Moses command one to give a certificate of divorce, and to put her
away?" (v. 7). In his response, Jesus set the record straight by indicat-
ing that Moses commanded no such thing. Jesus said to them, "For
your hardness of heart Moses *allowed* you to divorce your wives"
(v. 8), a concession by which these Pharisees together with those Jews
stood condemned before Jesus' witness that "from the beginning it
was not so." In this debate over casuistic exceptions to God's will,
Jesus sided neither with the liberal School of Hillel which permitted
husbands to divorce their wives for a minor "indecency" (such as

spoiling the dinner) nor with the more strict School of Shammai which allowed it only for major offenses (such as adultery). Instead of spelling out any casuistic exceptions, Jesus took the order of marriage out of the legal debate altogether and placed it into the proper framework, the will of the Creator, to which he referred those who sought to "tempt" him with compromise solutions that would justify their sin by legalizing it. Jesus then concluded the debate by saying to them: Whoever divorces his wife, except for unchastity, and marries another, commits adultery" (v. 9). Whatever the clause "except for unchastity" means, it cannot imply that Jesus annulled what he had just maintained—that he compromised the position he had just defended over against the Pharisees, that he contradicted what he had just established—namely, that divorce and remarriage is sin. This is evident not only from the immediate context but also from the unequivocal parallels in Mark 10:11-12 and Luke 16:18 (not to mention I Cor. 7:10f.) which have no "except" clause.

THE IMPLICATIONS OF THE NEW ETHIC

A conditional statement in Matthew could not be reconciled with Jesus' unconditional prohibition of divorce according to Mark and Luke (on the assumption that the latter reflects what is ideal and the former represents what is expedient) unless we assume (as many do) that the unchastity clause does not originate with Jesus but was added by Matthew.[3] But the problem only arises when we read more into this text (Mt. 19:9) than we ought. Jesus did not say that when a wife commits adultery her husband is "innocent" and therefore free to divorce and remarry without sin. Precisely this false assumption that when a marriage breaks up one party is always innocent, and the husband at that, is what Jesus refutes in Luke 16:18, Mark 10:11-12, and Matthew 5:32. And, even if the husband were innocent (which is unlikely), it does not follow that Jesus would have him take full advantage of it by remarrying and thus excluding the possibility of reconciliation with his repentant wife. Jesus left no explicit instructions as to how husbands should deal with unchaste wives, but might we not find a clue in that he himself forgave the woman caught in adultery though "in the law Moses commanded us to stone such" a one (Jn. 8:5)? Could not Matthew 6:14 ("If you forgive *men* their trespasses your heavenly Father will also forgive you . . .") apply also to repentant wives? Is not this what it means to practice the Golden Rule (Mt. 7:12) and to apply the test of goodness (Mt. 7:15f.)? Does not Jesus' warning that we shall be judged of God by the judgment we pronounce upon others (Mt. 7:1) apply here also? Is not this why the gate is so narrow and the way so hard that leads to life (Mt. 7:14)? Is our unwillingness to receive such high truth and our inability to live by it reason enough to modify or evade it? Jesus did not specify how much true fidelity can bear nor where one's responsibility ends. Paul, who claimed to have the mind of Christ (I Cor. 2:16), reminds us that "love bears all things, believes all things, hopes all things, endures all things" (I Cor. 13:7).

Of course, this kind of ethic does not make sense to "natural man"; it never has and never will. These words were not intended for unbelievers but for those who know that with God all things are possible. Unbelievers have always justified divorce. They who justify breaking covenant with God also justify breaking covenant with each other. But a believer is one who holds entirely to the covenant faithfulness of God by whose abounding grace man in Christ becomes the faithful covenant partner he was meant to be.

In counseling believers, Paul refers directly to the teaching of Jesus: "To the married I give charge, *not I but the Lord*, that the wife should not separate from her husband (but if she does, let her remain single or else be reconciled to her husband)—and that the husband should not divorce his wife" (I Cor. 7:10f.). Paul explicitly cites Jesus' prohibition of divorce and then adds—in case there be any doubt on the matter—that the separation of one partner does not release the other from the marriage bond. But what if one spouse is an unbeliever? Precisely then, says Paul, is the Christian partner to persist in covenant faithfulness in such a way that the unbeliever and the children are "sanctified" (I Cor. 7:12-16). If separation takes place, it will be because the unbeliever refuses Christ and therefore refuses to live with a Christian. But neither Jesus nor Paul suggests that a believer whose spouse has left is free to remarry. Paul conceded second marriages only upon death of the original spouse and then only reluctantly (I Cor. 7:39). The sum of the matter is that neither Jesus nor Paul conceded divorce as a Christian option. Whatever, therefore, the rationale for temporary separation (whether on account of sickness or sin) the believer will live in hope of reunion and reconciliation. As for the rest, Paul honored marriage by comparing its mystery to Christ's relation to his Church (Eph. 5:32), but recommended celibacy "in view of the pending distress" (I Cor. 7:26) even as Jesus had acknowledged eunuchs "for the sake of the Kingdom" (Mt. 19:12).

MARRIAGE IN THE POST-APOSTOLIC ERA

While the post-apostolic age no longer discouraged marriage on account of the imminence of the Lord's return—Lactantius had advanced the "Day of the Lord" by two hundred years and Hippolytus by an additional one hundred—it was nevertheless discounted for other reasons. The Gnostics branded procreation a work of Satan, Tatian held marriage to be fornication, and Marcion demanded either celibacy or continence within marriage. Many of the Church Fathers, however, took a more favorable view. Clement of Alexandria held the succession of children to be as necessary as corks which hold up fish nets both for the maintenance of the country and the perfection of the world.[4] Tertullian penned one of the finest descriptions of Christian companionship in marriage: "Where the flesh is one, one also is the spirit. Together husband and wife pray . . . together perform their fasts; mutually teaching . . . exhorting . . . sustaining. Equally they are found in the Church of God, equally in hardships, in persecutions and refreshments. Neither hides anything from the

other, shuns the other, or is burdensome to the other. . . . Between the
two echo psalms and hymns; and they mutually challenge each other
which shall better sing to their Lord. At such companionship Christ
rejoices for where two are in this way He Himself is."[5]

After the age of apocalyptic expectation waned and persecution
ceased, the Church under Constantine and Theodosius acquired the
status and dignity of the official religion of the Roman Empire with
the effect that its moral fibre softened. To save their souls the devout
withdrew from worldly society. Especially for the clergy, Eusebius of
Caesarea advocated celibacy as the higher way of complete dedication to God and regarded marriage as an accommodation to a lower
level of morality for the laity.[6] The ensuing monastic movement further exalted virginity and depreciated marriage with the effect that sex
often became an obsession for the monks who studiously avoided any
encounter with women. "When a mother came to visit her seven sons
in their desert retreat, they shut the door and responded to her remon-
strance with the consoling prospect of reunion in heaven. Even to this
day Mount Athos harbors only tomcats."[7] Jerome went to every
extreme to disparage marriage. In support of his view that sex was
God's one mistake in creation, Jerome noted that God refrained from
blessing the second day of creation, the number two "pre-figuring the
marriage-tie. . . . Just as in the account of Noah's ark all the animals
that enter by twos are unclean."[8] For him, the only rationale for marriage was that it produces virgins to populate heaven. But even on
earth the contemplative ideal ought not to be compromised by the jab-
bering of children and the cares of family life. If we marry we will not
be able to pray without ceasing on account of the embarrassments of
wedlock.[9] Only the rigorous study of Hebrew enabled Jerome to sub-
due his own turbulent passions.[10]

Augustine held procreation to be a gift of marriage which
God instituted not merely to replenish the earth but that "He might
people His city with the fixed number of citizens which His wisdom

foreordained." What Augustine so much lamented was the fact that, since the Fall, procreation was no longer possible "with calmness of mind ... without the disease of lust . . . without the seductive stimulus of passion . . . and corrupting of the integrity of the body."[11]

During the Middle Ages, the influx of Northern barbarians tended to demean marriage in Western Europe. Being more chaste than the Romans, these Goths emphasized property rights more than mutual affection in marriage. Betrothals were contracted to unify families and estates at too early an age for consent to be a factor. King Louis of France betrothed his infant daughter in 1158 to a thirteen-year-old English prince. In 1207 a son of the Count of Brabant was affianced at birth to the daughter of Philip of Swabia, and St. Elizabeth was engaged to twelve-year-old Ludwig of Thuringia at the tender age of four.[12]

THE ROMANTIC CULT

Partly in reaction against the influence of the church which enforced fidelity in many loveless child marriages irrespective of feelings of personal aversion, there arose in twelfth-century Southern France the cult of courtly love idolizing woman and idealizing romance. Romantic courtship presupposed that the beloved be superior to the lover who was her vassal. Consequently, love was held to be an exhilarating but ever uncertain quest nurtured by jealousy. Since the romantic adventure of this unfulfilled exhilaration was held to be impossible in marriage where love between equals was taken for granted, the cult of courtly love became in effect the cult of adultery. This motif is typified in the old Celtic legend of Tristram and Isolde, the essence of which is that love should not be gratified and that the only possible reconciliation is death. Hence, the cult of courtly love came to be equated with negation of life.[13] It is small wonder that, at the eve of the Reformation, celibacy continued to be exalted as the Christian ideal.

LUTHER ON MARRIED LOVE

Against the romantic influence of the Troubadours, on the one hand, and the ascetic ideal of the monks, on the other, Martin Luther exalted matrimony above virginity or license. From his own experience in an Augustinian cloister, he concluded that enforced continence for those who have not the gift of chastity is contrary to the order of nature. Since few are able to repress their sexual impulse without being plagued by the obsession of passion, Luther decided to leave the cloister and return to the world, not because the world was better but because monasticism was itself a form of self-deceit. Since it is not in man's power to be without woman, Luther took to wife a former nun and established a home, not on the assumption that marriage entailed no sin, but on the conclusion that it involved no more sin than any other alternative. It is our nature and to resist it leads to perversion. Therefore the Pope can no more forbid marriage than eating and drinking. Luther held that God willed procreation despite the fact that original sin is transmitted by it. He even allowed divorce in case of impotence and condoned bigamy as an alternative to promiscuity. But, by his own example, Luther exalted the home as the school for character and for the cultivation of Christian virtues. Speaking for himself, he described marriage as the sweetest, dearest, purest life above all celibacy and singleness. Marriage for Luther was, however, not uniquely Christian but an order of nature valid alike for nonbelievers, Jews, and Turks without first requiring any religious rites to make it so.

THE COMPANIONSHIP IDEAL

Perhaps the happiest balance between the austere sacramentalism of the Catholic Fathers (who exalted marriage primarily for the sake of progeny) and the unrestrained naturalism of Luther (for whom marriage was a worldly affair) is found in the Anabaptists, the Quakers, and the later Puritans who, like Tertullian, stressed companionability as the prime ingredient of Christian marriage. In their concern lest love for the spouse cool one's desire for Christ, they placed religious devotion above private affection. And, since they put God first in their lives, their togetherness was characterized by a mutuality that was not overly self-conscious. Their understanding of marriage as an expression of one's relation to Christ (Eph. 5:32) gave to their earthly "conversation" a heavenly ardor of affection.[14]

TOWARDS A THEOLOGY OF MARRIAGE

On the basis of textual and historical observations, we venture the following theological conclusions.

1) Marriage is dialogue. The human image of God consists in capacity for dialogue. One becomes a person through dialogue. Where dialogue ceases one's humanity is eclipsed. The structural basis for dialogue is our bisexuality (Gn. 1:27): In the image of God He created male and female.[15] That God fashioned Eve from Adam's rib (Gn. 2:21f.) means that she is his counterpart. It is through her that his own humanity finds its completion. This is how man comes to be a free and responsible person in community. Milton discovered, by default, that "in God's intention a meet and happy conversation is the chief and noblest end of marriage."[16]

2) Christian marriage is not a natural or worldly affair but a divine mystery (Eph. 5:32). Essentially, it is not a sexual but a spiritual reality. (Sexuality for its own sake apart from coexistence is a demonic affair.) In the New Testament, marriage acquires new significance, not within the context of procreation, as in Israel, but within the context of re-creation in Christ. Like the mystery of the Incarnation, marriage in the New Testament stands between the order of creation and the order of redemption. With few exceptions, the wedding feast motif is cast in an eschatological framework.

Christian marriage derives its inner meaning from the fact that God elected us to be the "Bride of Christ." The inner meaning of the exclusive love between husband and wife is to be sought in the covenant love of God in Christ. Christian marriage is therefore not a sort of "natural falling" into love but a total commitment of one's self in a human covenant whose meaning lies in the divine covenant.

3) Marriage is not an obligation for Christians. In Israel, she who was unable "to be fruitful and multiply" was considered accursed. In the Church this is not so. Why? Because the genealogy through Abraham and David fulfilled its purpose: achieved its destiny in the birth of the Messiah (Mt. 1, Lk. 3). With the coming of Christ, a new era began in which the new birth by the Spirit carries ultimate significance (Jn. 3). Central to the New Testament is not physical Israel but "children of God born, not of the will of the flesh nor of the will of man, but of God" (Jn. 1:13). Since the fullness of time has come in which God sent forth His son, born of a woman (Gal. 4:4), marriage is not a general command of God to the Church as it was for Israel. Jesus was not married. He said there would be no marrying in the resurrection (Mt. 22:30) and reminded his disciples that some are eunuchs "for the sake of the Kingdom," adding, "Let him who can, receive it" (Mt. 19:12). The Virgin Mary is reason enough for Christians, including Protestants, not to expose virginity to contempt (as is so often the case in Mennonite society). Paul advocated renunciation as a "special gift of God" (I Cor. 7:7). While marriage is a Christian option, it is, however, not self-evident but presupposes a holy and special gift and calling.[17]

4) While marriage is complete without being fruitful, it is intended to be fruitful but not unrestrictedly so. The command to multiply and fill the earth (Gn. 1:28) does not apply to the Church in an age of population explosion. In the New Testament we find no beatitudes comparable to Psalm 127:3f.: "Sons are a heritage of the

Lord, like arrows in the hand of a warrior. Blessed is the man who has his quiver full of them." Procreation is an order of creation, not a means of redemption. While deliberate sterility within marriage may be a refusal of a divine offer, it is a mistake to take procreation for granted as the way of all flesh. To have a child is a responsible decision under God, which in our day of population explosion and nuclear threat is not self-evident. To have a child is an act of faith and trust in life. An act of faith is not an accident. The supremacy of accident is not to be regarded as reverence for Divine providence.[18]

Marriage is Christian to the extent that it expresses God's own YES to humanity (in creation, incarnation, and re-creation) and to the extent that it reflects the fidelity of God's own covenant love.

Published in 1966 by The Committee of Welfare and Public Relations of the Pacific Conference, Mennonite Brethren Church (13 pp.).

[1]Cf. the comprehensive historical survey by Roland Bainton, *What Christianity Says About Sex, Love, and Marriage* (New York, 1957), to which I am greatly indebted.

[2]On exegesis cf. Lohmeyer/Schmauch, *Das Evangelium des Matthaeus, Kritisch-exegetischer Kommentar über das Neue Testament* (Göttingen, 1962), p. 129f. and for bibliography cf. Rudolf Schnackenburg, *The Moral Teaching of the New Testament* (London, 1964), p. 132ff. and especially Kittel, *Theologisches Wörterbuch zum Neuen Testament* (Stuttgart), Vols. I:646ff. and VI:579ff., 737ff.

[3]The alternative is to limit the "except" clause to illegal incestuous marriages.

[4]*The Ante-Nicene Fathers*, II:378.

[5]*Ibid.*, IV:48.

[6]C. J. Cadoux, *The Early Church and the World*, p. 469.

[7]Bainton, p. 29.

[8]*Nicene and Post-Nicene Fathers*, VI:77.

[9]*Ibid.*, p. 31.

[10]*Ibid.*, p. 248.

[11]*City of God*, Bk. 14, chaps. 22-26.

[12]Bainton, p. 48.

[13]*Ibid.*, p. 62.

[14]*Ibid.*, p. 88.

[15]Cf. Martin Buber, "Ich und Du" and "Zwiesprache" in *Werke*, Schriften zur Philosophie, Bd. I (München, 1962); Nicholas Berdyaev, *The Destiny of Man* (London, 1948); and especially Karl Barth, *Church Dogmatics*, Vol. III, in particular III/1:288-324.

[16]Bainton, p. 100.

[17]Cf. Barth, III/4, Sec. 54.1 and Emil Brunner, *The Divine Imperative* (Philadelphia, 1936), chaps. 31, 32.

[18]Barth III/4:367. Cf. also Kahlil Gibran, *The Prophet* (New York, 1923), "On Children."

COMMUNION:
HISTORY, MEANING, MYSTERY, REALITY

HISTORY

The first Anabaptist communion service was held on January 22, 1525 in the simple peasant setting of Jakob Hottinger's house in Zollikon-Zürich. Conrad Grebel, founder of the Swiss Brethren, and a few new converts were present. It was a crucial moment in their life, for they were in serious trouble with the law which required all infants to be baptized within eight days of birth. Conscience had compelled their dissent from this unscriptural practice. Now they were anxious and very much in earnest, for they sensed their future would be bitter.

After searching the Scriptures and calling on God to show them the right way, ordinary laymen took bread from the kitchen table, broke and distributed it along with household wine to all who were present. That simple act, along with baptism performed with a water dipper, marked the beginning of the Free Church. And our Mennonite meeting here today still reflects the spirit and form of that event 452 years later.

The revolutionary significance of this event lay in its apostolic simplicity and spontaneous genuineness. Zwingli and the Reformed preachers were still celebrating the Latin Mass in all its ceremonial grandeur on the altars of the *Grossmünster*. The common people everywhere were given to understand that the substance of the wafer was supernaturally transformed, so that communicants literally ate Christ's body while the priest alone drank his blood. Even for Luther, the words, "this is my body," were too mighty to break the spell of sacramentalism.

The Anabaptists were outspoken in exposing this sophistry, insisting that the early Christians sought Christ not in the bread but addressed their prayers to him in heaven. The bread they held to be pure bread and the wine nothing but wine, for Christ was incarnated not to be eaten of men but to atone for their sins. Generally, the Anabaptists adopted the symbolic view, cautioning not to confuse the sign with what it signifies. Occasionally they cited Karlstadt, explaining that in saying, "This is my body," Jesus pointed not to the bread but to himself.

MEANING

What did breaking bread together then mean to them? Hans Oggenfuss testified it was done with the intention "from now on to live and keep a Christian life." Jörg Schad confessed they broke bread together "that they might always have God in their hearts and think of Him." Hans Denck explained that to "eat my flesh and drink my blood" signifies how it must happen spiritually and not carnally so that, just as bread and wine unites itself with human nature to maintain the life of the body, so we may become entirely one with God in the joy and love of the divine life. The Schleitheim Confession declares that "he who is not called to the one faith, the one baptism, the one Spirit, and the one body which all God's chil- dren have in common, may not be united with them by one bread as it ought to be where one desires to break bread in truth and according to the command of Christ."

This symbolism of divine unity within human community first occurs in the *Didache* of the Apostles which asserts that "as each kernel of grain gives up its entire substance to become one flour and each berry from the vine gives up its entire substance under the treadmill to become one wine and one cup . . . so also we who once represented many destructive and unfruitful opinions and faiths as we made our appearance from the wild thornbushes . . . give ourselves up under the millstone of divine righteousness to endure the Word of the Lord and say in faith: Here I am, a maidservant and a manservant of the Lord. May it be with me according to Thy Word. From that hour we are one body, one plant, one growth, one mind and opinion inaugurated into the will of Christ. . . ."

Peter Riedemann interpreted this apostolic parable to mean that, when Jesus broke bread and bade his disciples eat, he signified they would be partakers of his death to fulfill in their bodies what was still lacking of his sufferings. Hans Langenmantel exhorted that "he who does not believe and follow the sign of the crucified cannot ultimately be in the covenant. Therefore, let everyone examine himself whether he lives for himself or for God and His Church." Pilgram Marbeck admonished the *Bundesgemeinde* that participation in the *Bundesmahl* (covenant meal) means that our relation to each other is one of true covenant love, that we are prepared to die for one another as Jesus died for us, and that we pledge ourselves to witness to the truth unto death.

MYSTERY

Bread and wine symbolize the spiritual dynamic of divine Presence at the core of human experience. The reality of the

body of which Christ spoke consists in the intention which bread
and wine signify: to sustain the life of covenant between God
and His people in the spirit of Jesus. From the immense fragmen-
tation and dissolution of life we produce the bread of our toil and
the wine of our pain. Yet, in the very depth of our human condition, God intends to make us one in the divine perfection of His
own unity.

Communion is mystery because the material is the only medium in which we can know and express the spiritual. Communion is
miracle as the sharing of goods becomes an experience of true
friendship. This is the event of theophany for which we hope and
wait. Its nature remains a mystery, but the place where it happens is
called community.

The spiritual intention behind the "accidents" of matter, bread
and wine, is that we might be touched by the mystery of the divine
Presence throughout the entire universe. Sometimes we experience
it like the radiance of a falling star, not knowing whence it comes
nor whither it goes. As we discern the infinite perspectives hidden
beneath the smallness and closeness of our being and relation, we
come to realize that, whether we ascend to heaven or descend to
hell, the divine Presence permeates and consecrates the whole of
reality, leaving no place where darkness could cover us or where His
hand will not hold and lead us. In the certainty of God's Presence,
there is no secular place for those who love Him above all things
and see Him in all things.

His Presence enables us to be present where we are within the
time and space He has willed for us. His Presence makes all of life
and nature a sacred gift in response to which we long with our
whole being to be truly present to one another in His Name, whoever and wherever we are.

REALITY

Our life together is a spiritual struggle for the reality of communion. There is no way to communion. Communion is the way. Communion is where communion happens. We cannot force it to happen, but we know that it has happened, pray that it may happen, and trust that it will happen as we allow it to happen. And when it does, it happens as the paradox of Christian being: in losing we find, in dying we are born, in giving we receive.

The quality of togetherness in *koinonia* far transcends mere coexistence. Community implies covenant, not contract. It is not a means to an end but the end itself. *Sanctorum communio* is the reality of eternity in the midst of time. It is experienced as the reciprocity of giving and forgiving, as vital dialogue of life, as testing and confrontation which demand the full investment of the authentic self. Communion is the pledge of the whole self in response and responsibility to the highest truth. Community cannot be taken for granted. It is God's gift and our task, a divine possibility constituted as a human actuality embodying the spirit of Jesus within the history and destiny of a gathered fellowship. Communion is not a human ideal but a divine reality, a spiritual and not merely social event.

In breaking bread at his last supper, Jesus did what he always did: he gave himself. That is what he invites us to do: to share the spiritual essence and material substance of our real life with others so that together we might have the one thing for all—our common life in him. We live by what we give each other in the significant encounters of our life, those times of interaction when a new spark of meaning, a new flame of truth is ignited within us, or when our dimming light is rekindled by some deep experience of listening each other into life in a humble stillness grounded in the depth of peace.

The breakthrough to communion takes place as we confess our faults to one another before God, asking Him to forgive as we have forgiven. The confession of a broken and contrite heart enables the breakthrough to the Cross, to new life, to certainty, and to victory over sin. Confession prepares us to freely receive the costly grace of communion with joy and peace as the bond of Christ's forgiving love knits us together in a wholly new alignment of personal relation.

> ALMIGHTY GOD,
> unto whom all hearts are open,
> all desires known,
> and from whom no secrets are hid,
> cleanse the thoughts of our hearts
> by the inspiration of thy Holy Spirit,
> that we may perfectly love thee
> and worthily magnify thy holy Name,
> through Jesus Christ, our Lord.
>
> Amen.

Reprinted with permission from *The Mennonite*, Feb. 1/77, 65-67.

STATEMENT OF FAITH

WHAT I BELIEVE

Through pondering the wisdom of Jesus in *Exegesis*,
researching the genius of Anabaptism in *History*,
examining the lives of the saints in *Discipleship*,
debating the mystery of life in the *Classics*,
exploring the meaning of faith in *Theology*,
and evaluating the human condition in *Ethics*,
I came to realize that
1) life is a loving struggle for meaning,
2) in creative silence one recovers the reason for being,
3) truth exists in boundless communication,
4) authentic life is lived in awareness of death,
5) Jesus frees us from human authority,
6) we may live in complete openness to God,
7) the whole world is full of God,
8) to believe Jesus means to follow his teaching,
9) true community is based on mutual respect and genuine humility,
10) we do only that well which is done with joy,
11) faith and life can be pure and simple.

DEO JUBILATE.

SPIRITUAL CHARGE

Dear Graduates:

You have attended many classes, heard many lectures, and read many books. If you learned your lessons well you know that education is not accommodation and accreditation by degrees but authentic illumination and growth into being, a process not coterminous with the time lapse between registration and graduation but one which commences throughout life.

When we leave seminary we take with us some of the same questions with which we came but with higher consciousness and deeper commitment. These life questions include the following:

1) What can we know?
2) What may we believe?
3) What might we hope?
4) What shall we do?

WHAT CAN WE KNOW?

Much secular knowledge is self-knowledge rooted in the Greek dictum 'Know Thyself', which presumes one does not need God to understand oneself. The Bible, however, professes knowledge of the God who speaks and acts, who is for us and reveals Himself to us in creation, reconciliation, and redemption. In more than a thousand ways the Hebrew Bible proclaims "I AM THE LORD YOUR GOD," requiring our total allegiance, redeeming us from all duplicity and complexity, and from all illusions of self-sufficiency. Dostoevski reasoned, If God is not, everything is permitted but this: To say or think that I am. And conversely, If God is, one thing is not permitted: That one should be ignorant of Him.

To know anything is to know that God comes first. Consequently, the meaning of our existence is not synonymous with the fact of our existence, but confronts our existence. The meaning of life is not merely the self-expression of existence nor a projection from existence. We may discover or recover life's meaning, but we do not invent it. Jesus differed from others in that he really knew who God was and hence knew who he was. Such knowledge of God and self in the concreteness of life constitutes sonship and discipleship. While we cannot experience God apart from experiencing ourselves—for God is not only external to us but also the moral condition within us—knowledge of God is born of God encounter, not self-encounter. There is a difference between 'My will be done' and 'Thy will be done' and that difference matters.

To know God is to experience God as *Thou,* not as concept. To know God is to recognize that God loves us and to love Him back. We cannot preserve the idea of God apart from our relation to God, without which knowledge about God implies eclipse of God.

Philosophy investigates the essence, religion inquires about the Way. Philosophy is preoccupied with speculation, religion is committed to covenant. Philosophy thinks and demonstrates, religion feels and knows.

In answer to the question What can we KNOW? I charge you as graduates to remember that we can know God as our truest friend who is there for us, enabling us to be there for others.

WHAT MAY WE BELIEVE?

To believe means to trust. Because we believe Jesus we believe in his Church. A Christian needs others because of Jesus and comes to others through Jesus. *Sanctorum Communio* is the historical reality of Christ's eternal presence. It happens here and there, now and then, and when it happens it is for real. It is not a human possibility but a divine reality. It is not psychical but spiritual, not an ideal but a given. It is not a means to an end, but an end in itself. It is covenant not contract, functional not institutional, and, as such, both visible and invisible: we see it everywhere in faith but comprehend it nowhere apart from love. Christian community is rooted in the Cross, realized in resurrection, and actualized through Pentecost. The Church needs men and women of vision, courage, and fortitude who will live deliberately, freely, deeply, and simply, who will give of themselves fully and unreservedly, and who will fulfill themselves in the adventure of faith, hope, and love.

In answer to the question What may we BELIEVE? I charge you as graduates to remember that we believe in the reality of Christ's Church as the mystery and miracle of our life in his Name.

WHAT MIGHT WE HOPE?

Amid human depersonalization, family disintegration, environmental exploitation, war, famine, and nuclear threat, what is the nature and content of our hope for the future of humanity and for the earth?

Can the Gospel only interpret the process of history or might it change it? If so, how, where and when might we hope to recognize God within our history and destiny?

Evolutionary optimism and apocalyptic pessimism fail to realize that God has not promised us Utopia, but His Presence and

Spirit. This new reality depends for its actualization not on possibilities inherent in nature and history as such, but on our freedom to resolve the tension between promise and fulfillment by our own obedience to God's commandments. The new reality is not part of the old process but transpires as fellowships of hope embody the Divine Presence in the world through their commitment to overcome evil with good.

Mountains rise and fall and so do nations and generations. We are not responsible for the cosmogenesis of countless future galaxies in infinite space and time but for our immediate human relationships here and now. Awareness that God cares for us frees us from debilitating anxiety over our own life and death and hence from the necessity of defending against all others our own place under the sun. Beyond that, nature itself is not closed to progress. We have no reason to dismay if the light on the horizon remains motionless, so long as it is not going out.

The future of humankind lies not with scientific analyses that break down all syntheses and destroy the soul, but in recovering the lost resources of our spiritual center. Our hope lies in the personalization of life from this center. All fragmented life seeks this wholeness by the inspiration of God's own universal love deep within the nature of all things.

In answer to the question What might we HOPE? I charge you as graduates to remember that, "Life from the center is a life of unhurried peace and power. It is simple. It is serene. It is amazing. It is triumphant. It is radiant" (Thomas Kelly).

WHAT SHALL WE DO?

We realize the meaning of our being not in what we ourselves do but in what God does through us. Before doing anything, we need to understand the relation between doing and being—to be liberated from the heresy of sheer activism. We can give to others only what we ourselves are, and whatever we do is empty unless it binds us to others and to God.

Like Moses, we need a barefoot encounter with the Holy: we need to take off our shoes—the comfort and security of our domesticated spirituality. Like Zechariah, we need to endure in silence the noise of solemn assemblies so as to recover the right to speak a real word that says something. Like Jesus, we need to experience the wilderness of God's presence and power within our calling and vocation.

Then, we shall follow Jesus to become with him the poorest of the poor upon whom he pronounced his first blessing. We shall discern the mystery of redemption as we are compelled by God's love to be consumed by the world's pain. We shall make Jesus' teaching our design for living, exemplifying God's loving will for man.

In answer to the question What shall we DO? I charge you as graduates to live in complete openness to God, to recover a new spontaneity and integrity of spirit, of language, and of lifestyle, and to answer that of God in everyone.

God's Peace be with you always. Blessed be His Name!

Presented to the 1984 AMBS Commencement. Reprinted by permission from the newsletter *In Search*, Vol. 2, No. 4, Aug., 1984.

HOLINESS: THE DIVINE IMPERATIVE

In the Bible there are two parallel imperatives which express the same divine intention from complementary perspectives: "BE YE HOLY, for I, the Lord your God, am holy" (Lv. 19:2) and "BE YE PERFECT as your Father in heaven is perfect" (Mt. 5:48). Simply said, to be holy is to be whole and to be perfect means to be complete. By instructing his disciples in the way of perfection, Jesus reaffirmed the holiness which God required of His people. The quest for meaning and being is essentially the quest for holiness. We attain the reason for living as we embrace the beatitudes of Jesus and keep the commandments of God. In so doing we participate in God's own life and will.

The quest for holiness is the pursuit of authentic meaning and being for oneself within the world as it is and within the Church as it ought to be. The way of holiness leads via isolation from the world to involvement in the world through transcendence of the world. We experience the metamorphosis of holiness in the awareness of being at once "sons of men" as "sons of God"—an incarnational awareness which fully opens us to the world while enabling us to be independent of the world. To be holy means to live in constant awareness of God's guidance. This guidance may take the form of a burning bush, an angel, or an oral commandment. But, for the most part, divine guidance takes the form of an intuitive awareness rather than an audible voice or visible sign. The goal of our calling is to *ascertain God*.

The Hebrew *kadosh* and its cognates (which appear over 800 times in the Old Testament) are used to designate holy places (as Mt. Zion) and holy times (as the Sabbath) which constitute special relation to God portrayed as sanctified or sacred without blemish or fault, that is, perfect or flawless (*tammim*). The idea of holiness is also related to *kabodh* suggesting radiance and splendor. The concept of the holy is invariably associated with the sphere of divine power to redeem the roots of religion from all ambiguity and duplicity, all desecration and contamination effected by the profane.

In Sinai the ground around the burning bush (Ex. 3:5) is holy, as are Gilgal before Jericho (Jos. 5:15) and especially Jerusalem (Is. 48:2, 52:1, Neh. 11:1, 18), the site of the temple and the temple itself together with everything pertaining to it within its chambers and courts. At holy places one experiences holy time and action which awaken consciousness and inspire moral obligation to realize the divine commandment and to fulfill the human commitment. Through this divine intention the holy acquires the meaning of divine and thus becomes an attribute of God (Is. 5:16, 6:3, Hos. 11:9). The causative form of *kadosh* conveys dedication of the self, not to the cultic ritual but to the personal reality of God to whom the consecrated person now exclusively belongs. The Old Testament emphasizes the holy Name of Jahwe which was disclosed at Sinai in the covenant relationship through which Israel became the people of God.

In post-exilic Israel the concept of holiness develops along "two intermingling streams, the priestly cultic, on the one hand, and the prophetic and ethical, on the other." The cultic emphasis on the holiness of the Sabbath, the altar, garments, candelabra, swords, priests, books, and so on is complemented by emphasis on the holiness of heaven, of the angels, and of the Spirit. Later, in intertestamental Judaism the Scriptures also were called holy. Indeed, they formed the new pivotal point for the system of holiness in Judaism, thereby replacing the temple (TWNT, 227). Since the Holy Spirit speaks in and through these holy Scriptures, the scribes and their pupils and all who obeyed the Torah were designated as holy, a phenomenon resulting in a consequent shift in emphasis away from cultic temple holiness ritual to the exposition of the wisdom of the Torah as it pertains to moral holiness in daily life. The awareness of the holiness of Scripture as the Word of God is reflected in the miraculous accounts of certain rabbis being encircled by fire as they studied Torah. Since Scripture is holy, so also is the individual scroll, hence the writing of it is itself sacred and thus the admonition of generations of copyists: "My son, be careful in thy work, for it is a work of God." This explains why scrolls copied by heretics should be burned, "because they are not written in holiness" (i. e., by a strict Jew with sufficient care). Those who lived by the Law and who by their suffering demonstrated their steadfastness were referred to as saints (I Mc. 1:46). This self-designation as God's holy people is especially noteworthy in the Qumran community in which the ordinances of purification were obligatory not only for priests but were made binding upon all the members.

In the New Testament the concept of holiness is determined by the Holy Spirit, the gift of the new age, with a shift from the cultic to the prophetic so that the sacred no longer belongs to things, places, and rites but to manifestations of life produced by the Spirit. Jesus was endowed at his baptism with the Holy Spirit and was driven into the wilderness for forty days by the Spirit before he performed his first miracle (Mk. 1:21f.). Jesus was holy, that is, filled by the Holy Spirit from his conception. In all these considerations holy means belonging to God and authorized by God. After Christ's resurrection, the Spirit is imparted to the disciples at Pentecost.

Hallowed be thy Name, the first petition of the Lord's Prayer, implies the consecration and consummation of all human being in the holiness of God. God and not man is the sanctifying subject. "His Name is His person, which is holy in itself and is to be revealed in its holiness." "When God's deity is revealed to man in the mystery of worship (cf. Is. 6:3), then God is sanctified to him.

The cultic element is here absorbed in adoration in which God's deity is felt in contrast to all creatureliness" (111). "Even the world and mankind are only elements in the process of sanctification in which God sanctifies Himself" (C. Brown, 73).

With the outpouring of the Holy Spirit there arises as new people of God within the old a *sanctorum communio*, a kingdom of priests, a holy nation (I Pt. 2:9), a reincarnation of the divine mandate of Leviticus 19:2. Now the commonwealth of Israel together with the covenant of promise is extended by Christ to the whole world, so that gentiles, once pilgrims and strangers, now belong to the household of God as fellow citizens and saints, for they have access in one Spirit to the Father. Jesus in the Sermon on the Mount already fills the requirement of sacramental purity with ethical content. The life of Christians is meant to be a living sacrament, holy and acceptable to God (Rom. 12:1). In Paul, nevertheless, justification overshadows sanctification which he applies passively rather than actively. For Paul sanctification is a divinely effected state rather than a moral action on the part of man.

DESERT KENOSIS

Invariably, the way of holiness leads through the desert. (Strictly speaking, there is no way *to* holiness, for holiness itself is the way.) Even Jesus was led into desertedness there to confront his deepest opposition. One goes into the desert in quest of existential isolation and spiritual concentration. It is in the vast emptiness and haunting loneliness of the God-forsaken barren desert that one is illumined and disclosed clarity and integration of one's inner calling. Though the harshness of that austere environment may be conducive to prayer and fasting, desert spirituality need not always be inseparably linked or limited to a vast and remote place or space. Though the spiritual intention may be significantly affected by the geographic dimension, it is not determined by it.

Indeed, we will find in our choice of *Poustinia* (Russian term for desert) what we bring to it in anticipation and inner preparation. Spiritual devotees have found it meaningful to reserve for prayer and contemplation a small room within their home, a holy place dedicated to this effect. Wherever it may be, "Poustinia stands for prayer, penance, mortification, solitude, silence, offered in a spirit of love, atonement, and reparation to God." Poustinia is a silent, lonely place where one can pour out one's heart in prayer and penance before God. It is a place where one can recover the courage to speak words of truth, where one can be cleansed and prepared for this task "like the burning coal the angel placed on the lips of the prophet" (Doherty, 30).

Before establishing a personal Poustinia, one should examine oneself, stand still, and look deeply into the motivations of life to discern whether the foundations of sanctity can be built on them. Everyone within the providence of God has been born to be a saint, and, if there is but one tragedy in death, it is this: not to have realized and fulfilled one's messianic calling as a follower of God, not to have manifested the *Imago Dei* as the guiding light of one's earth time. Amid each day's outward clamor and inward disunion a central interlude for contemplative assessment must be fostered to invite God's Spirit to absolve and set free from all fear, selfishness, greed, and narrow-mindedness so that we might thrive in holy integration according to God's will and order for blessed living.

"Nourished by the waters of [such consecrated, holy] Silence, *caritas* will [then] begin to sing its song of love," enabling all persons to spend themselves for others. Catherine Doherty describes how poustinik pilgrims "stole away at dawn or in the dark of the night, leaving a message that they had gone on a pilgrimage . . . to pray to God for their sins and the sins of the world, to atone, to fast, to live in poverty, and to enter the great Silence of God" (33).

Catherine poignantly relates how Peter, family friend and millionaire, after reading the Gospels decided to sell everything and give all to the poor. Going to the bank, he converted all his holdings to gold and silver, loaded the coins in sacks onto a horsedrawn wagon and proceeded directly to the poor of Petrograd. "There, family by family, house by house, Peter distributed his gold and silver. When the dray was empty, Peter said: 'Now I have in some small measure ransomed the thirty pieces of silver for which God was sold. And now I must go.' " Upon returning home, he took a loaf of bread, some salt, a gourd of water and a staff, and proceeded walking to the outskirts of the city onto the country roads. The last her father saw of him was "just a silhouette against the setting sun—a man in a long garment with a staff in his hand. He had no cash in his pockets (he had no pockets), nor in his bag. He had only some bread, water, salt, and a staff. Not even shoes. That was all."

Years later, Catherine's father met this pilgrim in Kiev at the Church steps, begging, before Mass. "With matted uncombed hair, tattered garments, he looked like a fool, a retarded person." Nevertheless, recognizing him, her father inquired: "Why have you chosen this vocation of idiot?" Peter responded: "I am atoning for those who called Christ a fool during his lifetime and during all the centuries thereafter" (35). It is said that even today the forests of Russia are full of pilgrims and hermits, poustiniks who have emptied themselves of the debilitating clutter of life in quest of a deeper spiritual integrality.

MOUNTAIN TRANSCENDENCE

At the other end of the spectrum, the spiritual quest for holiness is scenically dramatized by the soaring Himalayan Mount from where the guru magnificus instructs the novice in knowledge of the heart by inspiring within his consciousness the fountain of truth through silent intuition. This quest for higher ground—whether at

Mt. Sinai where God gave Moses the Decalogue or at the Galilean Hilltop on which Jesus proclaimed his beatitudes, whether glimpsed through Noah's Ark on Mt. Ararat or Jesus' transfiguration before his disciples on Mt. Tabor—the mountain motif represents the quest for self-transcendence and metamorphosis.

Coerced to peak experience at death, one aspires ultimately to become one with the Lord of the Universe. But it is the intention of mountain contemplation to transpose that lofty awareness into the Center of life, there to bear spiritual fruit for all seasons.

One of the first lessons about holiness which the swamis teach is 'the gospel of nature'. One begins by listening to the music emanating from birdsong, the blossoming flowers, the growth of the smallest blade of grass and thorn of the bush. In everything dwells evidence of the beautiful. If one does not learn to listen to the celestial music of nature and to appreciate her beauty, then that which impels one to seek Love at its fountain may be lost in remote antiquity. The gospel of nature reveals that empathic knowledge through which one learns Truth and beholds the Good in all its majesty and glory. If the human soul has been trained to love nature, then "a revelation comes peeping through with the dawn. When the sun rises, the pain and miseries of life disappear with the darkness and the mist. Mortality finds its way in the awareness of immortality. Then a mortal being suffers no more from the pangs and sorrows which death seems to shower upon him . . . [for] at death man learns to become one with the infinite and eternal." In the depth of silence is hidden the source of Love. The eye of faith alone can unveil and see the illumination of that Love. The discovery of the sages binds the whole of humanity in the harmony of the cosmos.

The way of perfection begins with the desire to meet and know God directly. It is not truly satisfying to possess knowledge acquired from others even if one were to master the whole of universal publication. How then can one become enlightened? The wise throughout history have agonized undauntedly to know Truth directly. "They were not satisfied by the mere opinion of others. Nor were they frightened off from this quest by the defenders of orthodoxy and dogma who persecuted and sometimes executed them because their conclusions were different" (Rama, 80).

"When you know the truth directly you do not need to ask your neighbors or your teacher. You don't have to seek confirmation in books. Spiritual truth does not need an external witness. . . . Tread the path of direct experience . . . until all your doubts are resolved. Direct experience alone has access to the source of real knowledge" (80).

MYSTIC IMMANENCE

The Mystic finds ultimate meaning not in the ecclesiastic institutions which history describes, not in theological creeds formulated to satisfy intellectual demands, nor in cultic forms through which organized religion perpetuates itself. Rather, the heart of religion is found in one's consciousness of God.

This religion does not crystallize, it transpires as a vital fluid awareness of the Divine Presence. By some deeper principle of perception than that which transpires in our sense-world, mystics discover and renew their lives in God. They understand themselves to be living individual cells within the larger whole of infinite being which, like inlets opening on the boundless sea, "feel the shoreless tides beat in" (Jones), an awareness of the Divine Presence experienced not merely as a moment of truth but essentially as a permanent habitation. This decisive and immediate, immanent and all-pervasive consciousness of God is not something to be conveyed by words whose meaning might be extrapolated by linguistic analyses. It is much more an overpowering intuitive awareness of having been chosen and called by God Himself to partake of the noödynamics of God's own vital Divine life.

This Divine-human reality reveals the triumph of the Spirit in personal life. It was the particular greatness of Christ to have fulfilled his calling by leading people to God so that they might truly live by fulfilling their own life with him. He did so "by showing us the Father, not as a Sovereign, not as a stern Judge—but as Infinite Lover who yearns over us and who suffers through our sin and blindness. . . . It is the reproduction of this type of Divine-human life which Christ manifested" (Jones).

Paul, the earliest interpreter of the Gospel, in describing his new life says: "It pleased God to reveal His Son *in me*" (Gal. 1:15-16). "It is no longer I that live, but Christ lives *in me*, for I bear in *my* body the marks of the Lord Jesus" (Gal. 6:17). Paul refers to this mystery of "Christ in you [as] the hope of glory" (Col. 1:27). "For you have died, and your life is hid with Christ in God" (Col. 3:3). The faith insight underlying Paul's marvelous optimism is the awareness that God desires to inhabit people, win them, dwell in them, join them to Himself in One Spirit. And the heart of Paul's gospel is the good news that God is realizing His Presence in the life of humankind. The Kingdom of God comes as soon as anyone does God's will and is reborn into the holy family to partake of the perfection of God.

The fullest expression of this Divine-human reality is conveyed by John, who frequently refers to our being of God, born of God, and begotten of God. "He who believes in the Son of God has this witness in himself" (I Jn. 5:10). The Divine life is appropriated through faith. Jesus insists, *You must eat me*, to express how the Divine life is appropriated as the vital energy is assimilated. John speaks of *knowing* as a process of appropriation, of partaking. "This is eternal life, that they [might] *know* thee" (Jn. 17:3). To receive eternal life or to receive God means the same thing. As we abide in God, God indwells us. We abide in Him because we love Him, and we love Him because we are born of Him. This organic interrela-

tionship is described by the vine and its branches to express this
vital union of spiritual life as the Divine seed expands into the
knowledge and reality of the mystery and history of our Oneness
with God and produces the spiritual fruits of the Spirit in the perfection of holiness.

These mystical meanings "convey the idea of a reality con-
cealed by surface appearances but at least potentially manifest to all
Christians," "a secret knowledge communicated in an extraordinary,
personal experience" (Jones). Consider the disciples' response to
their mysterious encounter with the risen Lord: "Did we not feel our
hearts on fire at his words?" The mystical way opens up a special
religious perception of reality "in which the various functions of the
mind, the affective as well as the cognitive, become united in a
uniquely harmonious and often intensively experienced manner"
(Jones). "Already the Gospels stress the continuous, intimate presence of God to Jesus. The mystical quality of a life so thoroughly
penetrated by God's own life receives a unique emphasis in the
fourth Gospel. The presence of Jesus' Spirit turns that quality into
promise to all true believers, for 'we all reflect as in a mirror the
splendor of the Lord; thus we are transformed into his likeness from
glory to glory.' In the center of faith stands the 'mystery of Christ'—
not a secret, but a revelation to be assimilated by the Christian ever
more intimately until his or her life coincides with the Divine life"
(Jones).

SAINTLY STIGMATA

God is experienced as the Being who pours Himself out in
unending lovingkindness and leads us similarly through the passions
of such self-giving to humanity in order that earth's pain and love
may be joined in holy redemption. To participate in this com-pas-
sion is to be a saint who is a lover: one who loves God, loves life,
loves the world, and loves the enemy.

Initially, to be a saint means to love *God* with all one's heart, soul, and might (Dt. 6:4). A saint is in dialogue with the Mind of God, committed to the Will of God, inspired by the inner and outer Word of God, empowered by the Spirit of God to reflect the Image of God, to embody the Mystery of God, and to do the Works of God. A saint prays without ceasing.

Next, a saint loves *Life* and partakes of God's own: Life eternal and hence temporal, spiritual and thus material, real and therefore actual. A saint identifies with the spiritual potential within the carnal which then constitutes incarnation.

Then, a saint loves the *World*, that is, the cosmos of John 3:16, and forever contemplates the dimensions and intentions of its providential temporal and spatial boundlessness in the awareness that the whole world is full of God who is present to all His creatures through all His creations. Saints are not saved apart from the world but in, with, and through it. This world is the place where God speaks and acts through infinite meaning. A saint loves the world as God loves it and embodies God's holy presence within its secularity.

Further, to be a saint means to love one's *Enemy*. Spirituality without pacifism is a farce camouflaged by a patriotic theology of cheap grace. He who does not take his cross and follow me is not worthy of me (Mt. 10:38). When German guards at Auschwitz hanged a ten-year-old child, an old Jew groaned, "Where is God?" Then Elie Wiesel recognized God's presence in the sad angelic face of that child. Somehow God and man had exchanged places. Throughout all, be very still and know that I am God. For by God's love man becomes wholly deified as God in him becomes fully humanized. A saint completes in his own body the sufferings of Christ.

To be a saint means to be able with Jesus to say in one's last breath at the final hour of one's life: It is finished. That is, my life is complete; it has been fulfilled.*

---

*The same expression *tetelestai*, as uttered by Jesus on his Cross (Jn. 19:30) and in the Sermon on the Mount (Mt. 5:48).

Gerhard Kittel, ed., *Theologisches Wörterbuch zum Neuen Testament* (Stuttgart: W. Kohlhammer, 1932); Vol. I, 88-115.

C. Brown, *The Lord's Prayer*, (1965), p. 73.

Catherine de Hueck Doherty, *Poustinia. Christian Spirituality of the East for Western Man* (Notre Dame, Indiana: Ave Maria Press, 1975).

Swami Ajaya, ed., *Living with the Himalayan Masters. Spiritual Experiences of Swami Rama* (Honesdale, Pennsylvania: Himalayan International Institute, 1978).

Rufus M. Jones, *Pathways to the Reality of God* (New York: The MacMillan Company, 1931).

SPIRITUAL DYNAMICS OF HOLY SILENCE

One can imagine a world without speech, but one cannot imagine a world without silence.

Silence has no dimensions or extensions, yet we experience it extensively and intensively.

Silence is inaudible, invisible, and intangible, and yet silence is as self-evident as life and death.

Silence precedes time and is independent of time, yet it is the soil in which the seed of time is sown.

Silence is not only endless but needless in the utilitarian sense of being good for something.

Silence is not a means to an end but a formative reality in its own right. We can feel its presence and describe its existence, yet we cannot comprehend its essence.

Silence constitutes the mystery surrounding every word and sustains the truth within the word.

Without silence there is no communication and no community—no forgetting, no forgiving, and no loving.

Silence heals and makes whole what is fragmented and dissipated.

In silence one recovers the autonomous meaning of one's being.

Silence is more than mere absence of noise; it is a primary reality in its own right which points to a life beyond the word and hence beyond the self. Silence is a positive, free phenomenon which we cannot produce at will simply when we stop talking. Absence of speech does not create silence, it simply makes it more apparent. Silence is not merely the nonexistence of something else, such as noise, speech, or music, as though it were only a negative condition. Silence is a formative and independent condition of being. Therefore, it is possible to speak about silence in the same way it is possible to make assertions about any other positive reality.

Silence is as self-evident as life and death though it precedes life and exceeds death yet envelops both even as it constitutes the mystery surrounding every word and sustains the truth within the word.

Encounter with silence as primal reality confronts in us the divine potentiality of recovering the original meaning of being.

Silence precedes speech and legitimizes speech. Only a word derived from silence has something to say. What it says is conveyed by the silence within the word. The power of silence to create speech gives infinite breadth to real conversation as a reciprocating awareness that resonates through the universe of knowing and being.

In the beginning God spoke the first word and then gave the word to us so we could be in dialogue with our Maker about the meaning of our being. The purpose of speech is to resonate throughout creation the infinite silence behind the revealed word, thus answering that of God in everyone by naming and addressing the divine mystery which otherwise remains nameless in all its wondrous forms as in the quiet of the dawn, the noiseless aspiration of the trees, and the silent changing of the seasons.

In music more than in speech the distance and nearness of space together form a gentle unity for the comfort and benefaction of the soul. In music one experiences the remoteness of infinity as simultaneously near at hand, an awareness that widens the soul to overcome all fear. True music enables the silent harmony with all things to become audible.

Silence exists without speech, but speech cannot exist without silence. As the mass of water exceeds that of land, so silence is more extensive than speech, but speech is more intensive than silence in its ontic dynamic. Silence is knowledge of the *Deus absconditus* who intends within the nature of being that speech be united with silence in a perfect contiguity even as the Word of God in Christ represents the silence within God Himself.

In silence, truth is passive and indefinite. In speech, truth is active and articulate. Without rapport with silence the word of truth would be too austere and exclusive, like a single truth denying the interrelatedness of all truth and lacking the natural basis of forgiveness and love.

In speech, the truth implicit in silence is made explicit by the logic of language. Though one cannot speak the whole truth in words, one often expresses more than one intends.

There is an inexpressible beauty in silence, a radiance which relieves it of its heaviness.

We live between the silence from which we emerge and that to which we return and seek to verbalize the meaning of being, of our origin and destiny, between these two worlds of silence.

Through many different languages man attempts to find the absolute word and express the one truth. In ancient languages there is more silence surrounding each word and also more between words as the linguistic architecture is more vertical than horizontal so that each radical retains its individual landmark of meaning within the sentence structure without losing its identity within an undifferentiated mass, allowing a new spring of silence to flow into the stream of the sentence after every word.

Those who embody the reality and incarnate the mystery of silence are not preoccupied with their own subjectivity. Neither are they fragmented by apparent contradictions between faith and reason, love and justice, beauty and truth, for they partake of life in the primordial wholeness of being rather than as incompatible Either/Or dichotomies.

Time is expanded by silence, but it is also absorbed by it even as it is completely consumed within the silence of eternity. When there is no more silence left in time, the race against time, which characterizes the nervous end-stage of existence, becomes a race against people and things.

There were meant to be little hills of silence on the earth so that our old tired words could sink down into them and arise completely reborn. As the hart panteth after water brooks, so speakers of many words need to return to the watering places of silence—the poustinias of the heart—to wait till they are satisfied.

Silence becomes holy as one returns the word to God from whence it came and then receives it back again as the original wonder of dialogical re-creation. Through such silent resignation and renewal, language is resurrected and the dialogue of faith reborn. When words lose their spiritual quality, all that remains is an acoustic quantity. The spirituality of silence is displaced by the materiality of noise, by a loud emptiness filling all space and time. When language degenerates to verbal noise, the words which constitute it lose their power of creativity and are reduced to meaningless-ness. Verbal noise displaces the spirit in the word and effects the psychic death of the soul. Even the noise of solemn assemblies can deteriorate to a mere cathartic function of trading in words without awakening to life. Verbal noise defies the intention of the word for response and responsibility: since no one is personally addressed, no one is really expected to listen. The noise of idle words is like a cloud of insects whose all-pervading buzz neutralizes everything.

When the silence within the word is violated and the space between the words is obliterated, the content of the word no longer matters, for the word itself is destroyed, and the faith and hope meant to be conveyed by it are shattered. When verbal noise dis-places dialogue, there is neither solitude nor community.

Unless we zealously guard the few remaining fragments of silence within our civilized life from verbal pollution and dissolu-tion, we forfeit the redemptive intention of the word within the world.

A world without silence is a world without meaning, a world from which the silent voice of God within the nature of things has been eclipsed by the monstrous ubiquity of incessant noise.

We need to recover oases of silence within the rhyme and rea-son of our active life, for it is in silence that we meet God face to face through the mystery of His contiguous presence within all things and through all relations. In God, word and silence are one, and that is how it is meant to be in us. Inspired by this holy intention, our word becomes a prayer arising from the silence of eternity to transform by that immortal perfection all things to their divine origin.*

---

*Abstractions from Max Picard: *Die Welt des Schweigens*.

SILENT MEETING: DIMENSIONS & INTENTIONS

There was silence before the world was created and there will be silence after it is consummated. There was silence before we were born, and there will be silence after we die. All of which is reason enough to explore the meaning of our being within the context of "silence"—in our life and in our worship.

The outer transition from speech to silence demands an inner transition from rhetoric to intuition, from speaking the outer word to hearing the inner word. Sometimes, especially in our worship, we may need to break both the cerebral barrier and the sound barrier to become inwardly gathered to listen each other into life—in holy stillness. We are so programmed by our verbal agenda and so accustomed to our deflated wordiness that we find it difficult to become outwardly still and impossible to become inwardly silent.

Sometimes inner stillness demands outer stillness; silence of the heart demands silence of the tongue. Particularly in our worship we need to become still—still before God, still with God, and still in God. We need to become still enough to find God in our worship, still enough to hear God in our worship, and still enough to enjoy God in our worship. Especially in our worship we need to pray: "Give us this day our daily silence."

In speech as in music, silence is the presupposition and framework of meaning. A musical note fulfills its intention only in proportion to the space and time of its surrounding silence. So it is with speech. Language conveys its meaning only as it words the silence.

The mystery of silence is unfathomable in its natural and supernatural aspects, its active and passive modes, its voluntary and involuntary nature, its inner and outer dimensions, and its epistemological and ontological intentions. Whether we think of natural silence, cosmic silence, or divine silence, we cannot speak *about* silence (as though it were an object) just as we cannot search for darkness with a torch in our hand. Nor should we speak *around* silence in order to circumvent it by words, and yet we can speak *of* silence.

Silence is a religious and ethical attitude. It does not signify an absence of intelligence nor an inability to function, but a capacity for discerning a higher form of knowledge that transcends the senses.

On the ethical level silence denotes control of the self, its senses and passions, and over the instabilities of our corporeality—a bridge over troubled waters, *Ataraxia, Gelassenheit*. That is why a well-balanced person speaks in measured tones, guards against speaking too much, and avoids speaking of inconsequential matters.

As an ethical concept silence signifies a strength of character, a victory of the mind over speech. Pythagoras imposed a five-year vow of silence upon his disciples so that they might purify their minds, and some Trappist monks take lifetime vows of silence in order to achieve a level of consciousness which lies beyond the dialectic of speech.

On the religious level the ground and need for silence is the transcendence of God beyond the world and hence beyond the word. Holy silence is therefore intuitively felt to be the highest human response to the divine mystery—hence the Jewish forbearance to verbalize the unspeakable divine Name and the early Christian reticence to publicize the holy mystery of our Lord's Prayer. Verbal prayer aspires to dialogical encounter with God as a person. Silent prayer ascends to a state of being in God beyond the realm of the senses.

Knowledge of God is not a matter of *saying* but of *being*, not of talking *about* God but of inward contact *with* God—through silence—as a process of epistemological and ontological interiorization. God is silence, and it is through silence that we participate in His being.

Ultimately the meaning of silence lies hidden in this realization that God is Silence and that His Word expresses that event. That is why His Word is creative, always new, surprising. Our words were also meant to convey this mystery, this power, and this life, but, as our speech becomes abstracted from His reality, it becomes powerless and deceptive. That is why only a word coming out of silence is a real Word and says something.

Our speech was intended to express the Divine Silence in the human word. That is what is meant by revelation, incarnation, and inspiration—by God's Word becoming humanity's word and by humanity's word becoming God's Word. That is why communication is a spiritual— not a vocal—exercise. That is why truth is not a matter of trading in words but of incarnation of *the* Word.

In exploring the relation of Silence to the Word, Bonhoeffer says: "Right speech comes out of silence and right silence comes out of speech. Silence does not mean dumbness as speech does not mean chatter. Dumbness does not create solitude and chatter does not create fellowship. . . . Real silence, real stillness, really holding one's tongue comes only as the sober consequence of spiritual stillness. . . . The silence of the Christian is a listening silence, a humble stillness. . . . There is a wonderful power of clarification, purification, and concentration upon the essential thing in being quiet. . . . Silence before the Word leads to right hearing and thus also to right speaking of the Word. . . ."

Silence as preparation for hearing and meeting God is not barren or dead but electric with expectation and anticipation, not only for hearing God's Word through one appointed ministerial spokesperson but for inwardly preparing each active participant for the divine eventuality of representing Christ in a vocal ministry. A fellowship that has disciplined itself in corporate spiritual stillness can thrive on the resourcefulness of many seeds of God sprouting the multifarious gifts of the Divine Spirit in fresh and vital messages that inspire and edify in a spontaneous and authentic way. Such a fellowship need no longer be solely dependent on the programmed ministry but can explore the boundless resourcefulness of the priesthood of all believers—so characteristic of the genius of Anabaptist beginnings—even without preprogrammed invocations and benedictions, without preinspired hymns, prayers, and sermons, and without musical preludes, interludes, and postludes to predetermine the inner state of the soul. But what would happen if all these props were suddenly removed? Wouldn't the result be a barren, stagnant, desolate silence? Obviously that can happen, but it need not happen. Structured worship too is not without its liabilities.

Silent meeting in the waiting ministry presupposes a certain maturity, self-transcendence, patience, and openness to the new. With some guidance and a little experience, constructive use of preparatory silence can inspire the unexplored resourcefulness of spontaneous unprogrammed meetings for worship. But if we hope to experience the truth and fruit of such silence we also need some preparation for the practice of silence. Such preparation demands humility of mind and heart. In the final analysis it is silence itself which prepares us for Silence. The hardest journey is the inner journey— also in our life together.

"For God alone my soul waits in silence"-Psalm 62:5.

Reprinted with permission from *The Mennonite*, Jan. 6/81, 2f.

REFLECTIONS ON SILENT WORSHIP

It is in creative silence that one recovers peace of mind and a renewed sense of the purpose of living. In the silence of religious experience the soul does not shut itself up in isolation but opens out to the Infinite. Silent meeting is a gathering in depth at the most profound level of existence, the Center from which we know God and discern what is true in ourselves and others. From such meetings arise our most valid insights, truest motives, and highest meanings. We meet to clarify our highest purposes in life and to strengthen our resolve to live by them.

We begin our meeting by silent intercession for ourselves and others until we find release from all frustration, anxiety, and selfish concern. We overcome outer and inner distractions and dispersions by focusing our attention on the one thing needful, our relationship to God, asking God for forgiveness, faithfulness, and strength to reweave or redirect our lives where necessary. We pray until we find the evil weakening in us and the good raised up, or as St. Seraphim of Sarov said: "We must pray only until God the Holy Spirit descends. When He comes to visit us, we cease to pray."

As we become engrossed and absorbed with God we reach a deeper level within ourselves and approach the spiritual center of our togetherness: to know and do God's will. In this state of openness before God and true communion of minds and hearts, we may experience an inner urgency to share a deep concern, recent insight, or personal experience giving fuller meaning to life. Vocal ministry may take the form of readings, prayers, Scripture, descriptions, reflections, or interpretations intended to further our understanding of God's will. Words spoken in meeting should aim to make explicit what is already implicit in the silence, thereby encouraging and deepening awareness of spiritual values. Allowance should be made for great variety of approach to religious experience and expression. Messages by different speakers may follow spontaneously, enriching and complementing one another like variations on a theme. In an unprogrammed meeting, an unfinished message often leads others to being inwardly inspired to complete it. What compels one to speak in meeting will be not so much the rarity or clarity of the insight as a deep inner glowing love for God and for His people. Ministry is a spiritual rather than a vocal exercise. For words to mean anything there must be a hidden life behind the speech the meaning of which language intends to reveal. The language of ministry is the foreground of reality behind which is the receptive sea of silent waiting on God for His word and call. Language abstracted from this background is powerless and deceptive. Words lacking the baptism of the Spirit reduce vocal ministry to a chatty conversation or a contrived homily. Truth is not a matter of exchanging words but of incarnation of God's word. Every opening received may not be suitable for immediate sharing. But that does not mean that it will be lost, for every seed from God bears fruit in its season once it has matured. It is in this process of maturation that one experiences the most creative moments of one's life.

Silent meeting is not the abolition of the ministry but of the passive laity, for it demands that every believer be his own priest and discern the ministry of Christ to and through others. In unprogrammed meeting where there is no music, responsive reading, or professional speaking, much more is left to each worshiper. It is possible to come to silent meeting and just to sit there waiting for someone to say something without fully realizing that everyone is charged with the responsibility for participation if the group is to function creatively. The importance of inner preparation for corporate silence on the part of each participant cannot be overemphasized. The authenticity of the vocal ministry depends on it. Nevertheless, no one should come to meeting paralyzed by a feeling of unworthiness, for "God is a God of the present moment" (Eckhart) and our very yearning for Him makes us resourceful. And silent meeting does not end when the period for worship closes, for those who have shared it will continue to live in its strength.

"Why are we so willing to talk and discourse with one another when, notwithstanding, we seldom return to silence without injury to our conscience. The reason why we are so willing to talk is that we seek comfort from one another, and we wish to ease our heart, wearied by many thoughts. But, alas! it is often in vain and to no purpose; for this outward consolation causes no small damage to the inward and Divine consolation. Therefore, we must watch and pray that our time may not pass idly away. If it be lawful and expedient to speak, speak those things which tend to edify."

Thomas à Kempis

"Many people seek fellowship because they are afraid of being alone. Because they cannot stand loneliness, they are driven to seek the company of other people in the hope they will gain some help in association with others. They are generally disappointed. Then they blame the fellowship for what is really their own fault. The Christian community is not a spiritual sanatorium. The person who comes into a fellowship because he is running away from himself is misusing it for the sake of diversion, no matter how spiritual this diversion may appear.

"Let him who cannot be alone beware of community. He will only do harm to himself and to the community. . . . But the reverse is also true: Let him who is not in community beware of being alone. . . . Only as we are within the fellowship can we be alone, and only he that is alone can live in the fellowship. Only in the fellowship can we learn to be rightly alone and only in aloneness do we learn to live rightly in the fellowship. . . . One who wants fellowship without solitude plunges into the void of words and feelings, and one who seeks solitude without fellowship perishes in the abyss of vanity, self-infatuation, and despair. . . . Blessed is he who is alone in the strength of the fellowship and blessed is he who keeps the fellowship in the strength of aloneness. But the strength of aloneness and the strength of the fellowship is solely the strength of the Word of God, which is addressed to the individual in the fellowship.

"The mark of solitude is silence, as speech is the mark of community. Silence and speech have the same inner correspondence and difference as do solitude and community. One does not exist without the other. . . . There is an attitude toward silence which misrepresents silence as a mystical desire to get beyond the Word. This is to miss the essential relationship of silence to the Word. Silence is simple stillness of the individual under the Word of God. . . . Silence is nothing else but waiting for God's Word and coming from God's Word with a blessing."

Dietrich Bonhoeffer

"Do you sit down in true silence, resting from your own will and workings, and waiting upon the Lord . . . until the Lord breathes life into you, refresheth you, and prepares you, and your spirits . . . for His service?"

William Penn

"As many candles lighted and put in one place do greatly augment the light, and make it more to shine forth, so when many are gathered together into the same life there is more of the glory of God, and His power appears to the refreshment of each individual, for each partakes not only of the light raised in himself, but in all the rest."

Robert Barclay

"I went to meetings in an awful frame of mind, and endeavoured to be inwardly acquainted with the language of the true Shepherd. And one day, being under a strong exercise of spirit, I stood up, and said some words in a meeting; but not keeping close to the Divine opening, I said more than was required of me; and being soon sensible of my error, I was afflicted in mind some weeks, without any light or comfort. . . . I then felt forgiveness for my offense, and my mind became calm and quiet. . . . And after this, feeling the spring of Divine love opened, and a concern to speak, I said a few words in a meeting, in which I found peace; this, I believe was about six weeks from the first time. And as I was humbled and disciplined under the Cross, my understanding became more strengthened to distinguish the language of the pure spirit which inwardly moves upon the heart, and taught me to wait in silence many weeks together, until I felt that rise which prepares the creatures to stand like a trumpet, through which the Lord speaks. . . ."

John Woolman

"In a truly covered meeting an individual who speaks takes no credit to himself for the part he played in the unfolding of the worship. . . . For the feeling of being a pliant instrument of the Divine Will characterizes true speaking 'in the Life'. Under such a covering an individual merges into vocal utterance, frequently without fear or trembling, and subsides without self-consciousness when his part is played. For One who is greater than all the individuals has become the meeting place of the group, and He becomes the leader and director of worship. With wonder one hears the next speaker, if there be more, take up another aspect of the theme of the meeting."

Thomas R. Kelly

"In the silence of the meeting for worship, thought becomes the servant of the searching spirit. With the longed-for direct communion of man with God, there comes a sense of guidance and a message from the Inward Christ. Sometimes this message seems purely personal; at other times it seems to belong to the meeting. The worshiper is then under a divine requirement to share it with his fellows, to contribute to the vocal service of the meeting. This responsibility of every member may lead to ministry which answers unknown or unvoiced needs of other seekers. A sensitive spirit often shares a vital 'opening' which brings worshipers to God and leaves them there."

A Book of Christian Discipline

"One never brings anything to meeting with the certainty of giving it there, but one tries not to come empty. . . . In (meeting) I have physically slept and again I have been terribly awake. In it my mind has wandered like a hummingbird on holiday and yet in it I have felt moments of intensity and concentration that have shown me what life could be like."

Douglas V. Steere

"Sit down in some place and turn in thy mind to the Light, and wait upon God simply as if none were present but the Lord."

Alexander Parker

"The meeting should be an opportunity for the circulation of life, of truth, of experience, of fresh and vital messages. The focus of emphasis ought always to be the refreshment and edification of the group, not the personal 'relief' or 'satisfaction' of an individual. Nor is the meeting a place for stereotyped 'sermonizing', for laboriously 'constructed' addresses. What is needed is a fresh, inspiring, illuminating, uplifting message, which opens the gates of life to struggling and discouraged souls. The meeting will be at its best when all that is spoken coheres and draws toward a single central purpose, so that it culminates in a unity of life."

Rufus M. Jones

This HERMITAGE is dedicated to the glory of God for the discernment of His will through contemplation and study.

It is neither a museum nor an asylum but a quiet path along the main road to being and service; it is not the solo virtuoso but a tone which accompanies, a note of grace which vibrates with unique divine inspiration, though hearing it demands a more delicate ear than is required to hear the dominant chord determining our religious melody.

EREMITICAL WISDOM

Just to be is a blessing, just to live is holy (Heschel).

Life is always an experiment. The essential thing is that we dare to immerse ourselves in it and let unlimited integrity govern our vision, our questioning and our answering (Jaspers).

Wiederkehren von allem gezweyten in das einig, das muss durch alles Leben gestudiert werden (Denck).

Great issues affecting mankind always have to be decided in the wilderness, in unmitigated isolation.

Our task is not to turn the world upside down, but to do what is necessary at a given place with due consideration of reality (Bonhoeffer).

Man muss Gott finden und lieben indem was er uns gerade gibt (*ibid*).

A person is ethical only when life as such is sacred to one—the life of plants and animals as well as that of people—and when one devotes oneself helpfully to all life that is in need of help (Schweitzer).

In solitude the soul develops senses we hardly know in everyday life.

Prayer is our answer to the inconceivable surprise of living (Heschel).

Only the illumined soul has no ignorance, no sense of ego, no attachment, no aversion, and no fear of death (Prabhavananda).

The only things worth worrying about are in ourselves, not in externals.

Learn to be peaceful and thousands of souls around you will find salvation (St. Seraphim).

Learn to live in the world according to your own spiritual way—like wild flowers!

It is impossible for a person to live honestly and at the same time comfortably in outward respects.

Blessed is he who cuts himself off from the world without hatred.

Never despise anyone, never condemn anyone, never speak evil of anyone and the Lord will give you peace.

Do not lose yourself in order to save another. Do not become a trader of words. Learn to control your tongue and your belly.

Two things a hermit hates: an easy life and vainglory.

Our work should respect the integrity of nature and not destroy its beauty and harmony. We must honor all living things with joy, love, and care lest in destroying that of God in creation we defile our own soul.

All true work of art is the fruit of a tree whose roots are charity, poverty, and prayer.

God's spirit is the ground of our meaning and being, the conscious inspiration for all that we do and are.